Dominion Theology

Dominion Theology

Recovering Our Social and Political Responsibility

BY
Michael Pòl Macneil

WIPF & STOCK · Eugene, Oregon

DOMINION THEOLOGY
Recovering Our Social and Political Responsibility

Wipf & Stock
An Imprint of Wipf and Stock Publishers
199 W. 8th Ave., Suite 3
Eugene, OR 97401

www.wipfandstock.com

PAPERBACK ISBN: 979-8-3852-6802-3
HARDCOVER ISBN: 979-8-3852-6803-0
EBOOK ISBN: 979-8-3852-6804-7

VERSION NUMBER 04/14/26

To Rev. Pauline Edwards of Bangor Pentecostal Church, North Wales: pastor, mentor, evangelist, friend, and fearless advocate for the wretched of the earth, for a life well-lived and for whom a crown of glory shortly awaits your departure. To so many memories of the last thirty-five years, I owe you more than I could ever pay, and one day, we will see each other in the presence of the Lord when we can discuss, if we are so inclined, whether this book remained "too wordy." Travel well, my friend.

"Whatever man may stand, whatever he may do, to whatever he may apply his hand—in agriculture, in commerce, and in industry, or his mind, in the world of art, and science—he is, in whatsoever it may be, constantly standing before the face of God. He is employed in the service of his God. He has strictly to obey his God. And above all, he has to aim at the glory of his God."

—Abraham Kuyper, from the Inaugural Rectoral Address at the opening of the Free University of Amsterdam, Oct. 20, 1880

Contents

Preface

THE MAIN MOTIVATION FOR me when I wrote the "Reformed" thesis upon which this book is based was because I felt an intellectual shallowness in my spiritual experience. I had heard a lot about "dominion" but knew there was much more that I was not seeing or understanding. At that point of spiritual dejection and despair, I went to a conference held by GPC in Glasgow, Scotland, where an elder of the faith Landa Cope (one of the founders of YWAM in the 1970s) was speaking. It was the first time I had heard someone talk about the arts, science, politics, and the "Old Testament Template" for the discipling of the nations—it was like "shoot this into my veins." It was intellectually like a five-course meal after living on McDonalds, pizzas, and kebabs for years, and it triggered a revolutionary change for me.[1] At the time, I was studying on a taught master's degree and decided to make it the subject of the dissertation, from which this book has descended.

So, what is the book about? In a time of prayer sometime later, I can remember being confronted by the Lord with the words, *where are strongholds?* If you have been spiritually brought up in Pentecostalism and radical Christianity like me, you instantly think of the spiritual princes of Daniel hindering Gabriel and Paul's great exposition of Eph 6:10–18.[2] However, he took me to 2 Cor 10:4–5:

1. You can find Landa's two main books on this subject in the bibliography. There is also extensive material on YouTube, and I will draw attention to other web resources of hers at various points in the book.

2. I hope my third book will actually be my first book, which I wrote way back in 1992. This explains my Christian experience as I was trying to explain it to others. A semi-revised draft from 2012 is on my blog at https://planetmacneil.org/Documents/Content/Macneils-Guide-for-the-Spiritually-Perplexed.pdf. Please note the trigger warning in the foreword!

> For the weapons of our warfare are not of the flesh, but divinely powerful for the destruction of fortresses. We are *destroying speculations* and every lofty thing raised up against the knowledge of God, and we are taking *every thought captive* to the obedience of Christ. (emphasis added)

Do you see the point? Strongholds are *in the mind,* and we take *every thought* captive. The fortresses and strongholds we tear down are *intellectual* ones. It is certainly very necessary to understand there is very much a spiritual dimension and reality behind these "thoughts"—these may indeed be "doctrines of demons" as Paul writes elsewhere.[3] However, the point remains, when we reeducate ourselves according to scriptural principles, we break those strongholds down, remove their authority to squat rent-free in our minds, and eject whatever spirits have held us bound.

So, the realms of spiritual authority, the armor of God in Eph 6, the fasting and prayer of Daniel in energizing the chief prince Michael have an important and significant place, but a dominion theology that lacks a coherent political and social program, with preference given to "governing in the heavenlies" by the operation of agnostic spiritual principles with no natural, physical outworkings or ethical and political commitments, is naïve and immature. Thus, the purpose of the book remains absolutely the purpose of the thesis, which is

> A manifesto for Christians who want to come out of the political closet and join the wider public square of broad cultural discourse.

To get down a bit more to the nitty-gritty, what *were* my frustrations with my Christian experience that provoked me to study dominion theology in depth? That is not hard to enunciate, and it is a long list, but one particular sore point from which a multitude of sins has flown admits special reference: a particularly obnoxious feature of late nineteenth-century and twentieth-century conservative Christian thought has been the cyclical obsession with the "rapture," and this has extended into our present milieu. The "rapture" will indeed be a glorious event, but as the posited rapture dates come and go, the obsession with it ends up discrediting Christian thought more generally as intellectually shallow and escapist.

For example, yet another viral hoax was perpetrated this year as a pastor announced Jesus had appeared to him and informed him of the date of the

3. 1 Tim 4:1.

church's departure.[4] Obedient congregants quit their jobs and accompany such prophetic ministers to the woods and mountaintops to wait for their catching away—only for it *not* to happen. Now you have the disgruntled, the distressed, and the disillusioned posting to YouTube, renouncing their Christianity. Other ministers have set the date only for it to pass and to excuse their failure by claiming it was because of their prayer and fasting that judgment was delayed and the rapture deferred.[5] Others have allegedly had the audacity to charge a "rapture fee" to their congregants to guarantee their place in heaven.[6] Similarly, the *Left Behind* media series primarily targeting the American evangelical market had amassed $41 million in sales at its midpoint by 2001 (it continued to 2007) and the creators were still milking the franchise with "behind the scenes" exposés in 2018; there was seemingly no limit to the appetite for the "coward's way out"[7]—exit the Tribulation on the first rapture-train to glory.

The aforementioned Landa Cope expressed my feelings about this perfectly when she said that "theologies of imminent return" emerge as a reaction in conservative Christian circles whenever their "radical" brethren have begun to assert themselves in the wider, especially political culture and this, in turn, militates against building a coherent Christian theology of involvement. In contrast, she pointed out that Scripture commands we are to "*occupy until I come*" (Luke 19:13 KJV) and that the definition of the Greek word translated "occupy" is best understood as a call to build and shape *all* the dimensions of culture, the arts and the sciences, the political and the social.

4. The pastor at fault this time was South African pastor Joshua Mhlakela, who has since publicly repented and stated he will never talk about the rapture again; that is to his credit. Isoje, "Times Pastors Predicted Rapture."

5. This was the infamous claim by Nigerian Pastor Metuh, who claimed the day of the rapture would be April 25, 2024. Isoje, "Times Pastors Predicted Rapture."

6. In Ekiti State, Pastor Ade Abraham of Christ High Commission made headlines after instructing his congregation to relocate to a camp where they were told to "wait for the Rapture." It was alleged he asked followers to pay a ₦310,000 rapture fee to guarantee their spot in heaven. Isoje, "Times Pastors Predicted Rapture."

7. This is a phrase I attribute to one of the most well-known and controversial of the British charismatic leaders between the 1970s and the 1990s, Gerald Coates, who led a thousand-member strong church (extremely large for the UK) and one hundred satellite churches nationwide at the height of his movement in 1997. He was one of the proponents of a charismatic form of dominion theology, "Kingdom Now," which we encounter later in the book. Coates, *What on Earth Is This*, 36.

In detail, the Greek verbal form used is πραγματεύσασθε (from pragmateuomai—Strong's 4231), which is in the imperative mood, middle voice aorist and has the literal meaning of "[you, yourself] trade, do business [now!]." Most modern versions translate the verse using this basic verbal idea of "doing business," but in this case (I am not a "KJV only" advocate!), the King James translators did a much better job in capturing the idiomatic sense in which the verb is being used. The context demands a stronger sense of the word: the master is going away and leaving his servants in charge until he returns; it is not just the narrow sense of "trading" that is intended here but the broader sense of taking care of the master's affairs by assuming a governmental position (in the passage, it is that delegation that causes the dispute). The account finishes with showing the diligent subjects receiving responsibility for entire cities, not just a financial reward. This building and shaping of culture is what this book is about and there were, in addition, some strong, motivating reasons for making the book happen at this time.

Firstly, with the untimely assassination of Charlie Kirk, there has been a muscular response, especially amongst those of college age, against any attempt to sideline, discriminate against, or push them out of the public discourse on the sole basis of their Christianity. Those young Christians are now making their presence felt both intellectually, politically, and socially. These recent events underline why Christianity is so desperately needed in the public square, not as the self-serving barons, lords, and kings of the medieval, Catholic hegemony but as the scientist, democrat, and merchant of Protestantism. That is, we are not, as is the frequent accusation against the Christian claims, seeking to impose a "theocracy." However, equally, we *do* need to understand then how to *apply* our Christianity in the public square in our pluralistic context, and this makes the availability of this work pertinent and appropriate.

Secondly, and this disturbed me most profoundly, many Christians, after rallying to the call to be culturally "relevant" in the 1980s and 1990s, had left their political closets but, by the turn of the new millennium, were retreating back to its safety and had even double-bolted the freshly refurbished closet door in the wake of the Trump phenomenon post-2016. This spiritual contagion was not just confined to the "denominational," renewed, or traditional churches that had just caught a whiff of revival during the heyday of Spring Harvest.[8] It was a global pandemic

8. Spring Harvest was a major British Christian festival that, becoming the centerpiece of the European charismatic renewal in the 1980s and 1990s, generated a huge

of evangelical, charismatic, and Pentecostal proportions. I was personally involved in an influential, cutting-edge "prophetic" fellowship who energetically prophesied us all back into the closet because of the foul-mouthed Trump and his coarse tweets, ignoring that he had also, like no president since Abraham Lincoln, *opened* the White House to the *evangelical* Christian world, rather than just inviting a token senior bishop as a "faith representative" to an otherwise ecumenical, multi-faith, Oval Office political pantomime. Such was my visceral reaction to this that I wrote the best part of 45,000 words in a month as a reaction to it and received the "left foot of fellowship" for my trouble.[9]

Thirdly, as a wider issue of Christian political ethics, it was a perceived dogma of the Enlightenment, oft repeated in political science classes and the hallowed halls of government, that the "religious" belongs to the sphere of the private and should not intrude into the realm of the public, where an indifferent pluralism was considered the binding norm. Indeed, with more than a hint of irony, it was considered *sacrilegious* for the private *to* intrude into the public. For, in my view, this "secularism" in the public square functions as would a religious commitment, and further, its adherents are known for their fundamentalism, seeking to delegitimize those who would oppose them and to exclude all "religious" distinctives that would challenge their orthodoxy. That is, in effect, we

---

number of new songs and showcased a generation of Christian musicians. It was rare during that period to see a house church without "Spring Harvest" collections alongside *Songs of Fellowship* and the legacy of traditional hymnals. Spring Harvest still exists today as an "interdenominational evangelical community": https://www.springharvest.org/.

9. Macneil, *Politics*. Explaining my colorful idiom, Paul and Barnabas received the "right hand of fellowship" from the Jerusalem elders in Gal 2:9 for the recognition of their ministry. A search on my blog (https://planetmacneil.org/blog) for "COVID" will yield how strongly I felt over this issue at that time, particularly the removal of our political and social rights. My censuring was in the early days of COVID, and there was lots of discussion among our Christian leaders that the correct application of Rom 13 provided the imperative of the accepting of government mandates, as did the Levitical laws of quarantine to justify lockdowns.

In my dissension to this view, in what I saw as the illegitimate abuse of Scripture, I found myself at odds with my elders to the degree it was made clear to me I had to capitulate or leave; it was *not* up for debate. After many months of reflection and being thoroughly convinced of the veracity and soundness of my position, I chose the latter. With the passing of the years and new, unrepentant publications on these issues from those same elders, I believe I was totally justified at the time in "obeying God, not men" (Acts 4:19), and my views have not changed regarding their capitulation at that time. I do not bear any personal animus towards them and would happily worship with them, but we certainly continue to differ when it comes to cultural philosophy.

have a choice of two oppositional religious points of view for the public square, secularism *or* Christianity, and it is appropriate *we* understand how Scripture is to be applied as the true religion, that we might not succumb in this generation, as so many of us have in previous generations, to the false narratives of the secular counterfeits.

Consequently, the book aims to fill in the knowledge gap for the nascent malcontents amongst the ranks of those young, rebellious Christian youth exiting their closets—and also a vitamin-rich, spiritual smoothie for those parents who were once filled with that same youthful vigor but became fat and indolent in their comfort as that tolerated oddity on the fringes of civilized society. For they have since found the closets have been auctioned off by the new political landlords: it is no longer possible for Christians to live on their parochial reservations. Now, full compliance to the political masters, with their digital IDs and their CBDCs, is being demanded on the pain of excommunication from civic society.[10] The book provides some theological and philosophical underpinnings to the legitimacy of the dominionist perspective, endorsing full participation in every aspect of culture, including the social and the political, and can thus be considered a work in the best apologetic traditions of Christianity.[11]

10. One particularly vivid account was from a personal friend who works in China. During the pandemic, their tower block had the main entry doors welded shut; when they had run out of pooled food, they began shouting from their balconies for help; a police drone then came and photographed them, with some receiving automatic fines to their bank accounts for "anti-social behavior."

This is the technocratic utopia being advocated by some of the most influential tech billionaires in the West; Larry Ellison has recently argued that the potential for 100 percent surveillance being offered by AI systems will ensure peaceful compliance to all laws, for we would "all be on our best behavior," and thus complete societal peace. Ellison should be commended for his technological achievements as the founder of Oracle and his current support of the IDF, but this aspect of his political vision I feel constrained to challenge. Straight Arrow News, "Oracle's Larry Ellison Sees AI Supervision."

11. By "apologetic," we do not mean, as in modern English usage, "saying sorry for being a Christian," but rather the discipline of philosophical apologetics, where we defend the faith from its detractors and opponents. More technically, the Greek word used by the apostles Peter and Paul is ἀπολογία (*apologia*), and quoting the Gingrich lexicon, defense as a legal technical term, a speech in defense of oneself: *reply*, *verbal defense* (2 Tim 4:16). Similarly, BDAG (the academic reference work for the Greek of this period), emphasizes this is a logical and structured *speech* of defense; it is *reasoned*, rather than inspirational or preached. Hence, Socrates made his *apologia* before the elders at Athens; it was a *positive* statement as to why he considered himself innocent of the charges leveled against him.

More specifically, the book examines "dominion theology" as a feature of Reformation thought, which had incorporated the late-Augustinian thinking of the patristic period as central to their worldview. The Reformers had frequently wrestled with what was the correct eschatological thinking regarding the triumph of Christ throughout the world, and it is appropriate that we start there.[12] We then move through the "modern period,"[13] where Christianity wrestled with the tensions between evangelism and wider social action, progressing to where in the last century we see modern revivalism and fundamentalism essentially rejecting social and political action as a

12. At first it might seem a breathtaking, sectarian move to leapfrog the entire Catholic period in moving from Augustine to the Reformation with little comment on the thousand years between them, particularly when there were some fine "Catholic" scholars. However, in many of the most important respects, we can consider Calvin to have re-expressed the patristic theology of Augustine in systematic form; Calvin was also extremely familiar with the work of influential scholastics such as Scotus and even non-aligned dissenting literature.

That is, the Reformation was a re-engagement with the primitive Christian foundations in their unadulterated form before their "infection" with first Plato and then Aristotle (where Aquinas, though brilliant as he was, might be considered a baptized Aristotle.) Whilst the argument to do it justice would need to be far more nuanced than this, even in this course form it still has substantial force and truth in it, for the brutal and tyrannical nature of some periods of the Catholic hegemony, and their violent opposition to protestant thought, is not something we need argue about, it is a matter of historical record.

13. By the "modern period," I do not mean our contemporary period but that which is argued to have begun with the Renaissance, the earliest dates being given as around 1250, with Italian figures like the painter Giotto and the writer Dante Alighieri. It was characterized by an increasing preeminence being given to the role of reason and the rejection of ecclesiastical authority, especially that of the papal dynasties. However, the Renaissance was in fact spread over many centuries and had both Christian and violently anti-religious movements within it; the Reformation shared the basic Renaissance position in rejecting traditional papal authority and was a distinctively Christian expression of it. Similarly, it was not until the early seventeenth century that Descartes is considered the first of the "modern" philosophers, and the "Jewish Renaissance" was not to occur in the parochial Russian Jewish communities until the mid-nineteenth century.

There are also considered to be separate movements of the French and German Renaissance, and as a matter of disambiguating the terminology, the "Enlightenment" is better considered that period of the later Renaissance where the focus on reason, science, and individual political liberty increased. Many history books argue that the Enlightenment chronologically followed the Renaissance; this is a gross oversimplification as they were different aspects of the same intellectual movement that asserted the right of men to think outside of ecclesiastical authority, free of the fear of sanction. Whilst the secular Enlightenment might cry "autonomy" in rejection of all religious metanarratives as a way of life, the Christian Enlightenment argued for the right of each individual to directly approach God without the need of a priestly mediator, the essence of a Protestant perspective.

distraction, with the result that conservative, Arminian Christianity essentially ghettoized itself for half a century.[14] However, in opposition to these obscurantist and fundamentalist movements, there was a separate stream within the neo-Calvinism of Abraham Kuyper that addressed the challenge of the same philosophical modernism and modernity very differently.

Kuyper, an enormous and underappreciated intellect of the second part of the nineteenth century, had offered a searching critique of *modernism* whilst embracing the technological tools of *modernity.* That is, Kuyper had rejected the *philosophical* modernism that he argued had terminated in the aggressive and bloody atheism of the French revolution, but had also advocated forcefully for "modernity" in the sense of embracing the scientific and technological advances of the period, founding the Free University of Amsterdam, two broadsheet papers, a political party (the Anti [French] Revolutionary Party), and serving as prime minister of the Netherlands between 1901 to 1905. As a result, he was at his most impatient with the religious conservatives suspicious of the innovations of the age.

Central to his philosophy was the concept of "sphere sovereignty," in which there are considered to be distinct modal spheres of human culture, in which the church had an ethical regulatory role, but to which it was not to dictate or censor.[15] This concept was itself a recapitulation and modernization of the Reformation emphasis on the legitimacy of and the equal value between the different "vocations" of human culture in opposition to the strict division between the religious and the secular, the priesthood and the laity, with its belief in the preeminence of the former. This tyrannizing over culture and the separation of laity and priesthood had been the cornerstone of the domination of culture by the Roman Catholic hegemony

14. As we shall see, modern revivalism is often associated with Charles Finney, and he is held up as the archetype and hero of the movement. However, Finney argued for and executed an aggressive presence in all the spheres of culture, most notably the political and the educational, serving as the first president of Wheaton College. He actively encouraged his followers to engage in political fights and to obtain political office, as can be read in his autobiography (which is public domain). Although he rejected the constraints that Calvinism had imposed on the ministers of the colonies, which he had viewed as the cause of their failures to maintain a Christian culture, his cultural philosophy was far closer to that of orthodox Presbyterian J. Gresham Machen, the founder of the Calvinist Westminster Theological Seminary, than the modern revivalists and fundamentalists who followed in his wake.

15. I consider his remarkable cultural and political achievements in Macneil, *Abraham Kuyper*, where I also offer an explanation as to why he is a figure that has been generally ignored outside the parochial boundaries of the Reformed world.

for almost a thousand years, with the absolute authority of the papacy in matters of cultural and scientific disputes.

This found further expression in J. Gresham Machen's work after his separation from Princeton and the founding of Westminster Theological Seminary in 1929. Kuyper had lectured famously at Princeton in 1899 and was one of the major influences on the conservative wing of the Presbyterian movement that had eventually coalesced under Machen. A distinct theology and, more importantly, a *praxis* of Christian involvement emerged from Machen's life and work in this period. He frequently addressed the US Congress arguing for the preeminence of biblical principles in opposition to the socialism of the great societal and economic reforms that were being enacted under the auspices of Roosevelt's New Deal. With his emphasis on the full societal involvement of the Christian community, Machen, I argue, is the historical precursor to what became modern dominion theology. However, it was to be after the Second World War, in the sociological, political, and theological upheavals of the period, that, in the work of one man, R. J. Rushdoony, a coherent Christian critique emerged. His subsequent development of a sociological program of reform is the first position that properly qualifies for the designation "dominion theology." He incorporated both Machen's practical orientation and fortified it with the seminal thought of Machen's first professor of apologetics at Westminster, Cornelius Van Til, who had himself been influenced by Kuyper's philosophy of sphere sovereignty.[16]

Following Rushdoony's pioneering work, the period of the 1970s and the 1980s was one of increasing political involvement of Christians in the political realm, particularly in the US. Conservative Christians generally had been particularly motivated by the 1973 Roe vs. Wade case that had "found" a constitutional right to abortion. President Jimmy Carter was the first to bring his faith to the fore and to make it a political issue in the 1976 presidential campaign. Subsequently, both Ronald Reagan and George Bush made their faith commitment a feature of their campaigns, and even Barack Obama, in 2008, made capital from his time in a liberal Chicago church, equivocating at the time on "gay marriage" that he might get the black evangelical vote. The charismatic revival of the period suddenly saw dominion theology becoming a feature of influential Christian leaders within the movement who were seeking an alternative to the traditional evangelical rejection of social action as being a feature of the

16. Van Til remained for over fifty years in that position.

liberal "social gospel." We will examine these related but distinct streams of dominion theology far from the Reformed roots of the movement. We then finish with an exposition of a Christian political philosophy for the contemporary period.

Importantly, the book extends and develops substantially the content of a thesis upon which it is based, partly because of the passage of time and improvements in my own understanding, but chiefly because the thesis was subject to a strict word limit of twenty thousand words.[17] That provided little opportunity to develop the argument beyond the narrow principal theme of establishing the orthodoxy of the position in response to its persistent portrayal as an extreme, fanatical form of Christianity, both from outside and within Christendom. I believe it provided, and still provides, an emphatic and coherent answer to that important historical question, but this constraint on its content was reflected in a question posed by an academic pastoral reviewer at the time, who had made the comment, "so what are you going to do now you have established this orthodoxy, what practical use is it?"[18] The additional material represents the broad contours of an answer to that question, and the book subsequently differs most substantively from the original thesis by

1. adding in what might be called the sociological and political application of the position by outlining what I call a "philosophy of Christian involvement."[19]
2. updating the content to include recent literature, developments, and innovations, both from within the Christian community and more generally in the wider Western political culture.

17. This book is an updated version of my Master of Arts (Studies in Philosophy and Religion) dissertation which obtained a Distinction at the University of Bangor in North Wales in 2016. My supervisor for the dissertation, now Emeritus Professor Eryl Davies, said that it would be *"an absolute tragedy"* if it was to remain gathering dust on the library shelves and encouraged me to publish it. That has remained frustratingly out of reach until now but post my doctoral studies and the successful publication of a book based on those studies (Macneil, *Foundations of Philosophy)*, I have been able to revisit, update and prepare it for publication, receiving further encouragement and assistance from Professor Davies and the current Head of the School, Professor Lucy Huskinson, to do so.

18. The questioner was the principal of a Pentecostal Bible college in Hungary, so I considered it worthy of consideration.

19. Stated most fully in Macneil, "Politics."

3. adding new material, rewritten sentences or paragraphs, or adding an explanatory footnote as directions to my further discussions of the issues in question where my thought and understanding have matured, particularly on those philosophical issues covered in depth within my doctoral studies (and I can better express what I was sometimes struggling to express in the thesis).

Finally, for my part, it has been very frustrating that it has been nearly a decade that this book has lain fallow on my personal website, where it was (and is still) in its thesis form (though it is being slowly migrated as I post drafts of this book!). But I am very pleased that the time has finally come to revisit and overhaul the work for publication in this revised and extended form. As all this time has passed, I decided to include this extensive preface to add some color and background. I believed, when I first wrote it and still believe now, that dominion theology is the most coherent form of Christian cultural thinking, and I commend careful consideration by the reader of what is written here. It represents a measured and critically thought-through response to those who, for whatever reason, be it fear, genuine ignorance, misunderstanding or maliciousness, have sought to misrepresent the position. It is very much a sister volume to my doctoral work and in this updated form, it is every bit as intellectually rigorous. It will provide substantive apologetic material for the believer seeking an intellectual defense of their faith beyond the pop-apologetics and cowardly dispensationalist eschatologies of our time.

Who This Book Is For and How to Read It

This book is indeed for everyone interested in the subject but does have some advanced passages, arguments, and discussions in places for the most demanding of readers. Sometimes, the language is philosophical or theological, and it is important not to get stuck or bogged down if you are new to the subject or want a more general overview. There is no need to understand everything you read the first time through, and there is no need to read the book from cover to cover; you can use it like a textbook or a reference manual—look at the contents, look at the indices, and read what you want to or need to, remembering you can always come back later if you want to dig deeper. There are lots of moving parts in dominion theology, with parts like the relationship to eschatology, the key historical figures, or the application in the modern political context, meaning that most of the chapters within the book are able to stand and be read on their own, according to the interests and requirements of the reader.

—Dr. Michael Macneil PhD, December 26, 2025

Acknowledgments

A SPECIAL THANKS TO Dr. David Sullivan (ret.) of Bangor University, North Wales, who was a masterful philosophical mentor during my master's level coursework. Thanks should also go to the current head of the department, Professor Lucy Huskinson, and the former head, now retired Emeritus Professor Davies, for being willing to support this book proposal. Professor Davies once gave me 30 percent for an essay that I thought was great, and we had quite a few in-class conflicts when I thought I knew more than he did and was a higher-quality Christian than he was; that taught me the valuable lessons: (1) always read the recommended sources of your professor, and (2) remember that being a legend in your own mind is an ever-present danger of the human condition.

Spiritual thanks also to Pastors Rodney and Adonica of the River Church, Tampa Bay, who continue to stand without apology. If it was not for discovering that "green desk," things might be very different today. Spiritual thanks also to Paul and Linda Fenwick of Byker City Fellowship for being "practitioners of dominion." Some of those days were the greatest of times.

A special thank you for the forbearance of my wife Sayuri as I pursue these writing projects; her love, support, and literary recommendations for how to improve my emotional intelligence quotient from its previous "unsatisfactory" rating six months after getting married have been invaluable over the last decade. I am repaying her by watching many hundreds of hours of Japanese dramas, a cultural revelation if ever there was one (the Japanese must think their men are useless and women would run things far better);

I would certainly recommend *Doctor X*. Thanks should also go to her sister Maki, too, for some great recommendations!

Thanks should also go to all at Wipf and Stock publishers for help in bringing this book to life. I am sure there will be a cover designer who has done an excellent job, a proofreader who has suffered long and endured much tribulation to enter into the kingdom, and a typesetter who has earned their wages. It is greatly appreciated that you have agreed to publish my work.

Finally, my greatest debt will always be to my Lord and Savior, whose arrest of me on a Friday evening in 2006 whilst having curry, beer, and watching TV, not remotely interested in studying philosophy or theology, is the ultimate cause as to why this book was written. Every step of the journey of this book was curated in masterful fashion, from the disillusionment with my spiritual life, the introduction to Landa's work, encountering the Reconstructionist movement, and the appreciation of the enormous legacy of the Reformation, to finally finding the right publisher decades later—*Soli Deo Gloria*.

Abbreviations

ACLJ	American Center for Law and Justice
ACLU	American Civil Liberties Union
AOG	Assemblies of God
BDAG	Bauer, Danker, Arndt, Gingrich: *A Greek-English Lexicon of the New Testament & Other Early Christian Literature*
BDF	Blass, Debrunner, Funk: *A Greek Grammar of the New Testament and Other Early Christian Literature*
CCC/CCFC	Campus Crusade for Christ (Cru in the US)
CMF	Covenant Media Foundation
COG	Church of God
COGIC	Church of God in Christ (not related to COG)
CR	Critical Realism
CRT	Critical Race Theory
CVT	Cornelius Van Til
DDR	Deutsche Demokratie Republik (Communist East Germany)
FV	Federal Vision
GPC/GPA	Glasgow Prophetic Center/Glasgow Prophetic Alliance
IMF	International Monetary Fund
JTB	Justified True Belief

MP	Member of Parliament (British designation for an elected representative)
NAR	New Apostolic Reformation
NGO	Non-Governmental Organization
NHS	National Health Service (UK)
OM	Operation Mobilization
OPC	Orthodox Presbyterian Church
ORU	Oral Roberts University
RC	Roman Catholic
RE	Reformed Epistemology
RTS	Reformed Theological Seminary
RV	Reasonable Verisimilitude
SM	Spiritual Mobilization
TA	Transcendental Argument
TAG	Transcendental Argument for God
UK	United Kingdom
UN	United Nations
US	United States (of America)
WCC	World Council of Churches
WEA	Worker's Educational Association
WMC	Working Men's Club
WHO	World Health Organization
WTS	Westminster Theological Seminary
YWAM	Youth with a Mission

Introduction

Overview

In this chapter, I introduce dominion theology and explain why I believe it constitutes a distinct concept rather than merely an addendum to the study of fundamentalism or evangelicalism. Nevertheless, I assert the claim to orthodoxy of dominionism by locating it firmly within evangelicalism, then workout the distinctives of dominion theology from within that general framework. I then outline the methodological assumptions and approaches of this book, finishing with a description of hypotheses examined within the book, and a brief outline of how the chapters attempt to address them.

Locating Dominion Theology

The subject of this book is dominion theology—its development and contemporary expression with a view to prognosticating its future within Christianity, and to demonstrate an application of it in political practice. To the layperson, the term "dominion theology," rather like the term "fundamentalism," has acquired a pejorative sense, and the designation has become so vague that there is often a struggle to understand what is meant. However, one *does* understand that, like the term "fundamentalist," it is associated with a fanatical and extreme interpretation of orthodox Christian beliefs. Indeed, the militancy associated with "dominionists" often result in a conflation with the fundamentalists by political liberals and liberal theological critics.[1] In my view, this is not a useful designation unless it is carefully qualified because, even as the movement grew and exerted its influence, many fundamentalist, evangelical, and Pentecostal leaders were most notable in their failure to credit the dominionist movement or in their open hostilityto it.[2]

The Relationship to Evangelicalism

In contrast to this generalizing proposition, a key presupposition of this book is that dominionism, like fundamentalism, is only correctly understood when considered within the context of a distinct and orthodox grouping within conservative evangelicalism.[3] I propose they are representative of distinct hermeneutical traditions within evangelicalism, resulting from a very specific historical context and a distinct set of philosophical and theological ideas.[4]

I wish to emphasize this principle here as there have, at times, been an intense polemic between dominion theologians and the more traditional evangelicalisms where the orthodoxy of dominionism is questioned or denied.[5] In return, dominionists have accused the fundamentalists of a rank "dereliction of duty," of servile "subordinationism," and it is *they*, rather than fundamentalists, that represent a return to the truly biblical Christianity.[6]

With such passion on either side, it is easy for this polemic to eclipse the important fact that the arguments between the parties are more accurately described as *ideological* arguments about Christian *praxis* resulting from a distinct interpretation of Scripture rather than more fundamental theological ones about the status of Scripture itself.

1. For example, Pelletier, "Movement," and PRO-S.O.C.S, "Righteous Revolution," respectively.

2. For example, in Dobson et al., *Fundamentalist Phenomenon*. None of the authors mention the most visible of the American dominionists at the time they were writing, the Reconstructionists, despite it being empirically the Reconstructionist program that they had adopted (e.g., political vision, Dobson et al., *Fundamentalist Phenomenon*, 186; and millennialism, 71). See also McVicar, *Christian Reconstruction*, 15.

3. Poythress, *Inerrancy and Worldview*, 13n1.

4. "It is what is nowadays called a hermeneutic—that is, a way of reading the whole Bible that is itself part of the overall interpretation of the Bible that it undergirds." Packer, *Introduction to Covenant Theology*, loc. 22.

5. Clapp, "Democracy as Heresy"; Lindsey, *Road to Holocaust*, 282.

6. For example, Rushdoony, *God's Plan for Victory*, 175–213.

Indeed, some pivotal figures of the dominionist movement were also recognized as significant within fundamentalist circles and were often misidentified as fundamentalists, owing to the shared commitment to the inerrancy and infallibility of the Scriptures.[7] Hence, it is within this understanding and theological framework that I assert that dominion theology *does*, in its purest form, belong to orthodox Reformed evangelical theology because it is understood in its broadest sense as having the following characteristics:

a. Christianity for whom the Scriptures, rather than church tradition or papal sanction, have the "ultimate authority in matters of spirituality, doctrine and ethics."[8]
b. Christianity that "confines and submits [itself] completely to the teaching of the Bible."[9]
c. Christianity that submits to the "fundamental and inalienable authority of scripture."[10]

Where it is distinctively different from other forms of conservative evangelicalism is in its view of Christianity's place in the wider culture and the discussions of the public square. Dominion theology is not content for the evangelical Christian faith to be a "deeply private matter" but argues its voice is legitimately applicable to the problems of the public domain and that its intellectual coherence warrants that it should be heard there. It is

7. Perhaps the most famous example of this conflation of categories was in Barr's *Fundamentalism* of 1977/84, where he wants to argue that Machen and Warfield were "fundamentalists." Probably, more than any other book, this critique of "fundamentalism" was highly influential because of Barr's enormous reputation as a biblical scholar and liberal-evangelical, but it suffered from some serious misunderstandings and failures to distinguish between the various forms of conservative evangelicalism.

In reality, Machen and Warfield were orthodox Presbyterians with beliefs highly divergent from the premillennialism and Arminianism that were not just distinctive of the early fundamentalists but demanded as a standard of Christian "orthodoxy." Some fundamentalists went as far to challenge Machen's orthodoxy on this basis; Warfield's progressive track in his eschatology, from classical postmillennialism to a more mystical conception of a triumph of the saints in heaven, and his rigorous commitment to the inerrancy and infallibility of the Scriptures made him much more amenable to and influential with the fundamentalists.

8. McGrath, *Passion for Truth*, 22.

9. Lloyd-Jones, *What Is an Evangelical?*, 42.

10. McGrath, *Passion for Truth*, 23.

this *practical* context in which dominion theology sees and positions itself that I believe explains the controversy surrounding the movement.

The Importance of Dominion Theology

For example, in 1988, one fundamentalist opponent of the youthful dominion theology movement described it as "one of the fastest growing movements amongst evangelicals today."[11] This use of the designator *evangelical*, and not fundamentalist, by a critic was in fact an admission of the theological orthodoxy of the movement. It was clearly exerting far more influence within modern Christianity than would a fringe radical group; it was clearly appealing to *mainstream* theological conservatives. Thus, it is necessary to carefully consider both the theology of dominionism and how it came to exert this influence and appeal.

The Approach of This Book

In light of our argument above, the approach of this book necessarily stands in contrast to the general historical, sociological, or psychological approaches that are characteristic of recent studies of what humanism has described as religious fundamentalism or religious studies.[12] These have typically employed a "historical-reductionist" critical approach based on the thesis that "fundamentalism" (of which dominionism would be a *genus*) is in fact a "trans-religious, trans-national and trans-cultural" phenomenon based on shared *ideological* assumptions and anti-modern worldviews irrespective of their particularist expression.[13] Typically, they may also assign a correlative psychological category specifically applicable to the fundamentalists in question.[14]

11. House and Ice, *Dominion Theology*, back matter.

12. Almond et al., *Strong Religion*. This was a particularly interesting book written in the wake of the decade-long fundamentalism project at the University of Chicago, especially significant as the authors had established the project. The project was an enormous analysis of fundamentalism working on the assumption there was a unifying conceptual basis for the category, a set of characteristics that all religious "fundamentalisms" shared. In fact, it is arguable it established precisely the *opposite*, and this book should have been written before the project ever started as the thesis to be tested by the project.

13. Macneil, "Fundamentalism as a Modernism," 1–2; Almond et al., *Strong Religion*, 9–14.

14. Barr, *Fundamentalism*, xi. Barr gave more attention to the psychological argument

Thus, the description is entirely naturalistic, and it neatly and completely sidesteps any theological dimension of the phenomenon. So, for example, once when attending a conference breakout discussion, the session leader corrected me by insisting the word "spiritual" be replaced with "religious," otherwise, we were not having a "scientific" discussion but a "theological" one. The implication was clear: theological language was clearly unscientific, and it certainly was not "queen of the sciences." For such thinkers, "dominionism" should be made a general political, sociological, or psychological category to assist in generating analytical models in this naturalistic way.[15]

In my view, the consequence of this reductionism and humanistic presuppositional approach is that there is an obfuscation and dilution of the salient conceptual distinctives.[16] The resulting pseudoscientific sociological or political analysis based upon these humanistic working assumptions can only ever neatly reclassify the entire movement as a "reaction to modernism," an expression of the "American political right," the alt-right, "Christian Nationalism," or another "conservative" movement.[17] Such an approach, I have previously argued, is rather like describing the Tyne Bridge to "Geordies" in terms of the number of nuts and bolts and the amount of metal it contains—this is accurate but irrelevant to its enormous power as a symbol of the city to those living there or in exile.[18] I argued there that

---

in this preface to his 2nd edition. He had become more hostile to the fundamentalists in the seven years between the editions.

15. The presuppositions of this method of thinking are forcefully critiqued by Plantinga, *Where the Conflict Really Lies*.

16. Lloyd-Jones, *What Is an Evangelical?*, 22–26.

17. Lawrence, "From Fundamentalism to Fundamentalisms," 88–101; McVicar, *Christian Reconstruction*, 9–12; Yurica, "Despoiling of America."

18. Macneil, "Holistic Context for Understanding," supporting PowerPoint slide 2. A "Geordie" is national slang for an inhabitant of Newcastle Upon Tyne in North-East England, a city 46 miles (74 km) south of the present Scottish border (the old Roman boundary between the nations was a wall that still runs through what is now the West-East route across Newcastle, "Hadrians Wall," which still has visible sections on the route through the city and is a tourist attraction along various sections of its 80 Roman miles.) It derives from the time when the people of Newcastle remained loyal to the English King George, when the Scots attacked the city.

Even though they eventually succumbed to the Scots attack, King George recognized their loyalty and resistance. To this day, Newcastle has remained strongly "English" in identity despite the enormous number of Scots and Irish who took up residence there for work during its heyday as a heavy industrial city. This actually made it far more "Celtic" than English (much like Liverpool), if by "English" you mean the culture of the "South"

whilst empirical profiling is useful and necessary, it is also in many philosophical and theological contexts, as Wittgenstein made clear, an approach that gives us no cogent epistemological or semantic benefit, "No fact (experience) justifies [dominion theology] and none can overturn it."[19]

Thus, my approach will be (without ignoring the insights of the humanistic mode of analysis when appropriate) to keep a focus on the distinctively *Christian* thinking and the progression of that thinking within the *Christian* tradition. I believe this is a prerequisite to understanding correctly *Christian* dominion theology. However, some elucidation to this principle should be made. The Christian tradition is broad and frequently at odds with itself; traditional Catholicism and orthodox Protestantism proceed on a substantially different epistemological basis. Orthodox Catholicism considers the natural law theology of Aquinas as normative. In contrast, classical Protestantism took its direction from Augustinianism, which denied such a natural theology was possible. We are arguing from the Augustinian presumption.[20]

Nevertheless, movements *do* exist at specific times in specific cultures, and it must be recognized that as history proceeds, the very success of a movement may mean the adoption and modification of aspects of their program by other conservative elements, as seen in the *Christian Manifesto* of Francis Schaeffer and the *Moral Majority* of Jerry Falwell.[21] There were sociological, political, and even psychological dimensions to these movements that are useful and even *necessary* to consider in *properly* comprehending them. Movements are more than ideologies, even if ideology gives a movement its basic character; the culture of the nation,

of England and the satellite shires who consider the "Northerners" like us barbarians that eat children for breakfast, and who need helicopters to drop off food for us in the winter (the latter a true story, despite Newcastle being a stopping point on the main North-South route between London and Edinburgh for centuries!).

19. Wittgenstein, *Culture and Value*, 50e.

20. I consider these issues in more detail in my *Foundations*. With the embrace of evidentialism within some sections of even the Reformed academy, and with the work of Christian analytic philosophers like Plantinga, Craig, and Swinburne, the distinction between Catholic and Protestant thought has narrowed. It is noted that some philosophers have explicitly moved from a Reformed position to a Catholic position. However, the point I make here stands: the *orthodox* or historical versions of the traditions stand substantially opposed to one another in terms of their basic epistemological commitments, i.e., the relationship between faith and reason, does reason provide a basis for faith (Aquinas), or does faith inform the basis of reason (Augustine)?

21. Wagner, *Dominion!*, 212–13.

international priorities, influences, and constraints will all affect the working out of a movement. This will most certainly be the case where "secular" appropriations have exerted a reverse influence on the praxis of parent theological movements and have even resulted in cooperation between or common cause with some non-Christian elements. History has shown that when a Christian organization enters the political arena, it often seeks self-conscious redefinition.[22]

Dominion theology has been particularly sensitive to these cultural factors. Christians around the world have responded dramatically differently to the advocation for a more muscular presence for Christians in the public square. As a rule, believers in the West, where Christianity has been tolerated on the outer rims of culture, have often opposed dominion theology, seeking earnestly again to be "quiet Christians." In contrast, those in countries that have had historically to contend for their freedom, such as in Central and South America or in parts of Africa, have frequently been far more aware of the need for a Christian reconstruction of *all* the institutions of the state. Thus, this book recognizes these variables and, alongside establishing its theological orthodoxy and philosophical coherence, argues also regarding the practical instantiation of dominionism.

Summary

I began by asserting and then proceeded to prove that dominion theology is a legitimate and distinct theological category. Owing to this status, I argued it is worth studying in terms of itself and warranting a coherent analysis to benefit both those within and those apart from the movement. Many *within* the movement are unaware of the history and theology of the movement. Many *apart* from the movement have simply collapsed dominionism into the fundamentalist category. I have asserted that my approach centers on a Calvinistic, Reformed theological analysis and is firmly philosophically Augustinian. We also observed that there are historical, sociological, philosophical, and spiritual variables to consider in our analysis.

In brief, going forward, we argue to elucidate the following two propositions and to answer the following two questions:

- Dominion theology cannot be understood apart from the historical situation or sociological context and movements that helped shape it.

22. Wagner, *On Earth as It Is*, 7.

- The emergence and dominance of secularism, scientific humanism, and scientism were major cultural factors in the development of dominion theology.[23]
- Does dominion theology continue to exist as a coherent movement or have its ideas been absorbed into the wider Christian movement?
- How are we to apply dominion theology to our lived Christian experience within our sociopolitical environment?

Chapter Outlines

Chapter 2: The Main Divisions of "Last Days" Thinking and Their Relation to Dominion Theology

Dominion theology is rooted in a specific view of the "last days" that is a specific *eschatological* understanding. This chapter gives an overview of the main divisions of eschatology (premillennialism, amillennialism, and postmillennialism) and identifies their relationship to dominion theology.

Chapter 3: The Precursors of Modern Dominion Theology

The context for the emergence of modern dominion theology was the cultural revolutions of the nineteenth and twentieth centuries. The chapter thus focuses on the identification of the cultural issues that arguably caused modern dominion theology to emerge as a *distinct* category during the 1960s.[24]

Chapter 4: The Emergence of Modern Dominion Theology

This is really the story of the work of one man, Rousas Rushdoony. His philosophy and theology are considered in depth, and it is demonstrated

23. Many readers will be unfamiliar with the rather technical word *scientism* and its relation to the concept of science. We will discuss this concept in detail at various points, but a good working definition of scientism is the belief that the only questions *worth* asking are those to which science *can* give an answer. Thus, according to this view, because "religious" and "spiritual" questions are outside of the purview of science, they are not worth asking or considering.

24. North, "Cutting Edge," 1.

how it became a coherent sociological program that envisaged an entire reconstruction of society on a Christian basis. It examines how he rejected the social gospel movement, how he developed a critique of the modern state, and how he argued for Christian "epistemological self-consciousness" from the apologetic theology and Christian philosophy of Van Til. It finishes with how he applied biblical law as the basis of societal reformation and reconstruction.

Chapter 5: The Dominionist Movement

The purpose of this chapter is to describe how the dominionist movement developed its program to the point of international recognition and presence within a diverse range of Christian practice. It examines how Rushdoony's Reconstructionist movement developed and the various emphases that emerged within different streams of the movement as it grew. It then examines how the ideas of the movement became influential more generally within Christianity.

Chapter 6: Critiques and Their Evaluation

Critics often accuse dominionists of "worldliness," because of the focus on the reformation of *temporal* culture, and of misunderstanding the relationship of the Old Testament Law to the New Testament dispensation in arguing for theonomy. I examine these core criticisms of dominionism, the responses of dominion theology to these criticisms, and evaluate their relative cogency.

Chapter 7: The Philosophy of Christian Involvement

Revivalism and fundamentalism progressively denuded modern Christian thought and culture of the rationale for active participation in the wider culture and, most specifically, in the political realm. This is where we examine how dominion theology should be applied in the cultural and political context of our present age and lived Christian experience.

Conclusion

I consider the degree that the statements and questions posed above have been answered by considering the current state and future prognosis of dominion theology.

The Three Main Divisions of "Last Days" Thinking (Eschatology) and Their Relation to Dominion Theology

Overview and Scope

IN THIS CHAPTER, ESCHATOLOGY is defined as the theological discipline of the thought regarding the "last days" and the three main divisions within it are outlined. It is not intended in this chapter to give a thorough review of the variations of eschatology within each broad category as they are vexed and nuanced but, rather, it is to identify some high-level philosophical and theological distinctives for each division, which are relevant to the closing discussion of the chapter and the wider analytical theme of the book. We are not concerned with these vexatious nuances held with searing passion by their advocates because this is not a book about the "last days" *per se* but, that said, you *cannot* avoid a discussion of the "last days" when analyzing and seeking to understand dominion theology.[1] This is because each eschatological viewpoint implies a particular philosophy of history governing the significance of the text of Scripture regarding not just the *final destination* of creation but also how the church *should exist on Earth*. By understanding this dynamic, it becomes clear as to why dominion theology has been predicated upon and historically associated with a particular set of eschatological views.

1. For example, questions within the premillennial view of "are you pre, post or mid-tribulation rapture?" are not of interest to us as they do not help us move the main argument regarding dominionism along, but they are certainly interesting questions if a full understanding of "last days" is your interest.

Definition

"Eschatology" from the *Koine* Greek *eschaton* is the doctrine of the "last things" or "last days."[2] Eschatological discourse has centered on the one thousand years ("the millennium") referred to six times in Rev 20. However, this is immediately subject to a hermeneutical caveat—*what* the millennium is and *when* it occurs or even *whether* it is "realized" (and not just a literary symbol) in the present age is a *function* of the eschatological view. In this respect, there are three basic divisions of eschatological thinking: *premillennial*, *amillennial*, and *postmillennial*. For the premillennial and postmillennial viewpoints, the millennium is normally viewed as a definite historical event that will occur at some point in the future.[3] In contrast, the amillennial view posits one, more, or even all of the following:

a. It has already been "realized"[4] in a mystical or symbolic way, fully in the *present* church age.

b. It is the growing presence of eternity in the present.[5]

c. It pertains only to the saints in heaven.

Thus, the millennial concept shapes the arguments regarding the significance and role of the church in the present with respect to the world. This is why it becomes so significant in the understanding of dominion theology, and it is appropriate to examine these perspectives more closely.

Amillennialism

Amillennialism is the largest of the eschatological groupings.[6] Various forms of amillennialism have enjoyed a continuing and serious presence up to and including the contemporary period, becoming firmly established

2. "Koine" or "common Greek" is the name given to the composite Greek dialect associated first with the conquest of Alexander the Great. As his army was drawn from throughout the Greek provinces, the nuances of the provincial languages tended to get lost in the name of military efficiency and the language became more explicit.

3. Walvoord, *Millennial Kingdom*, 4.

4. The term "realized eschatology" is associated with the work of C. H. Dodd, who first published his ideas in *The Parables of the Kingdom* (1935). Additional comments on this term are found in his revised 1961 edition, especially viii, 164.

5. Bultmann, "Problem of Eschatology (A)," in *History and Eschatology*, 38–55.

6. Price, "Millennial Issue," 7–10.

in the third century AD but with earlier pre-Christian historical precursors that we discuss shortly.[7] The Western Catholic church adopted Augustinian amillennialism and, subsequently, Reformed denominations were institutionally amillennial at their foundation, varying little from the Augustinian position as they sought to return to Augustinianism more generally in their understanding of the Christian church.[8]

That is, Luther, Calvin, and Melanchthon were *traditionally* thought of as amillennialist; Price noted an apparent oddness that the Reformers jettisoned almost everything of Roman Catholicism *except* its eschatological perspective.[9] However, this is readily mitigated in that the Catholic church had largely departed in many matters of theology and philosophy from Augustine to Aquinas's appropriation of Aristotle but *had* retained Augustine's eschatology; the Reformers sought to return to Augustine more *generally* and purge the scholastic incorporation of Aristotle in matters of theology and philosophy.

The Allegorical Method

Amillennialism, in all its forms, is founded on an *allegorical* view of Scripture—what is intended to be communicated by Scripture is something other than its "plain (literal) sense." In other words, there is some "hidden" or "eternal," "timeless," "deep meaning," or symbology employed in the text by the author to communicate beyond the limitations of the text itself. Although this might sound elaborate and sophisticated, it has been and remains very common as a literary device employed as long as there has been literature, occurring across people groups and eras, spanning

7. Notable modern amillennialists have been Bishop Christopher Wordsworth (b. 1807), Abraham Kuyper (b. 1837), Louis Berkhof (b. 1873), Albert Schweitzer (b. 1875), C. H. Dodd (b. 1884), William Hendriksen (b. 1900), and Malcolm Smith (b. 1940). Berkhof's amillennial *Systematic Theology* (1932 and 1949) was highly influential within modern Calvinism. A snapshot of this continuing influence can be found in this review of a digitization of his work: https://www.logos.com/product/5084/louis-berkhof-collection. William Hendriksen's *Israel and the Bible* (1968) is considered the "classic representation of replacement theology" (Horner, "Reformed Eschatology," 4); Malcolm is still living: his website is https://unconditionallovefellowship.com/.

8. Walvoord, *Millennial Kingdom*, 49–55.

9. Calvin was historically thought of as amillennial (Price, "Three Views") but has also been cited as foundational for postmillennialists (Bahnsen, "Calvin and Postmillennialism"). As noted shortly, some view the amillennial position as derived from the postmillennial position, with the millennium pushed into the distant future.

various genres of literature (including, very definitely, some biblical books such as Proverbs), and other Jewish literature of the same period. Indeed, some Jewish midrashic commentaries on the biblical Hebrew text argue that the most significant "meaning" of a biblical text is often one beyond the "literal" one.[10]

Thus, as a school, it cannot be summarily dismissed prima facie as some fundamentalists and other conservative evangelicals have done, and are still prone to do, when discussing it. The Bible is, after all, *also* literature, with a human as well as a divine history. It is also an important philosophical point that even if you accept *allegory*, it does not *necessarily*, in the logical sense, commit you to the amillennial eschatological view. Most commentators would accept that the book of Revelation uses allegory in *some* passages, regardless of their governing eschatological perspective or approach to scriptural interpretation.[11] However, the point remains that allegory is central to the amillennialist view and is applied most comprehensively within it.

10. To the philosophically minded reader, this might sound like "postmodernism." However, many postmodern approaches to texts, such as found in the deconstructionist movements, deny that a text holds *any* objective (or "inherent," or fixed) *meaning*. This approach to a text is clearly a far more extreme position and the logical consequence of this is that God could *not* use a text (in this case, the Bible) to teach the people his law or communicate spiritual truths. Though there were attempts to bring such "postmodern hermeneutics" into biblical interpretation, the weaknesses and limitations of the postmodern school is exegeted by philosophical theologians such as Thiselton, *Hermeneutics*, §§15–17 and postmodernism generally is comprehensively critiqued by Blackburn, both from an ethical perspective, *Practical Reason*, §9, and as a matter of epistemology (the possibility of knowing *anything* at all), *Truth*, 250.

Though such extreme views were very popular in the heyday of postmodernism (1980–2010) and will still find defenders today, few will argue that a text has such a "plasticity" of meaning that it must *always* fail to communicate what the author is saying. As Blackburn pointed out, the irony of postmodernists arguing about translations of their works exposes the ridiculousness of their own claims. The very reason why you write as an author is because you believe you *can* communicate meaning within your prose.

The secondary absurdity of the position is that it otherwise makes nonsense of not just religious literature claiming to be the word of God but all kinds of technical and instructional materials also. That is not to deny there is ambiguity; your skill as a writer constantly works to overcome it as you understand where your readers have misunderstood you. As the philosopher Wittgenstein noted, if we do our philosophy in the real world rather than in the abstract of the ivory tower of the academy, we avoid such indulgent and ridiculous excesses of belief.

11. Though there are many disputes as to how many passages are allegorical, the critical passages are Rev 18–20 (and perhaps 21); see Price, "Three Views" and "Premillennialism."

Historically, Philo (30 BC–AD 40) was first to develop the foundational allegorical hermeneutic and Origen (AD 185–254) was the first church father to apply it to eschatology in preference to Jewish premillennialism (considered later). This permitted his Hellenization of the biblical texts to reflect the primarily Hellenic context of the church after AD 100.[12] It permitted the spiritualization of potentially problematic prophetic passages regarding the future deliverance of Israel or the progress of the people of God as applicable to the church *only*.

That is, amillennialism allegorizes the church as the "kingdom of God" and it is *the church* that has become the putative heirs to *all* the promises made to Israel within the Hebrew Scriptures. The physical nation of Israel and the ethnic Jews have passed *entirely* from the purposes of God; the reformation in the twentieth century of a political nation-state called Israel was of *no* prophetic or spiritual significance. The church, in this dispensation of the kingdom, has inherited all the blessings of Abraham. Price, in discussing this view, offered this Scripture as the "proof text":

> For neither circumcision nor uncircumcision counts for anything; the only thing that matters is a new creation! And all who will behave in accordance with this rule, peace and mercy be on them, and on the *Israel of God*. (Gal 6:15–16 NET; emphasis added)[13]

With such a long history, there have been variations and important developments within amillennialism that we consider now, but they all share this basic identification of "Israel" with the church; that is, a "replacement theology."

Classical Amillennialism

In the classical amillennial system, the final judgment and eternity is viewed to begin with the second coming of Christ (the *parousia*).[14]

12. The first one hundred years of the church saw it move from a predominantly ethnically Jewish composition to a predominantly Gentile (non-Jewish) composition. This track is already seen in the narrative of the book of Acts, when Paul and Barnabas declare "they go now to the Gentiles" (Acts 18:6). The cultural separation from Judaism was accelerated when the Roman Emperor Nero understood "Christians" were not just another Jewish sect and removed from them the protection afforded to the "official" religions (of which Judaism was one).

13. Price, "Three Views."

14. *Parousia* is a direct borrowing from the original Greek word, with the literal

Importantly, it is not preceded by a literal thousand-year earthly reign of the Jewish Messiah, but the Church age itself is viewed as symbolized by the millennial concept. For Augustine and the early Latin church that followed him, this *numerus perfectus* (10 × 10 × 10) was a symbolic, indefinite period of time in which there is a perfection of God's law; it was the unfolding of the kingdom government of God in the Church Age.[15] Christ's reign is expressed through the church in the progression of *historia sacra* (sacred history) in which "radical regeneration takes place."[16] It is with his *City of God* (c. 412) that the view received its fullest expression.[17] Augustinian amillennialism envisaged increasing glory within the church ("the City of God") set against the increasing wickedness in the world but viewed the church as ultimately victorious.[18]

Augustine showed an astute awareness of previous "date setting" for the return of Christ in the early church (particularly amongst the *chiliasts*, the primitive premillennialists) and stated that, in principle, the Church Age is of indefinite duration:

> The sixth is now passing, and cannot be measured by any number of generations, as it has been said, "It is not for you to know the times, which the Father hath put in His own power."[19]

However, it is also clear that he *did* expect the return of Christ *before* AD 1000, perhaps as early as AD 650,[20] and it is this "failure" of his predictions that is believed by some twentieth-century commentators to have led to the changes within modern amillennialism: "It is the failure

meaning of "being present" in the sense of "arrival," and used in Christian theology for the return of Christ.

15. O'Daly, *Augustine's City of God*, 168. O'Daly speculates that ten is the number of the law.

16. van Oort, "End Is Now," 3–5.

17. Date of composition is given as 412–426/7 in van Oort.

18. It is this eventual triumph of the church that connects it with postmillennialism in the mind of some commentators and why some see it fundamentally as a degeneration from the postmillennial position in response to a collapse in cultural optimism and humanity's ability to reform itself. The reciprocal view is also held, that some view postmillennialism as modified amillennialism; we consider the reasons for both positions in the subsequent discussion of postmillennialism.

19. Augustine, *Complete Works*, loc. 23756 [1699].

20. Walvoord (1959) alleges 650, 1,000, and 1,044 in the iterations of post-Augustinian thought in response to the "failures" of Christ to return.

of amillennialism . . . to meet the facts of history."[21] The nineteenth and twentieth centuries were times of transition and change for amillennialism. There were conservative and liberal versions of modern amillennialism that took a very different approach in their allegorizing of Scripture.

Modern Conservative Amillennialism

As indicated above, it is often proposed that it was the perceived failure of Augustinianism that precipitated the changes in amillennialism. I believe this is only half of a half-truth, for the Reformation had reaffirmed the essentials of the Augustinian view despite these "failures," it was rather that the pressure for change came from a wider cultural crisis in late modernity, which is examined more specifically in the next chapter. For now, it is sufficient to say that for Western theologians, there was a crisis of orthodox faith *generally* in response to Darwinism and a crisis of confidence in the power of humankind to reform itself as political liberalism collapsed in response to the outbreak of major and brutal conflicts amongst the "civilized" Europeans.

Faced with this challenge, amillennialism generally became increasingly pietistic and pessimistic regarding modern culture. Though some like Masselink and Hamilton remained exponents of the traditional Calvinistic view of increasing victory within the church, by the end of the nineteenth century, Düsterdieck and Kliefoth had spiritualized the millennium as a "heavenly reality" to accommodate the perceived negative track of history.[22] Warfield also incorporated this idea of the triumph of the church as a *heavenly* event into his eschatology.[23] It was a solution that allowed the earth to atrophy yet maintained a glorious end for the saint, "a state of blessedness of the saints in heaven."[24]

21. Pentecost, *Things to Come*, 384.

22. Masselink, *Why a Thousand Years?*; Hamilton, *Millennial Faith*; Düsterdieck, *Kritisch exegetisches Handbuch*; Kliefoth, *Offenbarung des Johannes.*

23. Warfield was often understood as having a postmillennial orientation in his theology that emphasized the triumph of Christianity in history, which is why some consider amillennialism as a degraded form of postmillennialism, spiritualizing events traditionally viewed by the postmillennialists as realized on Earth. We examine this in more detail shortly.

24. Walvoord, "Millennium Issue," 430.

Modern Liberal Amillennialism

Liberal amillennialism was the second modern response to the failure of classical amillennialism. In general, it is known for its *secularization* of the biblical texts, such that the resurrection and the second advent are not considered *actual* events but *spiritual pictures* to be realized within the life of the church or by individuals alone. It, like conservative amillennialism, had both theologically optimistic and pessimistic forms:

a. The "social gospel" movement of Rauschenbusch was a positive, optimistic view with the emphasis on the church as salt and light within "the world."[25] Here, "the world" is taken to mean the social structures and sociopolitical processes. Salvation and kingdom-building was the salvation of society through both church and state rather than the individual. The socialistic emphasis of the model led to its discrediting as the practice of socialism in the twentieth-century Communist states became totalitarian.[26]

b. Dodd, Schweitzer, and Bultmann, to various degrees, represented the "liberal historicist" school. They maintained, in varying emphases and senses, a "realized" eschatology of the timeless and eternal manifested in the current age in space and time rather than in any future age.[27] This historicism waned with the twentieth century as logical positivism came to dominate many academic fields.[28]

25. Rauschenbusch, *Theology for the Social Gospel* and *Social Principles of Jesus*, both published in 1917.

26. Rauschenbusch, in his early work, enthusiastically endorses and defends a communist version of socialism, with private property viewed as a "transitional phase" of human organization. In his later work, this was far more muted, but it remains a fact of history that many subsequent advocates of the social gospel were socialist progressives politically. It is also notable, though, that he personally remained relatively orthodox in his view of the redemptive work of Christ and the need for personal salvation, in stark contrast to some of his successors that viewed "sin" as societal *against* the individual, rather than something the individual commits in offense to God. In our modern parlance, this is expressed when someone argues that many "criminals" are in fact "victims" of a society that has wronged them.

27. Schweitzer, *Historical Jesus*, 478–87; Bultmann, *Presence of Eternity*, 138–55; Dodd, *Parables*, 163–69.

28. "Historicism," more generally, was the view that there were deterministic "laws" that governed the course of history. History was moving towards an inevitable consummation. This view of history was associated most vividly with the "left wing," revolutionary Hegelians and was highly influential on Marx and his successors, who believed the destination of history was the communist utopia. As communism failed and

c. Niebuhr, though arguably neo-orthodox in his general approach to Christianity, was a major exponent of the liberal method of secularization of the biblical narrative and possessed a pessimistic view of human progress.[29] This pessimism became the dominant mode of thinking for the post-liberal theologian.

Contemporary Amillennialism

Thus, in brief, a cultural pessimism, particularly regarding the present age and an extended theological piety had become the *de facto* amillennial position in both its conservative and liberal forms during the 20th century.

Premillennialism

Premillennialism as Apostolic

Premillennialism was, according to the compendium of Peters (which cites a consensus of historical work), the exclusive position (though in a primitive form known as "chiliasm"[30]) of both Judaism and the early church fathers for the first 250 years of the church.[31] This is because the early believers, as predominantly Jewish, adopted the Jewish eschatology with some Christian reinterpretation. Jewish eschatology held, in an uneasy tension, the

---

philosophical positivism came to dominate mid-twentieth century science and thought, the historicist theses, with their metaphysical underpinnings, were viewed as fundamentally flawed and "nonsensical." See Macneil, *Foundations*, 62–67.

29. Niebuhr, *Nature and Destiny*. This was the archetypal post-liberal synthesis of Reformation and Renaissance ideas.

30. Peters, *Theocratic Kingdom*, 482–83 (this is a public domain work, and there are digitized versions out there of various quality but no official versions; the version I have is a scanned version of the book itself from a university of library). *Chilias* is Latin for "one thousand." The Latin word "mille" also means one thousand, hence the term "millennium" in modern parlance. The central belief of the chiliasts was a belief in a period of a thousand years known as the millennium. In contrast, modern premillennialism is a system of theology and is far more comprehensive, but chiliasts are still considered as representative of early premillennialism.

31. See Andrew, Peter, Philip, Thomas, John, James, Matthew, Aristio, and John the Presbyter (all these named as such by ancient historian Papias). In the period AD 100–200, the list includes Clement of Rome, Barnabus, Ignatius, Polycarp, and Papias (both disciples of John). In the period AD 200–300, Pothinus, Justin Martyr, Melito, Tatian, Irenaeus, Tertullian, Hippolytus, and Apollinaris. See Pentecost, *Things to Come*, 373–80.

ideas of the coming Messiah as *both* the suffering servant of Isa 53 and the glorious coming of the King with power and glory.[32] Which view prevailed at a particular point in history was very much subject to the conditions in the nation; during times of great prosperity and military strength, the conqueror was preferred; during occupation and subjugation, the suffering servant was thought to symbolize the nation, but there was still the hope that the deliverer would arise. This conquering Messiah vanquished Israel's enemies, oversaw a restoration of the Davidic kingdom, and the establishment of his earthly reign throughout all the world.[33] This was also clearly the expectation of Jesus' early disciples:

> So when they had gathered together, they began to ask him, "Lord, is this the time when you are restoring the kingdom to Israel?"[7] He told them, "You are not permitted to know the times or periods that the Father has set by his own authority." (Acts 1:6–7 NET)

So, Christian premillennialism interpreted Jesus' first advent as the suffering servant, and for classical premillennialism, his second advent was to be as triumphant king and judge in contrast to his "meek and lowly" first advent. This represented a distinct solution to the tension present in the Jewish eschatology and became the apostolic position, viewing the struggle of the church against the Roman Empire as an extension of the "sufferings of Christ"[34] but on the path to final victory.

The Decline of Premillennialism

Premillennialism waned with the "accommodation of Constantine" (AD 313), which fundamentally changed the way the church related to the Roman Empire as it effectively became the favored state religion.[35] The rationale of suffering and the Roman emperor as the antichrist beast of Revelation underpinning the premillennial eschatological formulation collapsed, with the result that it was virtually absent from the church from the sixth century to the early nineteenth century. It was also one of the few

32. Price, in "Premillennialism," argued that the tension was so strong that sometimes there was a split into two different events, or perhaps a Jewish and a Gentile messiah.

33. See, for example, Isa 2:1–5.

34. 1 Pet 4:13; suffering as a believer and the response to it is a recurrent feature of 1 Peter.

35. Wright, "Edict of Milan," 313.

areas of thought not revised as part of the Reformation tradition, which had generally followed the amillennial Augustinian position, with Calvin dismissing premillennialism with the few, curt words: "This fiction is too puerile to need or to deserve refutation."[36] Similarly, Luther had also explicitly rejected the "triumphalism" associated with some medieval scholars, viewing it as a "trick of the devil."[37]

Dispensationalism

However, premillennialism reemerged in the 1820s in a modern and radically distinctive form with, first, Irving and then Darby (the founder of the Plymouth brethren), which became known as dispensationalism.[38] Irving divided the age of the church into distinctive ages corresponding to the characteristics of the churches as described in the first three chapters of Revelation.[39] The final age, which Irving considered the church had entered, was the Laodicean or "lukewarm" era in which the church apostatized.[40] Darby developed Irving and formalized the rapture doctrine—a removal and rescue of the persecuted remnant church just before its final defeat. This is, at once, the most controversial and cherished doctrine of dispensationalism:

> [The] idea of a mass Rapture is considered by many to be the most preposterous belief held by Christians. At the same time, it is the Blessed Hope of many Christians today.[41]

Popular dispensationalist narratives of the twentieth century became progressively dominated with the imminence of the rapture, captured by Hal Lindsey's bestsellers during the 1970s and the 1980s.[42]

36. Calvin, *Institutes*, loc. 20132.

37. Joachim of Fiore (1135–1202) was the most important example of what is argued by some, such as Price, as the precursor for modern postmillennialism. We discuss this in more detail shortly.

38. Boettner, *Postmillennialism*, loc. 67 (this Kindle edition is an abridged form of the original print book *The Millennium*).

39. There is clearly some spiritual insight demonstrated by Irving here. You can even accept these passages as demonstrating features of the Christian and the Christian life without accepting they are a linear, historical sequence as he asserted.

40. MacPherson, *Rapture Plot*, 74; 124.

41. Missler, *Rapture*, loc. 28.

42. These are listed in the bibliography.

The second distinctive feature of dispensationalism is the church age as a parenthesis of history between the sixty-ninth and seventieth week of Dan 9:27, which was considered an interlude between the histories of Israel.[43] Dispensationalism is known for its support of the current state of Israel as fulfillment of biblical prophecy and a pessimistic belief in the increasing lawlessness of the age until the sudden appearance of Christ to rescue the chosen remnant who have not apostatized or succumbed to the antichrist's kingdom. The dispensationalist view was popularized in the Scofield Reference Bibles of 1909 and 1917, where it has since enjoyed substantial support within fundamentalist scholarship during the twentieth century. Indeed, for early fundamentalists, it was considered a test of orthodoxy, alongside explicit support for the reformation of the state of Israel as a prerequisite to Christ's return.[44] From there, its support was maintained in various movements influenced by fundamentalism, such as the main Pentecostal denominations and the later Word of Faith movement.[45] The later charismatic and "house" churches, originating within

43. Dispensationalists argue that the book of Revelation reflects this structure *literally* and *sequentially*—the first three chapters are the church age, followed by the rapture event of 4:1 ("come up here"), the resumption of the history of Israel paused in Daniel (the period of the antichrist being the "70th week"), a second coming in Rev 19, and final judgment in Rev 20. As we note immediately below, its most attractive, cohering, and distinctive feature is the straightforward mapping to scriptural events. It is of note in Daniel that the word "week" is often an interpretation by the translator of an unqualified Hebrew "seven," leading some, like Price, "Premillennialism," to argue that both years and weeks are intended—there were two distinct fulfillments of the passages, one using "weeks" that was fulfilled shortly after the book was written, and another viewed in terms of "years" after the prophetic clock had restarted.

44. Marsden, *Reforming Fundamentalism*, 198–200.

45. The early history of Pentecostalism is slightly contested, with many marking the beginning of the movement as the Azusa street outpouring of 1906–9, out of which many of the large Pentecostal denominations mark as their beginning. However, some Holiness churches had previously added the "third blessing" of speaking in tongues, the Church of God in Christ (COGIC) was founded in 1897, and the Pentecostal Holiness Church (PHC) was founded in 1898. The earliest Pentecostals were known as "Holiness Pentecostals" because of their connection with the Holiness movement.

The Word of Faith movement was most immediately associated with the ministry of Kenneth E. Hagin, who effectively founded it as an independent movement with the establishment of Rhema Bible Training Center in 1963. Though Rhema continues today with multinational campuses, many would consider Kenneth Copeland Ministries (founded 1967) as the "second wave" of the Word of Faith movement, though Copeland himself maintains strong, personal connections with the Rhema movement. However, importantly, the designation is not really denominational in the traditional governmental sense but rather reflects a networked association of autonomous organizations.

the mainline Protestant and Catholic denominations, tended to remain amillennial and rejected any support for the state of Israel during the periodic conflicts since its reformation.[46]

Premillennial Hermeneutics

The premillennial approach to Scripture and interpretation was one of its most attractive, cohering, and distinctive features. Premillennial dispensationalism employed a "plain meaning," "grammatical-historical method," which strongly emphasized a "literal" textual hermeneutic.[47] The overwhelming logic and self-confidence of premillennialism enjoyed by dispensationalists up until the late 1980s was summarized by Price:

> Most independent Bible scholars are premillennial [dispensationalists] . . . 80% of Bible prophecy has been fulfilled literally. It is

---

This lack of central authority has been both the strength and weakness of the movement, with some of the most egregious scandals originating in its ranks; but owing to this loose, voluntary model, they did not prove fatal to the movement. It should be emphasized that this model of decentralized organization is not confined to just religious organizations in the modern world but is now found widely in business and political contexts.

46. On occasions, the issue of the status of the modern state of Israel was an explosive controversy within these movements, with some influential magazines strongly arguing against the premillennial view and dismissing the need for support for the modern Jews of the state of Israel. Price, an influential member of the British House church movement, discussed this at length in his "Premillennialism" series, arguing that the shuttering of these publications was a direct result of their refusal to support the modern state of Israel.

It is of note that the issue is once again extremely politically sensitive amongst the Christian right because of the war in Gaza, with a clear separation between those that support Israel and those who do not. Having listened to many discussions on this subject, it is evident that even if the scriptural injunctions to "bless the Jews" are acknowledged, they seem to be sidestepped, either by

a. citing replacement theology, which, as we have already seen, recasts the church as Israel, thus granting no significance to a political state in the Middle East now known as Israel; or

b. separating the support for the government of the modern secular state of "Israel" from the support for the Jewish people.

I examine the Israel-Gaza war in detail here: Macneil, "HAMAS vs Israel."

47. Walvoord, *Millennial Kingdom*, 129. Here, Walvoord admits the necessity of permitting fundamentally symbolic language in the apocalyptic genre. Some other premillennialists, such as Price, reject this, insisting on a strict literalism.

illogical to view that the remaining 20% be allegorized and is not fulfilled literally.[48]

Dispensationalism as Heterodox

Yet, it should be clear that this dispensationalist view bears little resemblance to classical premillennialism, which had emphasized the corporate eschatology of the victorious messianic king, even if there was conflict and apostasy before his appearing.[49] In effect, the second advent is seen as a rescue from the kingdom of the antichrist rather than a triumphant return.[50] It is extremely culturally pessimistic, and its rapture escapism has been the source of criticism from within those who prefer a classical premillennialism.[51] Though successful and well established within the modern evangelical movement, it has been profoundly challenged as a clearly modern and previously unknown innovation in the history of the church.[52]

However, with the dramatic changes in human civilization in the last two hundred years, some consider the advent of novel doctrines in the "last days" as a fulfillment of Daniel's "increase in knowledge" (Dan 12:4) and so something "previously unknown" in the history of the church is not *a priori* dismissed. Even if we were to accept that, to be theologically responsible, the evidence for the inference would need to be overwhelming. That does not seem to be the case with the rapture doctrine; it is seldom argued in a systematic or rigorous fashion but is frequently sloganized, with any Scriptures speaking of the return of the Lord (which is not the issue) called in support of a rapture. However, those Scriptures are talking about the return of the Lord, additional strong scriptural evidence needs to be produced for the secret rapture, otherwise you are just assuming that which is supposed to be proved. Missler probably comes the closest there, but his reasoning is

48. Price, "Premillennialism," pt. 1, 02:00.

49. Rushdoony, "Postmillennialism 1 and 2."

50. The IHOP Church holds uniquely that it is the church that orchestrates the tribulation via a worldwide prayer movement and so remains closest to this victorious coming of the King Jesus after the pattern of the classical premillennialists. Although now "disgraced" because of historical sexual abuse allegations, the founder Mike Bickle spent an enormous amount of time in the book of Revelation and in expounding it.

51. Bahnsen and Gentry, *House Divided*, 365–66.

52. Gary North, "Publishers Forward," in Bahnsen and Gentry, *House Divided*, ix–lii. See also appendix B, "Late Jesus."

elaborate and granular; the previous perspicuity of the premillennial view is lost in his reinterpretation of it.

It is also a worthwhile theological observation that Paul also spoke to Timothy of "doctrines of demons" (1 Tim 4:1) manifesting as innovation of doctrine in the last days. Such a radical innovation of thought without precedent in the history of the church should be viewed as unsafe, without overwhelming evidence to the contrary.

Postmillennialism

In essence, postmillennialism is the belief that the church on Earth becomes more glorious as time passes and its influence grows until the entire Earth is Christianized; the government and rulership of God through the church is established throughout every domain of culture. The Earth then transitions into the millennial period and the Lord returns at the end of that period:

> They shall not hurt nor destroy in all my holy mountain: for the earth shall be full of the knowledge of the LORD, as the waters cover the sea. . . . Cry aloud and shout for joy, O inhabitant of Zion, for great [exalted, enthroned] in your midst is the Holy One of Israel. (Isaiah 11:9; 12:6; amplification mine)[53]

Thus, the postmillennial view has an optimistic and triumphant view of the church and is militant regarding its outreach to the world. It expects evangelism to succeed and nations to be discipled.

The Scholarly Rejection of Postmillennialism

With that brief synopsis, some introductory remarks are immediately necessary before we consider the details, owing to the scholarly prejudice against postmillennialism. The prevalence of amillennialism within the Reformed denominational churches and the domination of premillennial

53. Isaiah 11–12 are recognized as passages important to eschatological thinking. Premillennialists consider them a picture of the millennial period itself, in which there has been a renewed and transformed ecology. Some amillennialists would see it as a picture of the growth of the church age. Most postmillennialists would site this verse as supporting a postmillennial view. Here lies the challenge of the hermeneutic you bring to a biblical passage—prophetic passages sometimes do not have sufficient data to stand on their own and will be interpreted according to your framework of understanding.

dispensationalism within the modern evangelical movement has meant that postmillennialism has been largely ignored and dismissed by many biblical scholars in the nineteenth and twentieth centuries. Subsequently, there is a problem with accurately understanding and assessing postmillennialism because of its misrepresentation within the pietistic and pessimistic eschatology so prevalent during this recent period, Rushdoony describing the problem thus:

> Although postmillennialism has a long history as a major, and perhaps a central, interpretation, it is summarily read out of court by many on non-Biblical grounds.[54]

That is, just because it has had this minority status and was effectively excommunicated from scholarly discourse does not mean it is without merit or is illegitimate *in principle.* Just because a doctrine or experience was missing from the general Christian consciousness for centuries does not disqualify it from being legitimately Christian. We need only consider the Pentecostal experience of speaking in tongues, which was virtually absent for centuries of the church but reemerged in the closing years of the nineteenth century within the Holiness movement.[55]

54. Kik, *Eschatology of Victory*, vii–ix.

55. This is an obvious departure from the cessationism common within Reformed thought. However, having spent many years in churches and fellowships where the "spiritual gifts" of 1 Cor 12 were commonplace, this proposition is not problematic for me. Additionally, spiritual gifts are often characteristic of revivals and renewals in Reformed contexts, even if they are not acknowledged as such. Of rather more interest is the question as to why Calvin rejected the supernatural manifestations and the "miraculous," this helps us understand his position. He reacted against the reliance of the Catholics on "miraculous" signs, such as weeping Marys, levitating saints, and what he saw in the rituals of the "stage players" acting like the apostles in the laying on of hands, despite the obvious defectiveness and corruption of their doctrine and character.

I concur strongly with him that spiritual gifts and the miraculous have been and continue to be used illegitimately by those seeking to justify their entire ministry on this supernatural basis, and that the word of God should be the standard by which a ministry is judged. However, I would also argue that he was too quick to declare the gifts redundant, even on his own logic. See Macneil, *Foundations*, 76, 76n30.

The point I make there is that Calvin had assumed the church had spread to all parts of the earth and was thus established, and *therefore*, the gifts were redundant; that was and is not accurate. Conversely, because there were and are so many "unreached" ethnic groups yet to hear the gospel, the need for the gifts is as strong as it was at the foundation of the church. Each generation needs a demonstration of the power of God, or it, like the second generation of Israel that came out of Egypt, will turn away from God to idols.

So, our first observation is that the optimism and practical program of the postmillennial view is the exact conceptual opposite of the pietistic emphasis and the pessimism of the modern iterations of the alternative positions. This explains its marginalization and absence from many scholarly discussions rather than any implicit intellectual deficit or incoherence. Some have attempted to argue postmillennialism is fundamentally incoherent in response to the worsening of societal and cultural conditions, but such an argument is logically fallacious and reflects their own subjective biases and prejudices.[56] Just because a society is in a state of decay does not mean the church cannot become radical and militant, leading to a restored and prosperous world, fit for the King to inherit. You may not believe that, but that is not a matter of logic; it is a matter of belief and faith in God to change the world.

However, the decay of our society and culture is necessary to put in a proper context to build a reform program as dominion theology seeks to do, and the underlying cultural reasons for this malaise I engage within the next chapter. In this section, we want to give special attention to the theology of the view. The purpose is to describe how postmillennialism has been conceived and then to reveal what I think *really* characterizes the view so that it becomes useful for the closing discussion of the chapter.

Postmillennialism as Modified Amillennialism

For proponents of this view, postmillennialism was generated from the problem posed for medieval amillennialists by the perceived failure of Augustinian eschatology. As we saw, for neo-Augustinians, the problem of cultural decay is solved by reimagining Augustine's dualism. The cycle of falling away is matched by a greater cycle of revival. There is increasing victory in the church. Eventually, the City of God prevails throughout the whole earth. So, for example, Walvoord asserts that for the most literal of the postmillennialists, "[they differ] only from the amillennial concept [of the millennium] *in the idea of growing triumph and final victory before the Second Advent.*"[57] Similarly, the influential amillennial systematic theologian Berkhof identified a group of scholars in the Netherlands during the sixteenth and seventeenth century that he considered the first to be

56. See also Riddlebarger, "Princeton and the Millennium."

57. Walvoord, *Millennial Kingdom*, 25.

postmillennial on the basis of their envisaging of an eventual *earthly* triumph of the church in a far future.[58]

It must also be noted in opposition to this that the converse is also posited by both Walvoord and Riddlebarger.[59] That is, postmillennialism reverts to amillennialism under the weight of cultural decay. For Riddlebarger, it is seen as an innovation from the *historical* postmillennialism within the old Princeton school.[60] She then identifies Warfield as the transitionary figure representing its reversion into amillennialism by his supernaturalization of the glorious state of the saints to simply a heavenly, rather than earthly, reality. This seems the more plausible view, particularly with the parallel decay of triumphant classical premillennialism into culturally pessimistic dispensationalism.

Postmillennialism as Heterodox and a Product of Philosophical Modernism

For proponents of this view, the radical optimism that is said to characterize postmillennialism is viewed as rooted in the Enlightenment view of the inevitability of progress and the "early modern" confidence of man to solve his own problems with the application of the faculty of reason. So, for example, Price gives only a two-hundred-year window for its history and suggests Daniel Whitby as the founder.[61] Similarly, Walvoord identifies Whitby as the Unitarian founder and enumerates Snowden and Brown as embracing and incorporating the evolutionism of nineteenth-century science with its view of the inevitability human progress.[62] Both Price and Walvoord argue that the tendency of postmillennialism is towards theological liberalism and Price asserts that the postmillennialist sentiment is the precursor of both fascist and communist conceptions of a golden age.

Assessing Postmillennialism

To be theologically responsible, the question to be answered is whether the salient features of postmillennialism are seen throughout the history of the

58. Berkhof, *Systematic Theology*, 716.

59. Riddlebarger, "Princeton and the Millennium," 36.

60. The very fact that the major Princeton seminary was postmillennial in its outlook should also furnish evidence against it as only a minor school of thought.

61. Price, "Three Views."

62. Walvoord, *Millennial Kingdom*, 28–32.

church or whether it was simply, as suggested in the models above, generated by theological pressures and responses to the *zeitgeist* of the middle and late modern age. The latter is clearly a far weaker theological position than the former position. However, I believe the criticisms presented above are weak and inconclusive, and we can safely assert that postmillennialism has a solid, continuous presence in the great theologians of the church. Let us consider the weakness of these arguments and the refutations in detail.

Firstly, Whitby was not an orthodox Christian in any respect but was first a Unitarian and his liberal postmillennialism, which converged easily with classical political liberalism and the reforming priorities of amillennialism, reflected a general cultural optimism rather than a view arrived at through theological analysis and reconstruction.[63] It must also be said that from a logical point of view, even *if* the secularization or dechristianization of the millennial concept was applied within utopian fascist or liberal theological thought, that does not invalidate the *authentic* postmillennial position.

So, for example, in what was the twilight of British classical liberalism at the close of the nineteenth and the beginning of the twentieth centuries, it was not unusual to hold the political ideal that the "kingdom of God" could be *legislated* into existence by the "Mother of all Parliaments"; the British Empire would indeed "endure for a thousand years."[64] This figure

63. Walvoord, *Millennial Kingdom*, 22–23.

64. This phrase was made famous in the wartime speech of Sir Winston Churchill on June 18, 1940. The British Empire had already endured for around five hundred years, and the British believed it would endure as a matter of "Manifest Destiny." Thus, reading the speech, you can tell he was using a phrase from the consciousness of the British liberal elite of Europe for the previous century. An interesting window on this period of British history is found on https://www.britishempire.co.uk/. Equally compelling is the dramatic collapse of the British Empire and the power of Britain generally that was to occur in the subsequent decades to this speech, to the degree that, in 1976, Britain was reduced to an IMF bailout to stabilize its economy and suffered major social unrest until the Thatcher election of 1979, which dealt directly with the impact of large-scale immigration.

This ushered in a period of major reforms and recovery for the next decade, though punctuated with left-wing violence and unrest up to her reelection in 1982 with the largest majority for a peacetime leader; she then assaulted the hold of left-wing unions on public life and transformed the economic relations and expectations of the people. The election of Reagan in the US, who had similar "monetarist" and anti-socialist social ideals, began what was called the "special relationship" between the nations, though recent British prime ministers have burnt that bridge in their close alignment with the EU. An in-depth study of this period and the obvious resemblance to the current position of the UK, which is undeniably in political and social decline, is found in Chadha, "Might the

was a deliberate biblical allusion, and it was no coincidence that the Balfour Declaration, indicating the British support for a Jewish homeland, belonged to this period.[65] Thus, the clear distinction between the two is exemplified succinctly by Boettner:

> This [authentic postmillennialist] view is . . . to be distinguished from that optimistic but false view of human betterment and progress held by Modernists and Liberals which teaches that the Kingdom of God on earth will be achieved through a natural process by which mankind will be improved and social institutions will be reformed and brought to a higher level of culture and efficiency. This latter view presents a spurious or pseudo-Postmillennialism and regards the Kingdom of God as the product of natural laws in an evolutionary process, whereas orthodox Postmillennialism regards the Kingdom of God as the product of the supernatural working of the Holy Spirit in connection with the preaching of the Gospel.[66]

This failure to be granular in the treatment of postmillennial thought is surely sufficient to justify the proposition that so-called liberal "post-millennialism" is radically different from theologically conservative post-millennialism, and the former cannot be applied as an effective argument in rapidly dismissing postmillennialism *generally*. Similarly, Berkhof's remarkable brevity regarding the nature of *theological* nineteenth-century and pre-WWI postmillennialism and his equation of "modern" postmillennialism with the "social gospel" seems to be committing, and satisfied with, the same category error.[67] This is a serious omission as this period had been described as the previous height of its popularity by both Walvoord and Price.

Secondly, the general support for the thesis that the failure of Augustinianism generated postmillennialism seems very weak for the following reasons:

1. There seems little evidence of an immediate reaction to the failure of Augustinian expectations. To assert that Joachim of Fiore (b. 1132) was postmillennial seems to be another example of improper use of the designation. His eschatology was radically heterodox and is viewed by

---

UK Really Need."

65. Macneil, "HAMAS vs Israel," §4.2.

66. Boettner, *Postmillennialism*, loc. 74.

67. Berkhof, *Systematic Theology*, 794–97.

some postmillennialists as radically dispensationalist because of his conception of the ages of the Father (Law), Son, and Spirit (grace).[68]

2. Although suggested as a "post-Reformation" movement, history seems to show that the Reformation thinkers were content to adopt the view that they could resume the building of the kingdom *as envisaged by Augustine* now that a correct foundation had been restored.[69] Both Luther and Calvin believed that the progress of the gospel was inevitable once the proper ministration had been restored, which, of course, is well documented as the origin of Luther's polemic in the failure to convert the Jews.[70]

However, Riddlebarger's view of Warfield's position in proposing amillennialism was simply an aberration of postmillennialism is, at first appearance, stronger. Her assertion is accurate that though Warfield considered himself a postmillennialist, he certainly spiritualized postmillennial concepts, allowing some of his immediate heirs to move straightforwardly to an amillennial position.[71] Nevertheless, she neglects to mention that Warfield was *also* important to the developing fundamentalist movement and, in contrast, his putative heirs in that movement were dispensationalist premillennialists.[72] Thus, it would be contradictory to assert that his eschatology inevitably collapsed into amillennialism. Rather, it appears that with postmillennialism, we are dealing with a *distinctive* category, and it is to the analysis of this category that we now turn.

Postmillennialism on Its Own Terms

The counterarguments presented above are not considered to be definitive or exhaustive. They are simply posited to demonstrate that the original arguments were not sufficient to dismiss postmillennialism in the arbitrary manner it has been dismissed. Postmillennialism is at least *possible* to posit as a distinct analytic category. However, it is now expedient to

68. Joachim, *Expositio in Apocalypsim*; Rushdoony, *God's Plan for Victory*, loc. 119; Anderson, "Joachim of Fiore," 2.

69. Pentecost, *Things to Come*, 26–33.

70. Luther, "Efficacy of the Gospel" and "Vorrede auff die Epistel [Preface to the letter]."

71. Riddlebarger, "Princeton and the Millennium," 21.

72. Barr, *Fundamentalism*, 262–63.

advance the positive argument in and of itself to establish the strong case for postmillennialism as a distinct theological category. As part of our argument, we identify that modern iterations of eschatological thought have tended to obscure previous historical similarities and attitudes towards the "last things." Eschatological orthodoxies have become more like ideological prejudices to which allegiance is demanded; this prevents a recognition of there being far more in common between the positions than is often admitted in contemporary dogma.

At the most basic level, postmillennialism is the chronologically opposite position to premillennialism. It believes in the return of Christ *after* the millennial period. The millennial period is that in which the church had previously established the fullness of the kingdom on Earth, considering the Great Commission of Matt 28 as literally fulfilled. Disciples have been made of all nations in their entirety. Jesus then returns and is welcomed to take his place in the kingdom on earth, with the final judgment at that point and eternity beginning. There is no concept of a remnant or a rapture, for

> The LORD owns the earth and all it contains, the world and all who live in it. (Ps 24:1 NET)

> For there will be universal submission to the LORD's sovereignty, just as the waters completely cover the sea. (Isa 11:9 NET)

Gentry summarizes the postmillennial view in this way:

> [Postmillennialism is] the view that Christ will return to the earth after the Spirit-blessed Gospel has had overwhelming success in bringing the world to the adoption of Christianity.[73]

I would concur with Gentry here, but I would add that the evidence supports the view that the distinct and authentic contemporary postmillennial position reasserts the primitive triumphalism of *both* the early *premillennialists* and augments it with the kingdom-building spirit of the *amillennialist* Reformers. It is the recapturing of a common radical optimism, an engagement with the world to convert and reclaim it rather than retreat or separate from it. It is, in this important sense, part of the apostolic vision of the church at its foundation to "go into the world and make disciples of all nations."[74] Discipling is taken to mean a distinctive "Christian culture":

73. Gentry, *Dominion*, 79.

74. Matt 28:19; Mark 16:15. (This is my translation of the first clause of the Greek;

> If we believe that the main and final goal of the Christian life is heaven, or the salvation of our souls, we will be indifferent to history and the world around us. . . . The goal is God's Kingdom, His purpose for humanity and the world.[75]

Although allegory and spiritualization are widely applied in postmillennial hermeneutics, in contrast to the early period of the church, which we have already seen was premillennial in outlook, the task or responsibility of the church in Matt 28 is probably taken in the *most literal* and *emphatic* manner by the modern postmillennialists, in contrast to the cultural pessimism and cynicism of dispensationalism and modern amillennialism.

Postmillennialism is a presuppositional position of victory in every realm, not just the "City of God" as in Augustine. It *is* a much stronger hermeneutic than simply a general parallel progress of history the of world and a church *eventually* triumphant, as might be seen in Augustinian theology. Augustine was dualistic and this important philosophical distinction, I believe, classifies his theology as predominantly amillennial.[76] In contrast, postmillennialism uses the perceived triumph of Christ as a present reality within the life of the church on Earth, not deferred to heaven or considered as a spiritual picture as we saw in some of the modern Augustinians, such as Warfield. The church is not the ark of the Catholic church, the chosen remnant of the Protestant dispensationalists, or the mystical kingdom of the saints in heaven of modern amillennialists:

> If I believe that Christ will soon rapture me from this evil world, this will have a practical effect on my life very different from a belief that I shall see the world get worse and worse, and live through a fearful tribulation. Again, if I believe that the world will see the progressive triumph of Christ's people until the whole world is Christian and a glorious material and spiritual era unfolds, I shall be motivated very much differently from either a premillennial or an amillennial believer.[77]

BYZ/BGT are identical except for punctuation.)

75. Cope, *God and Political Justice*, loc. 359; Rushdoony, *God's Plan for Victory*, loc. 36–39.

76. Boettner, *Postmillennialism*, loc. 162. Augustine, in his younger days, had been attracted to Manichaeanism, which was highly dualistic and emphasized the polarities of good and evil, spirit and flesh.

77. Rushdoony, *God's Plan for Victory*, loc. 72–77.

Rather, it is the entirety of human culture that is to be redeemed and converted by Christian action in every sphere, not just the church:

> [It] is also an error to make the church central to God's plan and purpose . . . and therefore [see] the church as the sphere of victory. This led to a very high doctrine of the church, both in Rome and Protestantism. If our hope for the futures of man and Christ's world is only in the church, then we will stress the church as man's hope. The church will be over-stressed because it is man's only hope. Neither the state, the Christian family, nor the school, nor any other institution offers hope, and none are seen as therefore central or important.[78]

Postmillennialism argues for the complete and total victory of Christ in the current world:

> [P]ostmillennialism is the eschatology of victory. . . . The notion of defeat does not go well with the fact of an omnipotent God and a conquering Christ. [Postmillennialism] takes with total seriousness and a totality of meaning the validity of Romans 8:28, "And we know that all things work together for good to them that love God, to them who are called according to his purpose."[79]

It rejects, in its entirety, the apocalyptic dualism of Hellenistic Western Christianity:

> [T]here is an Implicit Manichaeanism in premillennialism and in amillennialism. The material world is surrendered to Satan, and the spiritual world is reserved to God.[80]

Postmillennialism, in common with amillennialism on this point, rejects the biblical literalism of premillennialism as inapplicable to prophecy as a matter of interpretative principle:

> [I]t must be noted that premillennialism violates one of the most basic principles of sound biblical hermeneutics. . . . The fact that so many other scriptures are interpreted to fit in with a particular [literal] understanding of Revelation 20 indicates that far too much weight is being placed on a single text [and] requires the book as a whole be interpreted futuristically. . . . The truth or

78. Rushdoony, *God's Plan for Victory*, loc. 44.

79. Rushdoony, *God's Plan for Victory*, loc. 58–60.

80. Rushdoony, *God's Plan for Victory*, loc. 204.

> falsity of amillennialism or postmillennialism does not [require] the futuristic approach.[81]

In this respect, Postmillennialists generally favor a partial-preterist view of the book of Revelation and of prophecy in general. It should be noted that preterism is not limited to postmillennialism but is a general view of prophecy. The full preterist view holds that "the tribulation" of Revelation occurred in our distant past, in the first century, and the millennium has already passed.[82] The former is accepted but the latter is rejected by postmillennialists. Postmillennialists view prophecy as progressively fulfilled or prefigured in previous ages and generally favor covenant theology, which posits a single continuing intratrinitarian covenant of redemption that structures history from the creation mandate of Adam to eternity.[83] However, postmillennialists agree with the preterists that a literalistic approach to prophecy is naïve and immature: "literalism leads to absurdity in Revelation."[84]

Thus, being also covenant theologians, postmillennialists are hostile to any form of dispensationalism that divides history up into distinct ages in which God deals with man according to a distinct set of principles in each:

> Dispensationalism limits the Bible and its relevance; it wrongly divides the word of truth. It denies the wholeness of Scripture, and the fact that God does not change, nor does His law, nor His plan of salvation, change from age to age.[85]

Postmillennialism also takes issue with the amillennial view about the nature of the interadvental period. It objects to both forms of contemporary amillennialism that either internalizes the "kingdom" as a spiritual entity or limits it to the heavenly state of saints in heaven:

> Scripture makes it abundantly clear that *this* earth . . . is a part of the kingdom. Christ's messianic authority and reign extend over *all* of heaven and earth. . . . Every nation on earth is presently under the dominion of Christ. . . . Amillennialism fails to deal

81. Mathison, *Postmillennialism*, 176–77. See also Boettner, *Postmillennialism*, loc. 95.

82. Ice and Gentry, *Great Tribulation*, 11.

83. Rushdoony, "History I"; Mathison, *Dispensationalism*, 13–19.

84. Ice and Gentry, *Great Tribulation*, 173.

85. Rushdoony, *God's Plan for Victory*, loc. 119.

> with these scriptural truths satisfactorily. . . . [It] fails to deal with the many passages that tell us about the progressive growth of the messianic kingdom . . . that grows to fill the whole earth."[86]

In contrast to the mysticism that finds its way into premillennial dispensationalism (particularly within the charismatic churches) and the spiritualization embedded in Old Princetonian amillennialism, postmillennialists who adopt the Calvinistic Reformation position tend to emphasize Christian humanism rather than supernaturalism:

> We don't have God-ordained prophets anymore. Jesus Christ was the final prophet, priest and king. . . . Yet all men have a prophetic task . . . [the] successful proclamation of the word [into] every sphere of life.[87]

Summary

So, we can see, even in our brief exploration of postmillennialism, that it stands on a far more robust theological and scriptural foundation than its opponents have been prepared to admit. We have written far more in our brief treatment above than some of the most influential systematic theologies of the twentieth century. It is of little surprise, then, that so little understanding of the tenor and the approach to Scripture of postmillennialism has been demonstrated in those works. Importantly, we also identified that the attitudinal orientation to and presumption of Christian triumph was historically common to most eschatological thought; it is a modern aberration that it descended into mysticism and pessimism.

Eschatology and Dominionism

The purpose of this section is to focus the previous explanations and to establish which of the eschatological viewpoints has served as the historical antecedent to the dominion theology of the twentieth century. It is only necessary to briefly examine the attitude of the modern form of each eschatological position to the concept of societal reconstruction within the twentieth century for it to become obvious which viewpoint was the

86. Mathison, *Postmillennialism*, 180. Emphasis added in first instance.

87. North, "Importance of the 700 Club." Of course, I can disagree with North regarding the spiritual gifts but agree with him regarding the prophetic task.

historical antecedent to the modern form of dominion theology, which began to emerge during the 1960s.

Premillennialism

In the previous section, it was seen that dispensationalist premillennialism viewed the closure of the age in apostasy and the time of the antichrist. This historical pessimism was seen most strongly in the early fundamentalists of the 1920s, who effectively withdrew from social engagement in American public life after the intellectual humiliation of the Scopes "evolution" trial.[88] Their radical dispensationalism created a "holy remnant" mentality that they were the holy faithful at the end of the age that would be raptured away.

Culture was considered apostate; the only hope was revivalism to save as many souls as possible before the imminent coming of the Lord.[89] Social action was considered a distraction from the real task of evangelism and the social gospel of Rauschenbusch as liberal-modernist apostasy.[90] Thus, during the 1950s, the premillennial dispensationalist and prominent radio preacher Rev. J. Vernon McGee declared, "You don't polish brass on a sinking ship."[91] The implication was clear—civilization was sinking, so social action was meaningless—the Christian should be concerned with revivalism alone.[92] Thus, it should be obvious at this point that twentieth-century dispensational premillennialism would be philosophically opposed to the cultural optimism of dominion theology and would consider it theologically heretical.

88. Barr, *Fundamentalism*, 349n6.

89. Marsden, *Reforming Fundamentalism*, 5–8.

90. Marsden, *Reforming Fundamentalism*, 71.

91. Quoted in Rushdoony, *God's Plan for Victory*, loc. 175.

92. Marsden, *Reforming Fundamentalism*, 7. This makes the interesting point of how social action was not always excluded from classic premillennialism. The dispensationalism of the fundamentalists is perhaps one of the key differences between conservative evangelicalism and fundamentalism. It should also be noted that some dispensationalists *do* now combine their revivalism with social action and political involvement; it is arguable that one of the biggest changes in the last decade since I first wrote the dissertation this book is based on has been an increasing sense of social responsibility amongst many believers of different traditions. We consider both issues further in a later section.

Amillennialism

Amillennialism, with its emphasis on the kingdom hermeneutic and its adoption by the Reformation churches, might be considered more amenable to the reformist program of dominion theology. However, during the twentieth century, the failure of classical messianic liberalism and the cultural pessimism regarding the possibility of human progress meant the direct heirs of Princeton moved from postmillennialism to emphasizing the pietistic aspect of Warfield's transitional eschatology.[93] This perceived cultural decay and lawlessness of the century favored the view of the "other worldliness" of the kingdom and the escape to the inner life of a believer, a pietistic rumination on the "kingdom" of the saints in heaven. During the 1930s, the pietistic emphasis gained almost complete ascendancy in modern amillennialism. Rushdoony characterized modern amillennialism thus:

> In reality, amillennialism holds that the major area of growth and power is in Satan's Kingdom, because the world is seen as progressively falling away to Satan, the church's trials and tribulations increasing, and the end of the world finding the church lonely and sorely beset. There is no such thing as a millennium or a triumph of Christ and His Kingdom in history. The role of the saints is at best to grin and bear it, and more likely to be victims and martyrs. The world will go from bad to worse. . . . The Christian must retreat from the world of action in the realization that there is no hope for this world, no world-wide victory of Christ's cause, nor world peace and righteousness. . . . The material world is surrendered to Satan, and the spiritual world is reserved to God.[94]

Hence, it should also be clear that though amillennialists may have once spoken the language of modern dominion theology with its emphasis on kingdom-building in the present Church age, it has retreated into mysticism and pietism. Its new emphasis is the kingdom within and among *believers*.

93. Riddlebarger, "Princeton and the Millennium."

94. Rushdoony, *God's Plan for Victory*, loc. 164, 202.

Postmillennialism

Thus, by default, we must look to postmillennialism as the true historical antecedent to dominion theology, and it is possible to establish, without question, that the burden of evidence supports this view. I proposed in an earlier section that distilled down to what it represents in attitudinal and theological terms, it is the recapturing of the primitive triumphalism of both the early premillennialists and the kingdom-building spirit of the amillennialist Reformers. This has been elaborated during its revival in the second part of the twentieth century in the work of Rousas Rushdoony. Rushdoony, considered the father of the modern dominionist movement, had an obvious postmillennial eschatology. He summarizes the interpretation of postmillennialism as the call to fulfill the creation mandate of Genesis by redeeming the nations and institutions of the world:

> [P]ostmillennialism . . . sees salvation as victory and health in time and eternity, it sees therefore a responsibility of the man of God for the whole of life. . . . People out of every tongue, tribe, and nation shall be converted, and the word of God shall prevail and rule in every part of the earth. There is therefore a necessity for [social and political] action, and an assurance of victory.[95]

A single qualification is worth mentioning here as reflected in our discussion so far. Though most dominionists *are* postmillennial in operational terms and in theology, there is no *logical* necessity that they be so; it is rather that postmillennialism remains the only *modern* position that encourages a positive psychological disposition to and faith for the future. We shall see as we progress in our discussion that there were and are dominionists who are *operationally* postmillennial but are not *theologically* postmillennial.

Summary and Concluding Remarks

We began this chapter by considering the definition and history of the three main eschatological views: premillennialism, amillennialism, and postmillennialism. We noted that postmillennialism had been dismissed as simplistic, naïve, mystical, and guilty of ignoring the realities of history because of its radical optimism.[96] I then asserted that those many critiques

95. Rushdoony, *God's Plan for Victory*, loc. 219.

96. Mathison, *Dispensationalism*, xi; Walvoord, *Millennial Kingdom*, 34–36; Rushdoony, "Postmillennialism 1 and 2."

miss the salient point that postmillennialism is recovering the triumphal emphasis of both the classical forms of amillennialism and premillennialism. Hence, it is possible to understand why Rushdoony and Mathison, both scathing critics of premillennial dispensationalism, can illustrate that the early historical creeds, including those of the classical premillennialists, viewed a triumphant king coming in glory and not, as in modern iterations of the positions, on a rescue mission to the remnant.[97]

Consequently, it was possible for Bahnsen to argue extensively for John Calvin holding a postmillennial, rather than the amillennial, view commonly ascribed to him. He cited recent scholarly research that emphasized his reforming role, both within the civic culture and within theology, was based upon a conviction of Christian progress and victory within history.[98] Mathison was similarly emphatic in this unwavering belief in the Christian triumph in history: "Today's newspaper is then [not] an excuse for anxiety or apathy."[99] Finally, owing to the mysticism and pessimism incorporated into the dispensationalist and amillennial view, it was possible for Rushdoony to argue that they have succumbed to the principle of reason and contemporary experience as the arbiter of all things, adopting the philosophical position from the Enlightenment rather than one rooted in a Christian philosophy of history.[100] In contrast, the proper use of reason by the Christian is to elevate the promises of Scripture as our expectation.

Thus, my key argument in concluding this chapter is that postmillennialism alone in its conservative form retains the historic vision of Christian victory as its central hermeneutic, that was once held far more generally within the Christian church. The concept of Christian victory is not a modern aberration peculiar to postmillennialism but had historical expression in premillennialism and amillennialism. However, it *is* the absolute opposite intellectual position to both in their *modern* forms, premillennial dispensationalism and amillennial mysticism. Though postmillennialism is conceptually distinct from dominion theology, it finds natural expression through the militant language of dominion theology because of the *practical implications* of the viewpoint. The next chapter

97. Mathison, *Dispensationalism*, 245–48; Rushdoony, "Postmillennialism 1 and 2."

98. Bahnsen, "Calvin and Postmillennialism," 32–96. It should be noted that Luther explicitly emphasized the wider salvific effects of the gospel on the culture, but rejected (according to Price, "Three Views") the postmillennial vision of the total triumph of the church.

99. Mathison, *Postmillennialism*, xii.

100. Rushdoony, "Introduction" in Marcellus, *Eschatology of Victory*, vii–ix.

examines how the humanistic component of the cultural equation emerged before considering, in the following chapter, how it combined with the postmillennial viewpoint to mark the emergence of dominionism.

The Precursors of Dominion Theology

Introduction

THE ARGUMENT I AM making in this chapter is that by thoroughly analyzing the changes, tensions, and contradictions within the metanarratives of the Western culture over the last two centuries, it becomes inevitable that a Christian counterculture of dominion theology would emerge. I was emphatic in the introduction regarding the importance of a cross-disciplinary approach to properly understanding the context and emergence of dominion theology. Consequently, this chapter is more like a mountain climb than the trail-walking of the previous chapters, but it should be a rewarding climb if you persevere. It is probably the most difficult chapter in the book and the most technical one and, as such, is probably not suited to every reader, so feel free to skip forward as required or even omit it altogether if your interest is more specifically with dominion theology.

Theology, Philosophy, and Culture

The first point to make is that it is a frequent fallacy of evangelical theologians to pay insufficient attention to the *zeitgeist* of their situation in time and to give an ahistorical account of the church in time, sometimes ingeniously described as "prophetically energized interpretation of historical facts."[1] Divine providence becomes a means by which one sidesteps their culture, whereas I have previously argued theology is strongly associated,

1. C. Peter Wagner, "Foreword," in Hamon, *Eternal Church*, 12. Though this book has much to commend it, it has a single sentence on Reconstructionism—hardly an adequate assessment of a major realignment in theology of the church.

influenced, and influences the intellectual and cultural milieu.[2] It is also an error of the late modern period, with its mythological evolutionary scientism, to desire to reinterpret the entire past in terms of the present with nothing but the "autonomous mind of man."[3]

We will comment more on this at the end of the chapter, but for now, the point we are making is that both modernism and postmodernism, modernity and postmodernity, collided in this era, and it is for this reason that this chapter undertakes a philosophical overview of the nineteenth and twentieth centuries to properly provide the historical context and intellectual diagnosis of the era.[4]

The Rise and Fall of Science

The early decades of the twentieth century in the Western academy were marked, perhaps defined, by the analytic philosophy of Moore and Russell, which argued for a rigorously empiricist theory of knowledge and was forcefully dismissive of any "higher way of knowing" by religious experience.[5] Russell went on to be a key personality within the Vienna Circle during the 1930s and in the development of the anti-metaphysical tenor of its logical positivism, which downgraded religious experience as non-cognitive nonsense.[6] The Circle had issued a manifesto entitled (when translated into English) "The Scientific View of the World."[7]

2. Macneil, "Scripture and Post-Darwinian Controversy."

3. Rushdoony, *Mythology of Science*, 1–4; Rushdoony, *Limits of Reason*, loc. 88.

4. "Modernity" and "modernism" are readily separated as distinct categories—modernity refers to the technologies of the era, those sociological aspects that result from the innovations of the era; modernism refers to the set of ideas and philosophy. With "postmodernity" and "postmodernism," this separation has not been maintained; most writers use the terms indiscriminately. See Lyon, *Postmodernity*, 6–7.

5. Russell's basic philosophical text that served as a primer for a generation of philosophy students is *The Problems of Philosophy*. Moore was famous for his rigorous analytic method and his *Defense of Common Sense*. He had an entire issue of the *Philosophy* journal published in his honor at his death; it was his rigorous *method* rather than his conclusions that had generated such admiration. See also Russell, *Western Philosophy*, 789.

6. It is important to distinguish *logical* positivism from the "paleopositivism" of Auguste Comte a century earlier, but both forms of positivism emphatically rejected metaphysics and elevated science to scientism ("the only questions that are legitimate and are worth asking are those that science can answer"); Ayer, *Language, Truth and Logic*, 56–58.

7. Carnap et al., *Wissenschaftliche Weltauffassung*, 75–116. This is the English translation

Science was to be elevated to *scientism*, and it was the application of the principles of logical positivism, *the* (not "a") scientific view of the world, which would solve *all* the problems of humanity by liberating it from its bondage caused by the metaphysical pollution of culture.[8] So, Russell was to assert in his apologetic that

> questions of fact can only be decided by the empirical methods of science . . . questions that can be decided without appeal to experience are either mathematical or linguistic.[9]

This was a form of what became known as the "verification principle" that a proposition in any sphere of culture (not just religion and science) was meaningful *if* and *only if* it was capable of *empirical* testing. This was a cathartic, intoxicating, and radical principle that, from the mid-1930s for the next two decades, exerted a huge influence across the humanities and the sciences; any proposition or theory that failed this test was jettisoned as "non-sense." Any talk of theological and spiritual matters obviously failed this criterion, an empirical test for God or for God's action in the world was precluded by the very concept of God, and the positivist summary of religious thought was it makes "non-sense" to talk about a being called God or of God acting in the world. However, the principle also caught the theories of the softer social sciences and the speculative or mathematical sciences, who struggled to find empirical ways of understanding their disciplines that they might be on the side of "sense." The purge was on, and it was real, but that was the price to pay to enter the New Age, where science was to reign.

Yet, its thousand-year reign was abridged to but twenty years with the forceful demonstration of Quine, one of the movement's own philosophers, that the principle itself was *self-defeating*. It had exempted the principle *itself* from the criteria asserted by the principle—we cannot go into nature

---

of the original by Stadler and Uebel.

8. This supreme confidence of the logical positivists that they were right and the *last* word in philosophy (Wittgenstein had famously retired from philosophy after "solving" all of its problems in his *Tractatus*) is captured in Ayer's foreword to the 2nd edition of his *Language, Truth and Logic* (1946). He had introduced logical positivism to the English-speaking world in 1936 after he had attended meetings of the Vienna Circle, who themselves had developed the ideas of Wittgenstein's *Tractatus* and Russell's logicism. He admits to being overzealous in the first edition and still later was to retreat from the veracity of most of what he had written therein, but maintained it had served a "valuable cathartic purpose."

9. Russell, "Logical Positivism," 367.

and find a "verification principle," so on that basis, it makes *no sense* to talk about a verification *principle.*[10] In fact, and this became a general realization amongst many of the critics, *any* rational principle was problematic on the verificationist basis, and attempts to relax or reformulate the principle to admit the common idioms of analytic thought and scientific practice were seen to either exclude too much or were too rigid, voiding its efficacy as a methodological basis for distinguishing science from "non-science" and "non-sense." In other words, logical positivism *itself* was exposed as a "thorough going metaphysics [denying] all metaphysics."[11]

It must be emphasized that Quine had, from *within* empiricism, offered this comprehensive rebuttal of logical positivism. He had demonstrated that the verification principle required working outside of the empiricist framework; it was a brutal self-contradiction, a metaphysical dogma.[12] Quine's essay really marked the end of the movement and the "tyranny of empiricism"; even though Quine himself remained a sophisticated empiricist, he argued that no theory could reach the level of sufficient attestation that it could be considered "true" in an objective sense, but as long as it was *useful* in solving problems or explaining the world, the theory might be maintained.[13] Quine's influence was itself enormous in the post-positivist era, with his development of scientific naturalism and epistemological holism, where he asserted that we always "see the world" in terms of a theory of nature. Furthermore, there are many *possible* theories of nature that have equivalent claims as adequate explanations of phenomena; as the "data" of phenomena builds up, some theories may no longer be adequate

10. Quine, "Two Dogmas." This is generally considered to be one of the most influential papers published in the twentieth century and is still mandatory reading for philosophy of science students and, in my experience, those of many other disciplines.

11. Rushdoony, *Limits of Reason*, loc. 111.

12. Quine was mentored by and collaborated with Rudolf Carnap, one of the most influential of the logical positivists. See Macneil, *Foundations*, where there is substantial attention given to Quine.

13. Though a point more suited for the philosophical discussions of my *Foundations*, Quine was arguing for something distinct from pragmatism, though you might argue the *practical* implications of his position would be similar. He was rather making a rational proposition: he was arguing that no one need *ever* relinquish their theory; they could always "reinterpret" any fact or new data to fit in with the framework of their theory or modify their theory in some way to accommodate anomalies and new facts. This absolutely destroys any claim that scientific theories give you *objective* accounts or truths about nature, or that one theory is implicitly better than another on a purely *rational* basis; the theory is always tested against the world.

and can be dispensed with. This was a radical departure from the mythology surrounding a science as the sole source of truth.

In short, there was a plurality of possible theories of nature: each might be considered "empirically adequate" in describing phenomena; none could be asserted ahead of time as being the "true" account. Equally importantly, other philosophers of science contemporary to Quine, such as Kuhn, further undermined the claim that *only* the *scientific* was synonymous with the *rational*. Kuhn had argued persuasively that science operated within a specific cultural context, was non-linear, and had unavoidable subjective dimensions; it was not *the* truth but merely represented milestones on the way to a better understanding of the world.[14]

That is, something of the "*tyranny* of science"[15] was arrested during this era, with many of the softer sciences and the humanities liberating themselves from the physicalism of positivism and the scientific naturalism that was replacing it. The argument had been reframed to a far more restrained and measured discourse regarding philosophical and

14. By "non-linear," it is meant that many traditional accounts of science had (and still do) present scientists as building on one another's work, e.g., Einstein built on Newton, who himself had said, "If I have seen further than other men, it is because I have stood on the shoulders of giants" (letter to Robert Hooke on Feb. 5, 1675, in the archive of the Historical Society of Pennsylvania). What was so radical in Kuhn was that he had asserted that Einsteinian physics had *usurped* Newtonian physics, and Copernicus had *usurped* Ptolemy, replacing the previous theory with an entirely new *paradigm*, frequently contradictory and *unrelated* to what went before it—it was a *revolution* of thought, not an *evolution*. Kuhn fully expected Einsteinian physics to be usurped by another *revolution* within the scientific community.

Kuhn's *Scientific Revolutions* is another example of required reading for the philosopher of science, and its basic thesis has been adopted by many outside of the discipline of science to "protect" their discipline from the tyrannizing instincts of the academic scientists. It is somewhat ironic that Kuhn's lasting legacy has been felt outside of science in the humanities, as subsequent philosophers of science highlighted the ambiguity, the implicit relativism, and the imprecision of his language in the *Revolutions*. However, it was cogent and persuasive enough to have been seen as broadly applicable to the other disciplines in defending them against the charges of irrationality in their rejection of the primacy of a "scientific" methodology for the grounding of their discipline. See my *Foundations* for a broader discussion of Kuhn.

15. A term most immediately associated with another highly influential and controversial philosopher of science, Paul Feyerabend. It was a theme he returned to repeatedly during his colorful career, stated first in his *Against Method* and in his last publication (a composite of a lecture series) the *Tyranny of Science*, before dying prematurely of a brain tumor. Few assaulted the elevated mythology of science in our culture so directly and described the dangers of unfettered scientism as Feyerabend, and he, too, is required reading for philosophers of science.

"scientific" naturalism, arguing that any concept of God is unnecessary and irrelevant in understanding or describing the natural operation of the universe in the latter half of the twentieth century; science was in fact "neutral" on metaphysical questions—it was beyond the *competency* of science to answer those questions.[16]

Yet, those questions were still asked elsewhere in the academy and one of the dominant critiques of religious thought originated immediately after the positivist era in the non-positivistic analytic atheism in the philosophy of Flew and Mackie.[17] Flew and Mackie were not so much "scientific" in their critique but were evidentialist and *rational* in their intellectual approach, arguing that the beliefs of theists and Christians, specifically, were *irrational.* Both had argued this on the basis of the argument from evil, that the existence of a good, omnipotent God was logically incompatible with the presence of evil in the world, a position first argued by Epicurus around 300 BC and emphatically restated by Hume in his *Natural Religion.*[18]

Their work was immediately attractive to the subsequent *philosophical* naturalism, so that even if *scientific* naturalism *could* be neutral, it was seldom true in practice by virtue of the prejudices of the practitioners, and they quickly began incorporating these critiques as part of the continuing assault on the plausibility of the God hypothesis. As religious groups began asserting their rights to be heard in the public square during the 1970s and

16. Plantinga, *Science, Religion and Naturalism*, ix.

17. Flew's *Theology and Falsification* is generally thought (and in his own words in the retrospective, *There Is a God*, ixv–xv) to mark the rebirth of analytic atheism and, paradoxically, analytic theism by pioneering a post-positivist manner of speaking about God. See also Mackie, "Evil and Omnipotence," 200–212. This was considered a rebuttal of the staple "free will defense" of the theist for the existence of evil; the issue that remains part of the atheist critique of Christian thought especially, though most philosophers would consider now Mackie's rebuttal itself successfully rebutted by Christian philosopher Alvin Plantinga in his *God, Freedom, and Evil.* See also Macneil, *Augustine and Plantinga.*

18. Epicurus's dilemma is stated thus: "If God is good, he would want a world free of evil and if he is omnipotent, he would use his power to remove it. The fact there is evil in the world, indicates either that God is impotent, or that he is unwilling, and therefore not good." Many a Calvinist would resolve the dilemma by adding in an additional premise to resolve the paradox, arguing if there is evil in the world, it is because it serves the purposes of God and God permits it. The *how* or *why* evil is permitted in that way remains hidden in the purposes of God, that is the extremely psychologically uncomfortable terminus (particularly from the perspective of those who witness or have endured severe abuse or hardship), which would also seem to be the central message of the magisterial book of Job.

1980s, culture generally never tired of pitting the enlightened practice of "science" against the bigotry of the religious fundamentalist.[19] It was not long before the duel with philosophical and scientific naturalism was given crude expression in "New Atheism"[20]—a "strong scientism," the belief that science provides the "*only* . . . source of knowledge of the world, or alternatively, that the *only* questions *worth* asking were those that science *could* answer."[21] For all intents and purposes, the academy and its apologists had reverted to the working premise of logical positivism that the concept of God was irrational and incoherent.

However, such dogmatism struggled for credibility in the postmodern world; few, now, find such scientism persuasive or compelling and New Atheism is already considered a historical movement, barely making it a decade in the public consciousness.[22] Most philosophers now admit sources of knowledge outside of the constraints of scientific naturalism. Indeed, Plantinga demonstrated forcefully that the premises of *philosophical* naturalism do not even support *theoretically* a comprehensive science but mitigate against it. Plantinga, in his critique, made much of "Darwin's doubt"; we might paraphrase it thus: If our reasoning, hence our science, is but a natural process, why should I believe the conclusions of my reasoning any more than that of the reasonings of a monkey? Or put another way, the boundaries of nature ensure we can never get outside of nature to establish an abstract science *explaining* nature.[23]

19. Professor James Barr published his *Fundamentalism* in 1977, with a substantive revision in 1982. This was perhaps the defining critique of the era, being freely quoted in many subsequent publications critical of "conservative evangelicalism" both academic and popular. Despite his substantial reputation, his analysis in this work was flawed in important places, and he failed to distinguish fundamentalists from other conservative evangelicals (considering the terms synonymous) as we were careful to do at the beginning of our discussion in this book. See also: Macneil, *Fundamentals and Fundamentalism*.

20. Taylor, "New Atheists."

21. Sam Harris, Richard Dawkins, Daniel Dennett, and Christopher Hitchens were affectionately known as the "Four Horsemen of the [atheist] apocalypse." New atheism was known for its supreme confidence in its views and its derisive dismissal of all who disagreed with them, even if their opponents, too, were arguing on an atheological basis about different models of evolutionary theory. See Macneil, *Foundations*, §3.3.5, 68.

22. It is even more noteworthy that Dawkins now describes himself as a "cultural Christian," in preference to the alternative of radical Islam.

23. For a much fuller discussion of these philosophical issues surrounding science, see Macneil, *Foundations*, §3.3.7.

Instead, epistemological pluralism and holism now stand in stark contrast to the crudeness of New Atheism. Most philosophers are far more cautious regarding the scope of our problems, which science *might* have the competence to solve, and for the purposes of our argument here, it was certainly no longer "unscientific" or "irrational" to hold to the Christian worldview.[24] Modern naturalistic science destroys itself as a system or purveyor of knowledge and reduces to logical nonsense. It is of little surprise that cultural confidence in science had collapsed to a large degree by the middle of the 1990s.[25]

The Collapse of the Liberal World Order

Disillusionment following the Balkan wars of 1912/13 and then World War I in 1914 in Europe precipitated the collapse of classical liberal optimism and utopianism, being replaced by the Nietzschean "will to power" as the replacement metanarrative in the cultural powerhouse of Europe, the German republic.[26] Even though Germany had been defeated in WWI and the settlement after had deliberately disadvantaged Germany, it only succeeded in radicalizing its intelligentsia and enabling the rise of the National Socialists, who then dramatically rebuilt the nation, economically and politically. It is a paradoxical fact that though the Allies went to war again with Germany, Lord Keynes agreed with the Nazi critique of Western economics and adopted it as fundamental to his economic thought postwar.[27]

24. However, much more would need to be said as to why the Christian worldview is the *only* fully rational worldview rather than just a competitor in the postmodern marketplace. This argument was the subject of my doctoral studies and is developed in my *Foundations*.

25. In the era of television advertising, certain domestic appliance advertisements removed the "scientists" with their white laboratory coats because of the public suspicion over science. The COVID pandemic was also another example of what happens when science gets tyrannical and out of control; see Macneil, "Great COVID Caper."

26. Nietzsche, *Wille zur Macht*. Elisabeth Förster-Nietzsche bridged the divide between Nietzsche and Nazism by assembling this work from fragments of Nietzsche's unpublished work. It should be noted than many Nietzschean scholars object to this association of Nietzsche with Nazism, citing his sister's "Nazification" of his work, but is undeniable that Nietzsche had a willing audience amongst the Nazis and the fascist movements, including Hitler and Mussolini. Kuyper was to write after the close of WWI, "The rising sun to the up-and-coming generation of Germany . . . today everything revolves around Nietzsche" (Kuyper, *Blurring of the Boundaries*, 366).

27. Quoted in Rushdoony, "Money, Inflation, and Morality."

The core belief was that totalitarianism was a natural and efficient means of delivering a new humanist world order free of bourgeois sentimentalism.[28] The universalizing ideologies of Nazism and Communism came together in a pact during the 1930s, precipitating the Holocaust as rite of passage. Their central modern premise was a complete belief in the power of reason to "create an ordered world in which the unpredictability and chaos of [irrationality] would give way to paradise."[29]

The New Humanist World Order

In this context, it is not accidental that Roosevelt's willingness to cede Eastern Europe to a friendly Soviet Union indicated the strength of his implicit support of its humanism.[30] An uncomfortable, barely remembered fact is that Soviet dissidents post-Second World War experienced mass deportations from the West to Russia after the Yalta agreement, regardless of their personal wishes, and more Russians died at the hands of Stalin *because of this agreement* than were *ever killed by the Nazis*.[31]

With such a common unity of purpose to create a New World Order, it is no longer a bare economic fact that American loans to the Eastern bloc

28. The pervasive influence of Darwinism here should not be underestimated, both biologically (in the eugenics movement, that still had strong, open support in the 1960s as a foundational ideology to the family planning movement), in historicism (in Marxism), and here, sociopolitically. Some, indeed, saw the working out of evolutionary processes with almost a metaphysical or religious pretheoretical commitment to Darwin, with one of the greatest evolutionists of the modern era, Stephen Gould, writing in his *Punctuated Equilibrium*, "It is a metaphysical commitment we make" (145).

This means that the evidence for evolution is that there is no evidence (Gould, *Punctuated Equilibrium*, 116).This was in response to the embarrassment, he describes, that the fossil record with all its large gaps does *not* support a view of a *gradual* change of species. He used the Marxist concept of "revolution," that the jumps in the record were periods of rapid change, followed by quiet periods of no change—hence the gaps in the fossil record. As I noted in my *Foundations*, §3.3.5, this is a master class in sophistry being beyond both proof and refutation, and the bitter feud between Dawkins, Gould, and their disciples continues to this day, despite Gould passing in 2002. Thus, my conclusion expressed there is that evolutionism is a metaphysical dogma in its *entirety*, despite its cosmetic dressing in scientific clothes.

29. McGrath, *Passion for Truth*, 182–83.

30. Dallek, "Roosevelt's Relationship [sic] Stalin," para. 1.

31. Bethell, *Last Secret*. Nicholas Bethell is better known as Baron Lord Bethell and was a hereditary pier in the British House of Lords until his death in 2007. See also, Rushdoony, "Christian Reconstruction 1 and 2."

communist regimes during the Cold War are evidence for many dissidents that "*America was the greatest ally to the Soviet Union.*"[32] Rushdoony was able to describe at book length why "*Washington is as humanistic as Moscow.*"[33] Western capitalism had lost its Christian humanitarian roots of creating and sustaining wealthy cultures, and by 1947 it became simply a means of generating as much profit as possible; the Western dream became one of unprincipled and unbridled materialism.[34] A militant secular humanism had become entrenched in both the Western and communist blocs, and it was inevitable that a reaction within Christian thought was to emerge.

Late Modern Christian Thought

Theology was in a state of flux as it wrestled with theological liberalism during the nineteenth century. The rise of an alleged scientific "rationalism" and the metanarrative of Darwinism in the West during this period had precipitated the crumbling of past religious certainties.[35] The choice was clear: embrace the new scientific world order or retreat into allegorizing Scripture and existentialism in an attempt to hold onto faith despite the "overwhelming" scientific evidence against it.[36]

Barthianism resembled the latter; fundamentalism was the "scientific" response of conservative Christianity.[37] Fundamentalism, once it had moved beyond its anti-intellectual populist beginning period, was characterized by one commentator as "modernists swimming against the tide."[38] It was rigorously methodical and rational with, in Warfield, a ring-fenced

32. Rushdoony, "Humanist Order."

33. Rushdoony, *Christianity and the State*, loc. 1430.

34. Cope, "Business and Economics."

35. Bahnsen, "Calvin and Postmillennialism," para. 1–5.

36. Bultmann, *Jesus Christ and Mythology*, 35–44.

37. It is perhaps more accurate to argue that academic Protestantism generated a scholarly response to theological liberalism in what became the 4-volume set edited by Torrey (1917) but had been published in various journals previously. This was eponymously named "The Fundamentals," but this does *not* seem to be the origin of the term "fundamentalist," which was rather coined by newspaper columnists around the same time and referred to a particular style of populist, non-academic evangelist. Many of the first generation of "fundamentalists" were anti-intellectual and vocally opposed to the academy as an expression of the harlot Babylon, which provides good evidence that the academy was not the origin of the term. I examine the issue of fundamentalism in my "Scripture and the Post-Darwinian Controversy."

38. Lawrence, *Defenders of God*, 27.

doctrine of inspiration that was beyond refutation, being based on an impeccable modern logical position bereft of any substantive appeal to religious experience.[39] It was about doctrinal purity and demanded, like the political movements, rigorous and uncompromising commitment to the normative creed.

However, ultimately, the effort was unsuccessful as modernism collapsed into totalitarianism and the *Fundamentals* of 1917 became the final statement of conservative academic theology within the mainstream universities before leaving the harlot Babylon to her inevitable judgment.[40] There followed cultural ghettoization and intellectual withdrawal of the dispensationalist fundamentalist movement proper from social and intellectual action for approximately the period of 1920–1970.[41] The Reformed seminaries did not fare much better with the split of Machen from Princeton over its embrace of theological liberalism and then the subsequent splits from Machen over even finer points of doctrine, leading to a fragmentation of Presbyterianism in the US; and it was again to be the 1970s before Rushdoony was to offer his reformer's vision.

Politically and culturally, secular humanism and its stepsister, the "social gospel" movement, were having it mostly their own way, and if there was an evangelical vision for culture "as a whole," it was simply to facilitate the preaching of the gospel by any means necessary before the imminent return of the Lord. Rushdoony describes this place of Christian history thus:

> Scripture is stripped of its total message and reduced to a soul-saving manual. Matters of law respecting crime, the use of the land, money, weights, property, diet, civil government, and all things else are set aside to concentrate on soul-saving only. If now Christian schools are started by some of these groups, too often their essential purpose is to further soul-saving.[42]

39. It should be noted that Warfield (contra Barr) was *not* a fundamentalist himself but an orthodox, conservative Presbyterian of Princeton Theological Seminary. However, his defense of the inerrancy and infallibility of Scripture became formative for the fundamentalist position. Additionally, the commonsense realism, so influential in the Princeton epistemology, meant it was very sensitive to the imperative of having a scientific respectability for the apologetic; see Macneil, *Foundations*, §3.5.4–3.5.6. See also Warfield, "Inspiration," in *Writings*.

40. Torrey and Dixon, *Fundamentals*.

41. Lloyd-Jones, *What Is an Evangelical?*, 49; Stott, *Involvement*, 13.

42. Rushdoony, *God's Plan for Victory*, loc. 185.

The Rise and Collapse of Postmodernism

So, in summary we see that within the political culture generally, the story of the early twentieth century for the West was an emphatic rejection of the religious metanarrative and a radical embrace of humanism and modernism in various forms as the century progressed. Yet, such positions were sustained only by what can be described as an *irrational* confidence in the absolute rationality of reason, and it was soon to be challenged:

> But what if reason or rationality itself rests on belief? Then it would be the case that the opposition between reason and belief was a false one, and that every situation of contest should be recharacterized as a quarrel between two sets of belief with no possibility of recourse to a mode of deliberation that was not itself an extension of belief.[43]

The "post-modernists" who first began to appear in the 1960s recognized this implicit circularity of an unqualified confidence in reason and balked at this as epistemological totalitarianism.[44]

So, who and what were the postmodernists? "Postmodernism," especially philosophical postmodernism, is sometimes considered as a post-WWII movement, but it had been used first in schools of art, which Lyotard, the philosopher of the later movement, claimed went all the way back to Duchamp in 1912. Duchamp posited that a *painter* need not make a *painting* to be an *artist*. Similarly, if the location of an object was in an art gallery, the institution of the gallery bequeathed upon it the status of "art"; it could indeed just be a pile of bricks or an empty room where the light switches on and off.[45] In other words, in common parlance, talk of "modern art" often refers to *postmodern* art.

However, philosophical postmodernism began finding its philosophical feet during the 1970s and was brought into focus and mainstream Anglo-American academia (it was already well-established in the "Continental"

43. Fish, *Free Speech*, 135.

44. For an excellent primer on postmodernism by someone observing it somewhat critically rather than being part of the movement, see Butler, *Postmodernism*. He echoes Docherty, whom we quote later as saying postmodernism is a "mood" rather than a movement, but brings out the link with Marxism concisely and well as "the Marxist presupposition that we are all in any case the victims of a 'false consciousness' brought about by 'bourgeois' discourse" (111).

45. Both of these are famous examples of "postmodern art" exhibits that won prestigious prizes. See Butler, *Postmodernism*, 1–4.

academies) with the 1984 publication of the English translation of Lyotard's *La condition* (Fr. 1979). At around the same time as Lyotard published in French, American Princeton philosopher Richard Rorty's *Mirror* (1979) was published as a repudiation of modern philosophy; he became one of postmodernism's most colorful, forceful, and iconoclastic advocates.

It was no surprise that the intellectual rebellion of the postmodernists came to the fore in the postwar period. It had just been preceded with the carnage of Nazism and Communism, and it was clear that modernism *was* having its own crisis by pursuing its own secularizing and universalizing presuppositions to their inevitable and logical conclusion in the Holocaust. The radical intellectual flight from reason in reaction to these failed promises of modernism gave special impetus to postmodernism in the postwar period. It first manifested in the rebellion and optimistic cultural spontaneity of the economic boom of the 1960s but rapidly descended into a sharp cynicism that was distinctive of the recession that followed in the West during the 1970s. Lyotard, considered the seminal thinker of philosophical postmodernism, would have surrendered all hope of certainty *on principle* (if he thought there were any principles to be had) but wanted us to stay hopeful nevertheless: "It must be clear that it is our business not to supply reality but to invent allusions to the conceivable which cannot be presented."[46]

Lyotard's cryptic and uncommitted aphorism is perhaps representative; postmodern discourse became exemplified in finding a way to use a lot of words to not really say anything formally, but that *was* the point.[47] It was the organic process of philosophizing that the conceivable might *appear.* Derrida's lectures became known for their long, rambling nature—if you were looking for a "point" to the lecture, you were already *missing* the point. As Lyotard makes clear, the rambles are still *allusions* to that which cannot be presented; paralogism was endorsed as philosophical method.[48] By design, we are supremely subjective and eschew even the possibility of objectivity as bourgeois false consciousness.[49]

46. Lyotard, *Postmodern Condition*, 81.

47. A fine exemplar of dense, postmodern prose is also found in the essay accompanying the English translation of Lyotard listed in the bibliography.

48. As a further point of philosophical criticism, if they are "allusions," it suggests there is still something *presentable* awaiting a suitable, analytic, alternative narrative. It is difficult to find coherence in Lyotard's assertion here.

49. Butler, *Postmodernism*, 2. Butler makes the point that the movement is a movement of the political left; hence, most of what is produced has a political message and

Thus, this can readily be catastrophic to scholarship, with its implicit vagueness and renunciation of analytic clarity, perhaps demonstrated well by the "Sokal hoaxes," where fake papers advancing bizarre "postmodern" theses *were* accepted for publication in leading postmodern journals. "Sokal squared" was a similar recently repeated exercise concentrating on the nascent gender and CRT disciplines. Despite the ridiculousness and lack of critical peer assessment exposed by the fakery (it would indeed be difficult to understand what the process of peer review might mean for the postmodernist journal other than censoring works with a cogent argument as bourgeois), the academics were unrepentant, labeling it "an attack of the Right."[50]

In what might be seen as the desire to avoid such excesses, Rorty took a different track than the abstraction of the Continental postmodernists and was the focus of an "Americanization" of the postmodern movement by combining it with Deweyan pragmatism. Rorty also demonstrated a strong desire to generate some kind of *ethical* program despite initially becoming and remaining famous as at the vanguard of the crusade against truth.[51] Lyotard was said to be unhappy with this turn but with Rorty, pragmatism, pluralism, and relativism entered the cultural mainstream and the denial of the possibility of objective truth became the working hypothesis of the academy. Rorty, I would argue, was the patron saint of postmodern *philosophers* (whereas Nietzsche might be considered the patron saint of postmodernism in general[52]). Liked and loathed in equal measures, he was the most-cited philosopher by the early 1990s, becoming known for his rejection of "truth" and a disdain of his own discipline. He migrated into a new field combining literary criticism and philosophy but remained the favorite philosopher of the Left up until his death (2007).[53]

Though Rorty tried to mitigate the Continental postmodern deconstructionism so influential in literary criticism by moving postmodernism in the direction of pragmatism, Rorty himself had described the human

---

that, perhaps, is its *point*.

50. I give the details on the Sokal hoaxes and explore the issue of peer review more fully in Macneil, "Fake (but Peer-Reviewed)."

51. Rorty, *Ethics for Today*.

52. A case argued effectively by Blackburn in *Truth*, §4: "Nietzsche, the Arch Debunker."

53. The movement was sometimes characterized as philosophers writing poor literary criticism, and literary critics writing equally poor philosophy.

condition as one of "irony."[54] However, for those less sophisticated in thought than Rorty, this "irony" all too readily decayed into a despairing negativity that life just happens, and we are powerless in any real sense to understand and shape the world. Of course, the *supreme* irony for the postmodernist is that implicit within their view is the reciprocal form of the very same truth fallacy from which they were seeking to escape: *to deny any concept of truth is stated as an absolute truth.*[55] This then functions as an effective axiom of their postmodernist framework.[56]

With all this paralogism celebrated and on full display, Lyotard prophetically foresaw that despite this effervescence of postmodernism during this period, there was a desire for the terror of the modern illusion of analysis, certainty, and objectivity to return, and the counterreaction of modernism, as postmodernists prophesied of its demise, was swift.[57] It was a particular totalizing and caustic counterreaction of modernism to its alleged demise, borrowing from postmodernism the dispensing of the nicety of reasoned discourse, to be replaced with, as we have previously seen, a relentless polemic and mockery of one's opponents. This was exemplified by the New Atheist polemic against *any* and *all* religion. Yet, now, there were the additional dimensions of cultural Marxism: deplatforming and censorship. Postmodernists were also identified with a refusal to challenge critically, with those opinions deemed unacceptable on unargued but "deeply held" *a priori* criteria. Indeed, with subjectivity as central to our understandings of ourselves, your position was valid because it was *your* position and any attempt to argue from principle against you was equated with a refusal to permit your fundamental right to psychic calm and was therefore "violence." The point being that if my belief was "deeply held," you have no right to challenge it, and it was "violence" to attempt to do so.

In other words, as postmodernism decayed into this crude cultural form, it manifested in identity politics and dispensed with the need to argue and justify your position. For the Marxist, verbal "violence" could be met with physical violence as a form of self-defense. Mixed with this kind of cultural Marxism, the most demanding of modernisms, this quickly degenerated into the simple division of "oppressed" and "oppressor" and the "othering" of those with whom you disagree. The postmodern component is

54. Rushdoony, *Limits of Reason*, loc. 91; McGrath, *Passion for Truth*, 163–200.

55. Rushdoony, *Limits of Reason*, loc. 1005–50; Fish, *Free Speech*, 135–36.

56. Rhodes, "Absolute Truth."

57. Lyotard, *Postmodern Condition*, 81–82.

the belief that you are so "othered" from me that we can have no argument because our language and worldviews are incommensurate.[58] The Marxist component is that this "othering" is your way of keeping me in a state of perpetual oppression and I must resort to revolutionary action to overthrow that, and we certainly do not have to have a debate about it.

This provided a lens through which to view all interpersonal and international relations, and the oppressed could use any means necessary, including violence, to liberate themselves. Thus, far from being a tool of hope and pluralism, freeing thought from modernist tyranny, postmodernism had paradoxically become an instrument of neo-Marxist apologetics that obviated the imperative to have an argued position and, instead, divided people on the basis of their immutable and incommensurate characteristics.

Put another way, the problem for the postmodernist is rather like the problem Wittgenstein (who is often viewed as helpful to the postmodernist cause in other respects) posited at the end of the *Tractatus*, that we have used this ladder to climb up to this place but then have to pull the ladder up after us because we realize that *if* what we have concluded is true, *then* it is illegitimate to have climbed up using the ladder that we did. This point was not lost on some postmodernists, who readily subscribe to a *paralogical* conception of reality, because starting from "logical" presuppositions, as Wittgenstein did, nevertheless terminated in self-contradiction. Life (and philosophy) is clearly more than logic, and I will architect it myself.

In summary, then, as a positive, postmodernism has some valuable insights that serve to reign in the totalizing modernisms of the twentieth century (such as fascism and communism). In its most holistic mode, work in the humanities and, to a significant degree, the sciences can be usefully assessed for its sensitivity to postmodernity and postmodernism; in such a mode, its influence is now much more measured, and it serves now to help us to recognize "the limitations of our modern premises."

However, as an overwhelming negative, postmodernism, when combined with cultural Marxism, as it often naturally has been, being a movement predominantly of the Left, has paradoxically exerted a *coercive* rather than a liberating influence on scholarship. It is woefully inadequate and poorly defined as a system of thought *in itself* as it denigrates "*systems* of thought." Rorty's attempted combination of postmodernism with American pragmatism provides something of a way forward for

58. Lyotard codified this in his work *The Differend* (1983). He considered this his most important work, but it did not find its way into English until 1990.

postmodern thought beyond the abstract, intellectual Continental deconstructionism. Yet, few in the movement have the erudition or intellectual nuance of Rorty, who, in later years, was content to be described as a "bourgeois" thinker and presumably an enemy of the movement he nurtured to adulthood. Rorty was an embodiment of the postmodern dilemma; it is rather like trying to argue that breathing is illegitimate, though all that time you are breathing whilst you delegitimize breathing through breathed words. So, in Docherty, for example, he describes postmodernism as a "mood, not a period," and woe to us if we are swayed too easily by moods![59] There is still plenty of postmodernism in culture at large, but it is philosophically incoherent (with some postmodernists "reveling" in this very feature), its limitations now well exegeted, especially by those whose disciplines it criticized so severely.[60]

Thus, if the choice before us is one of logic, or perhaps better, *logos* versus postmodern paralogism, then we, as Christians, must surely choose *logos*, and this is freely admitted as a metaphysical commitment—my faith informs my reason at this point.[61] Similarly, as an analytic philosopher, I argue you need to understand how to live according to the design plan *correctly*—yes, I believe in objectivity—to live a long life; you understand the rules of the game and play it according to those rules.[62] As a Christian, I view those "rules" as the law of God, and following those, you will succeed. This is part of the case we build in the subsequent

59. Docherty, "Postmodernist Theory," 479.

60. For examples, see Thiselton, *Hermeneutics*, 327–48; Blackburn, *Ruling Passions*, 279–310. Blackburn's *Truth* (2006) contains perhaps one of the most far-reaching critiques of the postmodern view, his critique even reaching as far as a footnote in Rorty's own work.

61. As many Christians will know, Jesus is described as the "Logos" ("Word") in the original Greek of John 1:1. It has an obvious relation to the word "logic," sharing the same root but is rather stronger. It refers to an overall rational principle of the universe, first appearing as a similar concept in the ancient Greek philosopher Heraclitus (c. 500 BC). The personification in Jesus of the concept is in line with what is stated in Col 2:3, 9 (NET): "In whom are hidden all the treasures of wisdom and knowledge. . . . For in him all the fullness of deity lives in bodily form." You might also say "essence"—what it is about God that makes him God dwells in Christ.

62. Macneil, *Foundations*, 222. Here, I discuss the relation of the Plantingian term "design plan," which connects our knowledge of the world with the faculty of reason. The basic idea is that for cognitive functions (including our reason) that are working correctly in a suitable environment according to the way God intended, they could be relied on to give you knowledge about the world.

chapters and is fundamental to the philosophical and theological underpinnings of dominion theology.[63]

Concluding Summary

This has been the most demanding and complicated chapter of the book so far, as we have been very ambitious in trying to decode the philosophical and cultural milieu of the last two hundred years. There will be plenty with the chronology and inferences that we have made that some will readily object to, but far fewer will argue with what we conclude here as we gather our thoughts. The state of human civilization as the new millennium approached was characterized by "autophagic capitalism" and the bloody Marxist wreckage of the "rotting offal of modernity."[64]

This absolute descent of secular civilization into two world wars, multiple further conflicts along ideological lines, the Cold War, the bankruptcy of academia, the rootlessness of postmodernity, and the correlative pessimistic and cynical turn of evangelical Christian eschatological thought demanded a response. The emergence of Rushdoony's Reconstructionism in this period was the movement in which intellectual and social discontent turned to action. It is to his role in the Reconstructionist movement and its formative nature for dominion theology that is the subject of the next chapter.

63. Revisiting this section a decade later after it was first written allowed me to reorganize, tidy up, and update what is an extremely compressed account of postmodernism, but even in this updated form, it might raise more questions than it answers for the philosophy student. However, in my defense, a critique of postmodernism was not the subject of *this* book, I am only seeking to draw out specific themes relevant to dominion theology, which could be investigated further by the reader if desired and are argued more fully elsewhere. In that respect, a great primer on postmodernism *and* its relation to faith, the interest of this book, is found in Thiselton, *Hermeneutics*, 327–348. For issues of Christian philosophy specifically, I would be amiss not to recommend my *Foundations* based on my doctoral studies.

64. McVicar, *Christian Reconstruction*, 230.

The Emergence of Modern Dominion Theology

Rushdoony and the Proto-Conservative Movement

It was at once the crisis within humanism and the collapse of evangelical Christian cultural philosophy that provided the moral imperative for the dominion theology movement first seen in the critique and works of Rousas Rushdoony. An insider charting the development of the dominion theology movement was to write,

> In 1962, there was no Christian Reconstruction movement. There was not even an outline of it. Over the next decade Rushdoony developed the fundamental theological and sociological principles of what later was to become a movement.[1]

The political context of Rushdoony's early work was the coalescing of diverse political and big-business reactions into a proto-conservative movement in post-Second World War America; it was as a response to the rise of American statism during Roosevelt's New Deal era (c. 1933). This had asserted the central federal authority against the individual states and fundamentally changed the relationship of the American citizen to the state.[2] This development of the American statism had subsequently accelerated greatly during the so-called "Warren Court" period of 1953–1969.[3] Federal and judicial power was increased dramatically over the elected legislature at state level:

1. North and DeMar, *Christian Reconstruction*, xiii.
2. History.com, "New Deal."
3. After the chief justice of the American Supreme Court Earl Warren.

> To many people, the idea of judicial *deference to the elected branches* lost much of its theoretical appeal in the 1950s and 1960s.[4]

In other words, the will of the community being expressed through its representatives was set aside for ideological reasons prioritized by the federal government agencies. The enormous moral imperative of the statist movement that lent it apparent legitimacy was the racial conflict within the Southern states that enabled the legitimization of aggressive centrist and federalist imposition on the individual legislatures who had resisted normalization of race relations. The actions were frequently sponsored or initiated by radical "progressive" lawyers of the ACLU, who rose in ascendancy through the equality and race struggles of this period.[5] The philosophical motivation of the ACLU was that of its first patron, John Dewey (d. 1952), an advocate of "intelligent social control or social action . . . as a requirement of positive liberty or individuality, in modern industrial conditions."[6] This was thinly disguised socialist elitism, a call for the enlightened social progressives to radical *state* action to address social problems at the federal level, rather than with individual community initiatives that had been peculiar to the American way.[7] The radical leftism of the federalists and the anti-Christian rhetoric of the ACLU was viewed by Rushdoony as evidence of their desire to marginalize Christians and an unconstitutional attack on First Amendment rights.[8]

For these reasons, Rushdoony had made common cause with the proto-conservative movement that began to coalesce after the Second World War around a pro-capitalist, libertarian agenda against the federalists. He initially worked during the 1950s with emerging voices of conservatism, such as *Spiritual Mobilization* publishing articles in their journal *Faith and Freedom*. *SM* warned that statism with its bureaucracy and social action usurped the "Christian principle [duty] of love [to your neighbor]" and

4. Sunstein, "Justice Breyer's Democratic Pragmatism," 3–4. Emphasis added.

5. Such was the perceived hostility to Christianity of this organization that the initials ACLU even today are known in some conservative American Christian communities to stand for *Anti-Christ Lawyers Union*; Ito, "Demanding Respect."

6. Festenstein, "Dewey's Political Philosophy."

7. Missler, "America's Challenge." This may now be unavailable but updated versions are available from https://resources.khouse.org/, specifically the "Strategic Perspectives" series.

8. The First Amendment of the American constitution is perceived to guarantee religious liberty and to prohibit state interference in the practice of religion, see Legal Information Institute, "First Amendment" for a detailed but accessible summary.

> replaced it with the collectivist principle of compulsion . . . clergy and laity needed to focus on the spiritual causes of poverty rather than on the social and political programs advocated by secular social reformers . . . and the . . . advocates of the Social Gospel.[9]

Fundamentally, these were organizations set on building a "big tent" conservative caucus around "traditional" Judeo-Christian values: individual liberty under a constitutional order and anticommunism.[10] It was the first attempt at a Christian response to the moral energy borne out of the New Deal era and the socialism of the social gospel movement, juxtapositioning it against individual liberty and a positive vision of capitalism as a legitimate means of building a Christian social order.

Rushdoony and the Social Gospel

The conservative movement as it emerged directed a sustained polemic at the Social Gospel movement. Yet, from the perspective of a vision for the entire transformation of society in Christian terms (which, as we shall see, gradually became distinctive of Rushdoony's program), it might be argued that there was substantial idiomatic and "common cause" between both movements to establish the kingdom of God on Earth. Rushdoony, early in his career, apparently had left-leaning views, and for these reasons, it is necessary to identify what is in fact the fundamental distinction between these movements despite starting from this similar idiomatic base.[11]

9. Toy, "Spiritual Mobilization," 80n9; Doherty, *Radicals for Capitalism*, 271.

10. McVicar, *Christian Reconstruction*, 48.

11. McVicar, *Christian Reconstruction*, 23. McVicar works from the assumption that Rushdoony was central to the development of American *conservatism*, and particularly the American Christian right. His work was robust and scholarly. Chalcedon had collaborated with McVicar on this his doctoral work and had a general positive response to the book at the time it was published. Although Chalcedon's in-house scholar Selbrede did write a lengthy section in his review of "what was wrong with the book," it seemed to concentrate on details rather than substance. One clear point of disagreement was addressed in the review in conjunction with McVicar where some excised material was republished in the Chalcedon magazine.

Interestingly, his son Mark Rushdoony, now the president of Rushdoony's Chalcedon foundation, felt more still needed to be said and has now published (2025) a biography of his father where he seeks to re-center an understanding of his primary motivation. This was based on extended articles he had previously published as early as 2016 to establish the record regarding his father, so he clearly felt McVicar's account needed some supplementation or correction.

Walter Rauschenbusch was the father of the Social Gospel movement and had come "face to face with oppressive poverty" during his pastorate in New York (1886–1897).[12] He argued for a theology with the intention of reshaping Christian belief and praxis such that "a clear-eyed and continuous reconstruction of society" might take place.[13] On that basis, his emphasis on a kingdom gospel that was relevant to every sphere of life is shared with Rushdoony. However, Rauschenbusch, taking his philosophical presuppositions from Dewey,[14] saw the state and church inextricably linked in a symbiotic relationship for the wider salvation of society.[15] Rauschenbusch even followed Hegel and assigned a divine quality to the state: "The State is the outer court of the moral law; within stands the sanctuary of the Spirit."[16]

My own feeling is taking McVicar with the review article and Mark's biography helps complete the picture of Rushdoony. As Mark himself writes in the preface, he really has a different interest and motivation to McVicar, and rather than refuting McVicar in any substantive sense, he provides some excellent new biographical material to help us understand his father better *beyond* his influence on the conservative and Christian reconstruction movements. See Rushdoony, *Rousas John Rushdoony*; Selbrede, "First Major Book."

12. Stott, *Involvement*, 25.

13. Rauschenbusch, *Christianity and the Social Crisis*, loc. 2986. Rauschenbusch *would* have been familiar with the postmillennialism of Augustus Strong (he had dedicated his own *Theology of the Social Gospel* to him), which perhaps explains some of the idiomatic similarity with Rushdoony in the expression of his program for societal reformation. However, Strong emphasized the "*Church militant*" and not, as in Rauschenbusch, the "*State militant*." See also Stott, *Involvement*.

14. It should be noted, though, that Dewey's relationship to Christianity is an interesting one; he grew up in an evangelical home and worked for a decade (1884–94) under the auspices of the church in Ann Arbor and the University of Michigan Christian Association, attempting to wrestle with the social and political challenges within a Christian framework. By the turn of the century, he had departed, literally and figuratively, from the church, becoming probably the most influential humanist and intellect, within the US, of the first half of the twentieth century, known for his philosophical pragmatism, instrumentalism, theory of education, political activism, and being the first patron of the ACLU. Many consider his pragmatism as defining the overall tenor of American culture; though I would say many of the great industrialists within the West generally were operationally pragmatic, if not philosophically so. I discuss the wide-ranging influence of Dewey in *Foundations*, §2.6.6.

15. Of course, it might be argued that the Eusebian theology emerging from the fourth-century merging of church and state after the accommodation of Constantine would be the historical and philosophical precursor of such a view. It was periodically attractive to Christian theologians until the state asserted its supremacy over the church.

16. Rauschenbusch, *Christianity and the Social Crisis*, loc. 5418.

He explicitly embraced socialism, believing it represented the inevitable evolutionary track of human progress:

> Here enters socialism. . . . Private ownership is not a higher stage of social organization which has finally and forever superseded communism, but an intermediate and necessary stage of social evolution between two forms of communism.[17]

This is where there is a radical divergence with Rushdoony, who writes to address this embrace of socialism directly:

> It is customary among ecclesiastical socialists to deny there is biblical warrant for private property. . . . Scripture . . . places property in the hands of the family, not the state. It gives property to man an aspect of his dominion, as part of his godly subduing of the earth.[18]

For Rushdoony, it was the family, rather than the church or the state, that represented the fundamental organism of society and where the authority and prerogative for change must come.

This difference became even more evident as the movement that Rauschenbusch spawned did not maintain the Christian nuances and commitment, to some degree, of Christian orthodoxy that were clearly in his work.[19] It became aggressively concerned with "social action" in the form of using the apparatus of the state preemptively. A modern social gospel defense that would recast "salvation" and "sin" as applying to a society rather than to the individual—the individual is more often considered as "sinned against" by the oppressive and alienating power relations of capitalism, rather than needing to repent for their "sin" as a matter of divine order. Stated this way, it was thus straightforward to see why an alliance was to develop between political "progressives," such as the Marxists and the liberals with the social gospel movement on an operational level, and this was reason enough for Rushdoony to reject it. As I have noted elsewhere, the bloody experience of the Russian revolution had an arresting effect, at least for a period, for those advocating for communism

17. Rauschenbusch, *Christianity and the Social Crisis*, loc. 5678, 5850.

18. Rushdoony, *Institutes*, 450–51.

19. Rauschenbusch attempted an exposition of his views in *A Theology for the Social Gospel*, which reads as a respectable attempt after the pattern of systematic theology. The dedication in that work was to Augustus Hopkins Strong, an influential Baptist theologian who was struggling to evolve Baptist theology in the light of Darwinism, whilst attempting to defend orthodox doctrines, such as the virgin birth. Strong was also described by Berkhof as a postmillennialist, which is particularly relevant to our discussion here.

as societal salvation, and any defense of communism was conspicuous by its absence in the later work of Rauschenbusch.

The parallel is almost exact with the liberation theology movement of Gustavo Gutiérrez, which was a Latin American movement beginning during the 1960s. It explicitly employed Marxist hermeneutics emphasizing that "God was undeniably on the side of the poor." Iterations of the liberation theology movement, as its influence grew during the 1970s and the 1980s, meant it became far less Christian and much more Marxist, to the degree that the WCC was alleged to have sponsored the purchase of arms for "liberation movements" around the world.[20] As its radicalism and Marxism grew untenable, the movement was partially censored by the Vatican under Pope John Paul II in the early 1990s; this marked the waning of its influence, but it exerted a lasting influence on Roman Catholic social teaching.[21] From this perspective, it is rather ironic that dominion theologians were once accused by the famous televangelist Jimmy Swaggart of "being liberation theologians in disguise."[22] It was precisely the rejection of "big government" statism and socialism that was one of the main distinctives of Rushdoony's reconstructionism.[23]

20. A colorful look at this support is found at Rhodesia and South Africa, "Terrorist Sponsorship." The WCC itself officially denied that such aid was made, specifying any allocated funds were for "humanitarian" purposes only. However, its moral endorsement provided an enormous incentive and stimulus for direct support of "liberation struggles" around the world by various *member* bodies; those members were free to do what they wish, and the WCC had "plausible deniability." The WCC was one of the strongest early supporters and embracers of Gutiérrez's liberation theology.

21. Pope Francis (pope, 2013–2025) as a Latin American native was far more amenable to liberation theology and was known for his social activism. The present Catholic bishops of the USA are similarly very "liberal," issuing a public condemnation of the immigration policies of the second Trump administration and advocating for operationally "open" borders in the name of social justice. Big columns of migrants were seen marching behind crosses on their way to the US border under Biden.

Most controversially, some Catholic NGOs during the same period had allegedly facilitated the movement of "undocumented" Catholic immigrants into the US and most certainly supported such immigration. Francis was notable in that he rolled back some of John Paul's censuring of the movement, but by this point it, is fair to say that it has lost its cohesiveness and distinctiveness; today, many activists claim allegiance to "liberation theology" with little understanding of the nuanced theology of Gutiérrez.

22. North, *Unholy Spirits*, 392.

23. The irony was compounded when Swaggart had recommended Gary DeMar's *God and Government* at a time when many Pentecostals and charismatics were reacting to Rushdoony's Reconstructionism in a negative and critical manner, only for him to later discover that DeMar was reconstructionist and an associate of Rushdoony.

Rushdoony and Anti-Statism

Thus, for the social gospel and liberation theology movements, the state had become the primary *means* of institutional and social change; for Rushdoony, the legitimate sphere was a narrow judicial one, ensuring the just interpretation and application of God's law.[24] The state only legitimately exists as the agency of the application and not the source of law:

> For a state to claim total jurisdiction as the modern state does, is to claim to be as God, to be the total governor of man and the world. Instead of limited law and limited jurisdiction [over] welfare, education, worship, the family, business and farming, capital and labor . . . the modern antichristian state claims jurisdiction from cradle to grave, from womb to tomb.[25]

24. Rushdoony, *Institutes*, 1–14.

25. Rushdoony, *Institutes*, 34. The creation of the British welfare state followed WWII and the election in 1948 of the first explicitly socialist British Labor Party government under Attlee; the motto was "from the cradle to the grave," the state was there to take care of you. The establishment of the British "National Health Service" occurred during this period with the explicit aim of making healthcare "free at the point of need," such was the largesse of the socialist zeal that non-citizens came from across Europe to receive free care. With the recession of the 1970s and the catastrophic collapse for a decade of the British economy, charges were introduced and the quality of care fell with the door firmly closed to "health tourism."

The NHS has been in a cyclical state of financial crisis ever since and has many major reorganizations since 1979; and as an early-retiring, disillusioned colleague of mine noted (when I worked in the NHS), it had been reorganized back into the original state it was organized out of because of the ideological dedication of some influential staff to the founding ideals, and the refusal to embrace efficiencies and best practices from the private sector (Mrs. Thatcher, in her second term, had attempted to inject a tier of middle managers to deal with waste and inefficiency, which caused a visceral political reaction on the Left and was loathed internally within the NHS). It remains the most cherished British cultural myth and the model of government-run healthcare, despite its innate unaffordability and its state of dysfunction.

A further point of note is that the original architect of the British welfare state, Sir William Beveridge (Beveridge, "Social Insurance and Allied Services") was a classical liberal and *not* a socialist. He viewed the welfare state as a "safety net" to support citizens in a *temporary* crisis; the expectation was still that the citizen would recover and work to support themselves, they could not live off the largesse of the government, courtesy of their taxpayers, via the benefits system, as is now the norm in many Western cultures. My wife, being Japanese (where the welfare state bears far more similarity to Beveridge's model with extremely limited support), said that her greatest shock moving to Britain was seeing that people *could* live off the government when they *choose* not to work.

For Rushdoony, taking philosophical inspiration from Kuyper's concept of "sphere sovereignty," sociological reality was separated into distinct spheres or domains, each of which had clearly defined boundaries and jurisdictions:

> The church, in terms of Scripture, has no jurisdiction and control over other institutions and spheres of life except a "spiritual" one, i.e., the proclamation and application of God's word and authority to every realm . . . the church must declare that every sphere of life must be under the rule of God's word and under the authority of Christ the King.[26]

The church was *to declare* the authority of God in every realm but *not* to govern directly. Rushdoony viewed the reformation of society in the "social service" of one another within the redeemed members of a reformed community of empowered "trustee families" aside from the state. This sociological approach was based on his experience during the 1940s when still in his twenties as a missionary on the Duck Valley Indian Reservation. To Rushdoony, government intervention and "welfare," with its culture of dependency on Indian reservations, had "destroyed Native American Culture."[27] He concluded that nothing short of a "broad Christian *communal* program" was required to facilitate the spiritual redemption and regeneration of the Indian peoples and the culture of the entire reservation.[28] This was to start with Indians on the School Board but was to embrace every facet of life on the reservation as they took responsibility for *themselves.* In other words, even at this early stage of his ministry, he had concluded that a complete *and* Christian reconstruction of society was necessary.

Thus, importantly, Rushdoony did not possess a high view of the church behaving as the papal state had in Roman Catholicism but saw the church as "one agency among many."[29] Each sphere was to be directed by the church to the law of God as revealed in the commandments of Scripture regarding that sphere. Each sphere would interpret and develop its own case law from the principles of the Mosaic prescriptive law. Only in that sense would a man's life be authentically Christian and the society submitted to God:

26. Kuyper, "Sphere Sovereignty," 461–90; Rushdoony, *Christianity and the State*, 137.
27. Rushdoony, "Noncompetitive Life."
28. McVicar, *Christian Reconstruction*, 1. Emphasis added.
29. Rushdoony, *Institutes*, 34.

> A man must be a Christian in church, home, school, state, vocation, and all of life. In going from one sphere to another, a man does not move from the realm of Christ, to that of Mammon, Baal, Molech, or any other "god." Similarly, neither the school, state, nor any other order of life can exempt itself from *the catholic or universal sway of God's rule and law.*[30]

This position was in radical contrast to how he viewed the total ineffectiveness of the church in dealing with the political, social, and religious challenges of the twentieth century. In the decades of mass evangelism that had seen the number of American Christians more than double, to the place they were a numerical majority in the country, their influence within society had virtually disappeared. This was evidenced by the unrestrained humanism seen in the stream of Supreme Court rulings culminating in the removal of prayer from public schools in 1962 and the *de facto* establishment of a federal "abortion on demand" precedent in the 1973 Roe vs. Wade judgment.[31] He described modern Christianity's relationship to the state as merely *tolerated* on the fringes of society, with no significance for public life. Churches were quiet and subservient, that they might not lose their tax-exempt status granted to them at the behest of the state.[32] The

30. Rushdoony, *Christianity and the State*, 9. Emphasis added.

31. It is important to understand that the US Congress had *never* passed legislation regarding the "right" to abortion or the "banning" of prayer in schools. It was established in a judicial fashion as a matter of precedent through the courts. The justices "found" within the Constitution such principles through exotic and elaborate reasoning. Such judicial overreach and subverting of the anti-centralism of the Constitution was a strong factor in Rushdoony's hostility to federal action. In recent years, the Trump's administrations were notable in the first reversals of such "federal" decisions, reversing Roe vs. Wade, thus delegating abortion as an issue for state-level jurisdiction, and dismantling of "Chevron deference," a foundational doctrine since 1984 that asserted the government agency's *primacy* when interpreting "ambiguous" statutes.

This had effectively given enormous powers of coercion to federal government agencies over state legislatures because Congress had often crafted "deliberately ambiguous" language in the bills. The Chevron doctrine then ensured the federal interpretation of such a statute would become normative; see Turrentine, "Supreme Court Ends Chevron Deference." The author of this piece was *defending* Chevron deference in the interest of "government efficiency," whereas conservatives such as Rushdoony were always intensely hostile to it.

32. In response to criticism and political opposition from Christians, Senator (soon to become president) Johnson surreptitiously inserted a clause within a much larger bill that made it an offense for 501(c)(3) organizations from participating in, or intervening in, any political campaign on behalf of (or in opposition to) any candidate for public office at the pain of losing their tax-exempt status.

separation of church and state was no longer interpreted in the founders' terms of ensuring the church was free from political interference but rather as the state's grant to the church:

> Religious liberty is . . . replaced by religious toleration. . . . Religious liberty has meant, historically, the freedom . . . from state control and jurisdiction. . . . Religious toleration has meant that the state claims the right to govern and control . . . to declare which . . . church has the right to exist. Religious toleration places the power in the hands of the State.[33]

The "Broad Social Program" and the Split with Mainline Conservatism

Although Rushdoony made a fundamental contribution postwar to the emerging conservative consensus, he was soon criticizing it for its lack of coherent philosophical vision.[34] Its ethos was only *generally* Christian. In contrast, Rushdoony was to assert that a Christian people must attain "[Christian] epistemological self-consciousness."[35] In other words, a comprehensive, distinctly Christian way of understanding, constructing, and *living* in the world.[36] This obviously went far beyond the simple libertarian vision of being able to live a life free from state interference in community and business affairs. This clarity of vision caught the attention of some wealthy patrons and in the period from 1957–62, he developed his distinctive program.

As a commentator noted, no one realized the clause was there until Johnson used it against his Christian opponents, but it subsequently proved a very effective *psychological* barrier to church participation in the political realm. However, much like the later alleged "ban on prayer in schools," Christians for decades surrendered more than was necessary; a church *could* still be involved, it would just pay taxes and probably just needed the service of a competent accountant to minimize their liability, much as prayer and Bible study could *still* occur in schools on a *voluntary* basis; the legislation was misrepresented for decades by humanist groups as having far stronger prohibitions than were legally present.

33. Rushdoony, *Christianity and the State*, loc. 219.

34. McVicar, *Christian Reconstruction*, 63–76.

35. McVicar, *Christian Reconstruction*, 87.

36. This was the locus of my doctoral studies and the book based upon them: Macneil, *Foundations*.

Such was the cogency of his formulation that he was hired as the effective leader of a major conservative organization known as the Volker Fund (which became the Center for American Studies in 1961) and attempted to move the entire organization to his explicit Christian program. However, amidst battles with non-Christians and the more moderate Christians on staff, he was fired by the new patron in September 1963. Though he had strong individual supporters within CAS, the consensus amongst staff regarding his program was that

> his entire . . . project . . . was a . . . religious exclusive [Calvinist] form of conservatism. . . . It would be "catastrophic for big tent conservatism and [its] pro-business agenda."[37]

Thus, the consequence of Rushdoony's uncompromising, distinctively Christian theological approach was his effective excommunication from the mainline conservative political and Christian organizations. It was to be about twenty years before mainline conservatism paid attention again to Rushdoony, as the Reconstructionist movement he built in his absence forced itself to prominence, and it is to the philosophical foundations of his distinctive movement that we now turn.

Epistemological Self-Consciousness[38]

The State as a Religious Institution

We have seen that for Rushdoony, anti-statism was fundamental to the sociological aspect of his program. Yet, this distinguished him little from libertarians and many conservatives. It is the particular claim that the state is a *religious* institution and the battle between church and state is between "rival religions"[39] of humanism and Christianity that provides us with the hermeneutic key to the philosophical underpinnings of Rushdoony's dominionism. The distinctiveness and strength of his program was that it was a coherent philosophical and theological program that he had described as

37. McVicar, *Christian Reconstruction*, 72–78.

38. What I sketched in outline in some subsequent sections regarding the philosophical underpinnings, I developed in detail during my doctoral studies, which formed the basis of my *Foundations*. For the reader interested in exploring any of the themes in this chapter in greater depth, I would direct them there.

39. Rushdoony, *Christianity and the State*, loc. 241.

"epistemological self-consciousness."[40] To understand this term is, in my opinion, to understand authentic dominion theology, and it is to an analysis of this concept that we must now turn.

Van Tillianism

The basis of Rushdoony's "epistemological self-consciousness" is Van Tillian apologetics. Van Til (1895–1987) became the first professor of apologetics at Machen's breakaway Westminster Theological Seminary and is generally accepted to have originated a distinctive apologetic method during his career.[41] Van Til broke with the evidentialism and rationalism of Enlightenment apologetics that had come to be identified with Protestant orthodoxy, even within the conservative schools. Traditionally, evidentialism and rationalism had come to treat theology as a "science" and was concerned with the "facts" of apologetics, i.e., the unaided reason of a man or woman should be able to evaluate "evidences" for God's operation in the world and by the *shared, common* human rational process be convinced by argumentation to a place of belief, vis-a-vis the "theistic proofs."[42] Such an approach was based on a natural theology and assumed a *common (intellectual) ground* was available to believers and unbelievers. In other words, facts could be considered "objective reality," which are equally available between men and between men and God; their meaning is in themselves—they are "brute [uninterpreted] facts."[43]

40. McVicar, *Christian Reconstruction*, 87.

41. Van Til, *Christian Apologetics*, 3. Van Til remained in-post for almost fifty years; though made Emeritus in 1972, he still taught until 1979.

42. For example, see chapter 1, "On Method," in Hodge, *Systematic Theology*. The treatment of "theology as a science" suggests presuppositions based upon Enlightenment humanist thought rather than Reformation thought. McGrath engages in a lengthy analysis of the domination of Enlightenment thought within the old Princeton in *Passion for Truth*, 163–200.

43. Rushdoony, *Limits of Reason*, loc. 234. As a matter of cross-reference, we were discussing earlier how philosophers of science were similarly rejecting "brute" facts and theories while Van Til was formulating his apologetic. He was arguing, like Quine, that "factuality" was intricately involved in your view of nature. He used a very different vocabulary (being from an idealist milieu) but had come to conclusions similar to these post-positivist philosophers of science. Van Til was not given sufficient credit in this regard as to how fine a philosopher he was (contra William Lane Craig), in addition to a theologian and a Christian. I discuss this in much more detail in my *Foundations*.

Van Til followed Kuyper by uncovering the assumptions and fallaciousness of this reasoning, which had, at its heart, the presumption of an objective and detached human reason capable of a complete and unbiased evaluation of the facts of the world. Kuyper had reasserted the position of one stream of Reformation thought that an *unregenerate* reason was fundamentally faulty. Luther had written in reply to Erasmus, "Lady Reason . . . a whore of sophistry . . . her babblings are folly and absurdity."[44] Yet, lest we then conclude that Calvin and Luther were anti-intellectual in some way, the key qualifier here is *unregenerate.*

Both Luther and Calvin *argued* and *reasoned* that the Catholic church was degenerate and had ceased to be faithful to the Scriptures and the apostolic tradition. Specifically, it was the persuasiveness and cogency of their *reasoning* that brought many to their side. Both Calvin and Luther argued that the unregenerate reason could never come to a revelation of God apart from his grace and intervention; the Reformation principle was a rejection of the natural theology of Aquinas. This commitment was strengthened in Calvin: it was an *impossibility* that the reason of fallen humankind might reach God.[45] It was always the sovereign act of God that revealed himself to humankind, and apologetic philosophy was thus subject to scriptural theology.

Kuyper, in the nineteenth century, had recapitulated and modernized this Reformation position by asserting that there was a fundamental "antithesis between belief and unbelief."[46] Knowledge and logic in their very form are structured differently, with the result that there is, in principle, no "common ground" possible for argumentation between the believer and unbeliever. Van Til was seen to assent to Kuyper's basic epistemological proposition, expressing it thus:

> There are two and only two classes of men. . . . There are covenant keepers and covenant breakers. In all of men's activities, in their philosophic and scientific enterprises as well as in their worship, men are either covenant keepers or covenant breakers.[47]

However, Van Til differed from Kuyper in that he permitted a conversation, the apologetic task, to communicate and create this self-conscious

44. Luther, "De servo arbitrio [Bondage of the will]," (para. 125, Latin) in *Martin Luther Collection.*

45. Holder, "John Calvin," paras. 7–19.

46. William Edgar, "Introduction" in Van Til, *Christian Apologetics*, 2.

47. Van Til, *Christian Apologetics*, 62.

awareness. This important and subtle nuance, which I consider further in my *Foundations*, is that although, in *principle*, we develop two separate sciences, which would seem to suggest no common ground exists (as was argued by Kuyper), in *practice*, the nonbeliever unavoidably imports in a Christian conception of the world, which *then* permits a conversation to be had because of the inconsistency within the unbeliever's worldview.

The apologetic task then becomes this task of bringing the unbeliever to that place of realization of the implicit dependence of their worldview on Christian presuppositions, of coming to "epistemological self-consciousness." His view of Scripture and natural revelation as "perspicuous" and "meaningless without one another" at once legitimizes philosophy and science but, at the same time, constrains it.[48] It is important to make the historical observation that, in context, Van Til's criticism was also directed at Barth and neoorthodoxy. He was the first within the evangelical community to expose neoorthodoxy's inability to argue coherently for an objective Christian conception of knowledge, for it placed the Christian conversion in a subjective, existential "crisis experience."[49] As Edgar commented in his introduction to Van Til's *Christian Apologetics*, this is no safer an epistemological basis to build an apologetic strategy than what it intends to replace because of the import of the Kantian separation between realms, which is traditionally understood as denying the faculty of reason entry into the realm of faith, thus denying the possibility of any objective proof for the existence of God and severely limits what, of faith, might be articulated using reason.

In contrast, for Van Til, although natural and theological "facts" both have no meaning in or of themselves, they become propositional when interpreted in terms of the framework of the covenant of God with the world:

> The Bible is thought of as authoritative on everything of which it speaks. Moreover, it speaks of everything . . . either directly or by implication. . . . It gives us a philosophy of history as well as history. . . . [T]here is nothing in this universe on which human beings can have full and true information unless they take the Bible into account. . . . [I]f one goes only to the laboratory . . . one will not have a full or even true interpretation.[50]

48. Van Til, *Christian Apologetics*, 62. Kant did attempt an exploration of this issue in his *Religion*, a work notable for an insight into Kant's undoubted spirituality and its infrequent mentions in Kantian scholarship.

49. Van Til, *New Modernism* and *Christianity and Barthianism*.

50. Van Til, *Christian Apologetics*, 19–20.

Thus, Van Til does not locate truth as an abstract concept that exists in a realm above both God and humankind, to which each is equally bound as in Hellenic Western philosophy (after Plato), but as to something that has its origin in and dwells in the creature of God:

> [If it is assumed] that God and man stand in exactly the same sort of relation to the law of contradiction . . . it is assumed [to think truly that] both must think in accordance with that law as an abstraction from the nature of either [God or Man]. . . . The consequences are . . . fatal.[51]

What is "fatal" here for the apologetic task for Van Til is asserting that if you admit the principle that "truth" is somehow abstracted into its own realm apart from God, "the basic principle of the non-Christian conception of truth cannot be challenged."[52] In other words, if the Christian accepts the concept that truth is apart from God rather than something God has as part of his ontology, there can be no discovery of final objective truth but rather, at best, claims of warrant, probable truth, or of reasonable verisimilitude.[53] The best the Christian could hope for is an admission from non-Christians that there is sufficient warrant for Christian belief.[54]

51. Van Til, *Christian Apologetics*, 33.

52. Van Til, *Christian Apologetics*, 33.

53. Plantinga, *Warranted Christian Belief*, xi.

54. Indeed, Alvin Plantinga's entire philosophical project might be to establish the "justification, rationality, and warrant for Christian belief"; Plantinga, *Warranted Christian Belief*, xi. He is firmly within what is, arguably, an *Aristotelian* externalist, epistemological model; see Plantinga, *Warrant and Proper Function*, x. His unique contribution to Reformed epistemology suggests a far more nuanced and sophisticated view, but his own words cited here of a debt to Aristotle show he is approaching the problem very differently than Van Til. However, Plantinga has also outlined an appeal for *Christian* philosophy in his seminal "Advice to Christian Philosophers" (reprinted in Sennett, *Analytic Theist*, 296–315), and his concept of "Christian self-confidence" in that address suggests there must nevertheless be an epistemic independence, which suggests a point of contact with Van Tillianism.

In updating this footnote after my doctoral work, I would now qualify further the assertion of a dependence on Aristotle given above; a careful reading of the reference to Plantinga's own words confirms this. It does not give Plantinga sufficient credit in his contribution to a distinctively *Christian* epistemology. It *is* true that, here, he acknowledges the cogency of Quine's criticism of modal logic (which Plantinga was defending) as in some way relying on Aristotelian essences. However, that is rather different than what I have suggested here, that his epistemology has a fundamental *dependence* on Aristotle; it is rather that he shares with Aristotle an *externalist* emphasis.

He is far more *directly* dependent on Reid, but even then, he refined and fortified Reid to the degree he was recognized by his peers as making a major original contribution to

Van Til refuses to accept this principle and is aiming to demonstrate we can most certainly know what truth is because truth is resident in God and is revealed to us via the means of his self-revelation in Scripture and in a revelation of our own selves to ourselves through our willful obedience. Humanity's very constitution and desire to dominion is there because it is there within us as a "law," in the sense of a principle of correct and innate operation, i.e., in accordance with its design. God has placed his law in the human will, and the human personality, to a greater or lesser degree, chooses to embrace the leadings of God's will within itself according to God's purpose, grace, and choosing. The will of God is established through the agency of the human will, but "it is the ultimate will or plan of the self-determinate God that gives determinate character to anything that is done by the human will."[55]

This is a supremely Reformed apologetic, where God works *through* the agency of human free will. As I write in my *Foundations*, human will *is* free but never *independent* of its creator; God can always invade the will of his creature for his purposes.[56] In contrast, the Arminian position would argue that it can be wholly independent, and it is the position maintained by most evangelical Christians outside of the orthodox Reformed churches. The logical problem of the Arminian position was made clear by Van Til, *if* salvation was but a possibility and dependent on the will of men, *all* men *could* have chosen to reject the salvation of God, forever separating God from creation, an untenable position. The question the Christian is then confronted with is do *we* choose God, or does *God* choose us? I am constrained to believe the latter, however uncomfortable the implications of that is for me.

In light of this logic of salvation, for Van Til, dominion theology is the *only* theology possible because God's first intention for the created humanity was dominion:

> [T]he will of man . . . depends for what it is ultimately upon a creative and sustaining act of God. . . . [M]an is bound to act, God has set his program [what we should want]. God gave this program by way of self-conscious communication at the beginning of history.

epistemology. Indeed, in part, my doctoral work explored the congruence of and differences between their philosophical approaches, asserting there is far more in common than is generally appreciated between Van Til and Plantinga, with both seeking an *explicitly Christian* epistemology, which, happily, I *do* mention above.

55. Van Til, *Christian Apologetics*, 36.

56. Macneil, *Foundations*, §5.2.

> Man's *summum bonum* (the supreme good, from which all others are derived) was set before him. . . . He was to subdue the earth and bring out its latent powers to the glory of God.[57]

Here, we arrive at the principle that was to form the foundation of Rushdoony's dominion theology.

Rushdoony and Theonomy

At this point, it should be clear as to why Rushdoony seeking a *theological* basis for any reformation of society insisted on a Van Tillian epistemology. What is distinctive in Rushdoony is that he *applies* Van Til by insisting that societal reformation must be theonomical (Greek: *Theo* [God] + *nomos* [law]). Culture is derived from the law of God as revealed in Scripture and not subject to the premises and prejudices derived from the autonomous (Greek: *autos* [self] + *nomos* [law]) reasonings of the human will. So, Rushdoony developed Van Til's apologetic in a very important way, and the novel character of this development is captured by North:

> Van Til was analogous to a demolitions expert. He placed explosive charges at the bottom of every modern edifice [and] detonated them. But he left no blueprints for the reconstruction of society. . . . This was not good enough for Rushdoony . . . he concluded that the source of the missing blueprints is Old Testament law.[58]

Rushdoony extended Van Til's philosophical theonomy into the sociological realm.[59] He posited government of the self and society by God's

57. Van Til, *Christian Apologetics*, 36. Amplification (n. 9) was Edgar's editorial note.

58. North and DeMar, *Christian Reconstruction*, xi–xii.

59. We will examine in the next chapter that there was a sustained conflict within the orthodox Reformed seminaries over whether Van Til was a "theonomist" in the sense of how Rushdoony, and contemporary Bahnsen, began to use the term in its sociological sense, which is captured by Bahnsen in the response to his critics that appeared in the revised edition of his *Theonomy*. However, Van Til *was* explicitly theonomical as an issue of theological principle: the only choice for men was *theonomy* or *autonomy*.

We will also see that Bahnsen and Van Til were extremely close, with Van Til indicating it was his desire that Bahnsen should replace him at his retirement and stated that Bahnsen had most clearly understood his position and, thus, was well placed to develop its social and political implications. Van Til's wishes were not honored and Bahnsen's time in academia was short, becoming an independent scholar and debater after a brief period at RTS, terminated prematurely over the controversy surrounding his *Theonomy*. Van Til also responded positively to Rushdoony in a Festschrift written in his honor at

law in contrast to autonomy, which, as we see in our analysis above, is government of the self and society by the judgments of human reason alone. Theonomy to Rushdoony is in the interpretation *and* application of biblical law, and he seeded the Reconstructionist movement with it as the first modern dominion theology movement:

> It is a modern heresy that holds that the law of God has no meaning nor any binding force for man today. . . . To attempt to understand Western civilization apart from the impact of biblical law within it and upon it is to seek a fictitious history and to reject [biblical law] . . . the historic power and vitality of the West has been in Biblical faith and law.[60]

Reconstructionism reflects the purpose to reconstruct every sphere of society according to God's law:

> What is our standard; by what standards shall we approach the problems of philosophy and the problems of everyday life? If we begin with anything other than the ontological Trinity, with the sovereignty of God as *intellectually applied and systematically delineated in every aspect and avenue of human thought*, we end with the destruction of Christian theology and the deterioration of Christian life.[61]

He sees no discontinuity or contradiction between law as expressed in the Mosaic Law and the law of Christ for the believer in the church era. They are part of the same theological concept of divine law:

> Man as covenant-breaker is in "enmity against God" (Rom 8:7) and is subject to "the law of sin and death" (Rom 8:2), whereas the believer is under "the law of the Spirit of life in Christ" (Rom 8:2). The law is one law, the law of God.[62]

Thereunto, it is *crucial* to recognize that for Rushdoony, theonomy is not a reversion to *legalism*; he is not claiming a man is *saved* by keeping the law. Rushdoony is rather emphasizing the sanctifying work of the law *after* the redemptive work of grace:

---

retirement (Geehan, *Jerusalem and Athens*, 348); Rushdoony was the earliest interpreter of Van Til to apply his work (*By What Standard* [1959]).

60. Rushdoony, *Institutes*, 2, 5.

61. Rushdoony, *By What Standard*, 203. Emphasis added.

62. Rushdoony, *Institutes*, 3.

> Christ's atoning work was to restore man to a position of covenant-keeping instead of covenant-breaking, to enable man to keep the law by freeing man "from the law of sin and death." . . . The law has a position of centrality . . . in man's sanctification (in that he grows in grace as he grows in law-keeping, for the law is the way of sanctification).[63]

That is, there are not separate dispensations of "law" and "grace" but a coherent continuity, which can be directly and explicitly applied. Rushdoony's *Institutes* presents the thesis that the Ten Commandments are the statutory aspects of the law and that the detail of the law found in the books provides a source of case law to illustrate the principles of interpretation and, thus, the basis of civil governance in *any* era. It is conceived as an explicit template for every sphere and aspect of human existence. Anyone who reads the Pentateuch will be struck with how many times the phrase "I am the LORD" appears after the giving of a statute or a commandment; this is not inviting a debate but is a declaration: "I am the boss, and this is the way it is going to be."

It follows that any *Christian* sociological order must necessarily be based upon the same principles and, sometimes, the details of God's law, where they are not peculiar to the cultural situation of ancient Israel. This is the moderate theonomical position argued by Cope in both her *Old Testament Template* and her *God and Political Justice*. This would also appear to be the New Testament position, as the apostles did not expect the gentiles to be bound by Jewish custom.[64] A clear distinction in Christian Scripture was made between the timeless moral content of the law and the specific cultural applications of it. The promulgation of biblical law in terms of the dominion mandate is thus the fulfillment of the original intent of God:

> The purpose of Christ's coming was in terms of this same creation mandate. . . . Christ died to make atonement for their sins. . . . The redeemed are recalled to the original purpose of man to exercise dominion under God . . . to "fulfil the righteousness of the law" (Rom 8:4). The law remains central to God's purpose.[65]

63. Rushdoony, *Institutes*, 3.

64. Acts 15 is an extended pericope on this very issue. Similarly, the theme of virtually the entire book of Galatians centers on contrasting the inward renewal and work of the Spirit with the outward manifestations and customs (Gal 4:9–11).

65. Rushdoony, *Institutes*, 3–4.

One of the most important qualifications Christians needed to apply is that we do not live in a theocracy where the Lord rules over us directly; the book of Acts gives numerous instances of the difficulties and challenges of dealing with rulers.

Summary and Concluding Remarks

In this chapter, we traced the development of the different themes that eventually formed Rushdoony's sociological program. We began by considering Rushdoony's involvement in the post-WWII conservative movement that proceeded on a big-tent, libertarian basis in response to the statism of Roosevelt's New Deal era and the federally driven imposition of legal precedents that reduced the power of the states in favor of the government. With Rushdoony's additional experience within the Duck Valley Indian Reservation and the destruction of Native American culture by welfare dependence, he came to believe in a *total* reform of the different layers of society on a Christian basis. This separated him from mainline conservatism and began the development in earnest of his own distinctive program of societal reform on a Christian basis.

The Christians of the social gospel movement were also arguing for total societal reconstruction in the interests of social justice, but Rushdoony viewed its promotion of socialism, its emphasis on government-driven action, and a deification of the state as ungodly and destructive. For Rushdoony, the appropriate form of Christian thought was where the community had thought through the implications of its Christianity to the place of explicit understanding of how Scripture applied to the spheres of culture. It was the families of the community that drove the reform, and the philosophical framework of that reform was taken from Van Tillian thought, the theonomical imperative. Within theonomy, the Ten Commandments of the law of God are seen as eternal principles, and the books of the law provide a source of case law and examples of their application. This is then viewed as a template for national reform.

So, Rushdoony's final position was that we would do well to pay attention to the principles, details, and practice of the law within our governments, but this needs to be argued for by our Christian community, its political organizations, and associations of professionals, that *consent* might be gained, rather than an imposition by a religious hegemony or by government fiat. This was envisaged as a bottom-up movement, not a top-down one. This meant literature, organization, legal advocacy, and a broad cultural engagement. How Rushdoony attempted to put these principles into practice to build that Christian social movement, how he transformed evangelical politics, and how he inspired the formation of other Reconstructionist movements is the subject of the next chapter.

The Dominionist Movement

Overview

THE PURPOSE OF THIS chapter is to identify the first generation of major thinkers within the dominionist movement founded by Rushdoony and how their collective intellectual force caused a paradigm shift within conservative evangelical Christianity. This represented perhaps the greatest reorientation of the conservative church in its history.

Reconstructionism

Three appendices to Rushdoony's *Institutes* were written by Gary North. North was supported by Rushdoony through doctoral studies and eventually hired to work at Rushdoony's Chalcedon foundation. With North came Greg Bahnsen. Both men were recognized as "brilliant students," and both had studied under Van Til at Westminster Seminary.[1] They worked closely with Rushdoony and developed the platform that became known as Reconstructionism and propagated his ideas into the mainstream of evangelical consciousness.

Greg Bahnsen and Theonomy

We saw in the previous chapter that theonomy was central to Rushdoony's philosophy and was built upon Van Tillianism. Theonomy was taken on and developed with great academic rigor by Bahnsen, who was really the

1. McVicar, *Christian Reconstruction*, 151, 157.

intellectual engine and popularizer, and the center of the controversy, of this central component of Reconstructionism. As it was such a large part of the movement and the foundation of so much of its program, it is worth considering Bahnsen's position and contribution in detail.

Van Til had wanted Bahnsen to replace him when he retired from Westminster, and Bahnsen had been asked by him to lecture for Van Til during a period of illness—such was his confidence in the student. Bahnsen comprehended the full implications of Van Til's apologetic and developed it rigorously. His first major statement was in the publication of *Theonomy in Christian Ethics*.[2] It is especially significant that Rushdoony wrote the foreword to the book and put it in the context of the dominion mandate. For Rushdoony, a failure to keep the law renders the church impotent because it denies God's holiness and separates humanity from God's power.[3] Bahnsen's thesis centered on an exegesis of Matt 5:17–20 and asserted that the Old Testament law was not abrogated in any theological or ethical sense by Christ's crucifixion and resurrection.[4] The law was to be kept "every jot and tittle[5] but, as with Rushdoony, it is important to understand that Bahnsen was not asserting legalism:

> The law does *not* save a man, but it *does* show him *why* he needs to be saved and *how* he is to walk after he is saved. Because God's moral nature, his holiness, is revealed in the law, the law accuses and convicts its reader of sin.[6]

The ethics for the Christian remain the same as for the old covenant believer, but how God enables us to keep the ethical law have changed; it is by the grace through Jesus Christ writing the law on our hearts:

2. Rushdoony's introduction to the first edition was written in October 1971. The publication was delayed until 1977 owing to "factors beyond Bahnsen's control" (North and DeMar, *Christian Reconstruction*, xiii). With the later acrimonious split in the Reconstructionist movement (we consider this shortly), some initially asserted that it was Bahnsen, rather than Rushdoony, that first articulated theonomy (Rushdoony's *Institutes* were not published until 1973.) However, the fact that Rushdoony was invited to write the foreword by Bahnsen strongly suggests he was inspired by Rushdoony's development of Van Til. Rushdoony and Bahnsen also reconciled quickly after the initial split when Bahnsen left with North.

3. Rushdoony, "Foreword" in Bahnsen, *Theonomy in Christian Ethics*, vii–ix.

4. Bahnsen, *Theonomy in Christian Ethics*, 39–88.

5. Bahnsen, *Theonomy in Christian Ethics*, xv.

6. Bahnsen, *Theonomy in Christian Ethics*, 127. Emphasis original.

> "Fulfilment' in [Matt 5:17] [is] not any sort of euphemism for "relaxation" or "invalidation" . . . far from being different from the first covenant, the ethical stipulations of that new covenant would be the same as the original law; God says He will write the law on His people's hearts, not change the law.[7]

Fierce reaction to Bahnsen ensued from within the liberal, evangelical, and, perhaps most surprisingly, from his own Reformed circles.[8] There was a concerted campaign against his ordination in the OPC, and after completing his doctorate, he only managed a brief controversial tenure at RTS, where the controversy surrounding his theonomical views within the faculty led to the termination of his position.[9] He was not again to hold a position in a major academic institution despite his brilliance and recognition as a skillful debater within mainstream academia.[10]

Yet, during this brief period, he inspired a group of students, including Keith Gentry, Gary DeMar, James B. Jordan, Michael Butler, and David Chilton, who became the next generation of Reconstructionist thinkers developing work on eschatology (Gentry and Chilton), pastoral theology (Jordan), political theory (DeMar), and philosophy (Butler). Between them, in less in a matter of a few years, they authored over sixty-seven books that were to force Christian Reconstructionism to the forefront of the evangelical consciousness. Bahnsen's legacy is still strongly represented by the output of the *Covenant Media Foundation*, which he began as the means to distribute his written and recorded materials.[11]

Greg Bahnsen and "Federal Vision"

After the premature death of Bahnsen, his CMF became influential in the propagation of the "federal vision" theology, which is viewed as a paradigm shift within classical Calvinism and effectively dilutes, if not denies, historical Reformed commitments regarding the Christian's relationship to the law of God.[12] Even its most enthusiastic proponents recognize it as a "paradigm

7. Bahnsen, *Theonomy in Christian Ethics*, 46.

8. McVicar, *Rushdoony*, 163; Bahnsen, *Theonomy in Christian Ethics*, xiv.

9. North, *Theonomy*, xiii–xiv; McVicar, *Rushdoony*, 160.

10. Stein and Bahnsen, "Great Debate."

11. It is notable that most of this material is now available free of charge: https://www.cmfnow.com/.

12. Bahnsen, "Auburn Avenue Controversy," 433.

shift" away from classical Calvinism and into a more legalistic framework.[13] Bahnsen's son indicated he believed his father would be sympathetic to FV, whereas other past students of Bahnsen have argued forcefully to the contrary.[14] Nevertheless, with James Jordan, a former pastor of Tyler's Reconstructionist Westminster Presbyterian Church firmly in the FV camp, FV is sometimes viewed as a distinctive development of Reconstructionism having a more moderate theonomical viewpoint:

> The strict Theonomists . . . say that [we] must implement the Mosaic law as it stands. The more moderate Christian Reconstructionists have said that the Bible as a whole, including the Mosaic law wisely applied in line with New Covenant principles, should be the guide.[15]

There is nothing controversial in this statement; indeed, it would be considered the mainstream theonomical position. However, this is *then* combined with the requirement to *keep* that law as a continuing *condition* of salvation. In contrast, Bahnsen's *Theonomy* had argued that the keeping of the law was a *consequence* of salvation: we are saved by "grace alone."

Thus, the chief theological argument concerns the interpretation of the relative positions of James and Paul regarding "faith" and "works," which have long caused problems of interpretation as their literal sense would appear contradictory.[16] However, the Reformed position, since Luther has always been clear—we are saved by *grace alone*—which is the Pauline principle; but our works *evidence* our faith, which Calvin then viewed as surely the correct application of James's polemic. Whereas Luther was initially less persuaded on this last point, Calvin was explicit in his exposition of it in his commentary on James. FV seems to be a

13. This was discussed at length by Otis in *Danger in the Camp*.

14. Otis, *Danger in the Camp*, 431–51.

15. Jordan, "Theocratic Critique of Theonomy," para. 1. As noted earlier, Cope argues for this more moderate position, and convincingly so. The real issue between the positions was the status of the penal sanctions, especially those mandating public execution. The strict theonomists argued for a literal application, an obviously controversial position.

16. Luther initially described the book of James an "epistle of straw" in his translation of the Bible, viewing it as contradicting *sola fide* ("through faith alone") and had relegated it to an appendix. However, after 1537, he removed this comment from his preface, suggesting he had come to see the matter differently. It is worth noting that he had also moved Jude, Hebrews, and Revelation to the same appendix, viewing the content and authorship as contested. Modern Lutherans have accepted these books as canonical.

retrograde iteration of this argument, taking a side against both Calvin's and Luther's positions; hence, the intense opposition to this position from within the Reformed communion, and it is correct to view it as an aberration and departure from New Testament orthodoxy.

Gary North and the Tyler Reconstructionists

Gary North was first hired to edit the scholarly journal of Rushdoony's Chalcedon foundation and published his seminal *Introduction to Christian Economics* in 1973.[17] North excelled at developing economic theory, becoming known as "the economist of the Reconstruction movement," and he distilled Rushdoony's dense narrative into practical tools.[18] He presented these through a mixture of popular, polemical, and scholarly publications targeted at the seminary, conservative political activist groups, and the layperson.[19] His Institute for Christian Economics (ICE) was primarily responsible for the vast literary output of the Reconstructionist movement during the 1980s and 1990s.[20]

His intention was for a relentless polemic and scholarly rebuttal of the movement's critics within academia and the development of practical programs and strategies to promote the Reconstructionist agenda at a grassroots political level.[21] He effectively founded a separate political, militant, and publishing wing of the Reconstruction movement based in Tyler, Texas, which also had an associated "prototype" Reconstructionist church and a divinity school.[22] This functioned in a similar but more aggressive fashion to Rushdoony's Chalcedon foundation. He was a guest

17. North and DeMar, *Christian Reconstruction*, xiii. North passed away in 2022, aged eighty. His website (https://www.garynorth.com/) is still active and maintained by some associates. It is an excellent resource for getting access to primary source material regarding Reconstructionism; he graciously replied to me when I found a dead link to his "free materials" when I was writing the thesis upon which this book is based.

18. Clarkson, "Christian Reconstructionism," entire issue. (Note this is *not* the British satirical *Public Eye* magazine but an American research journal.)

19. North et al., *Theology of Christian Resistance* and *Tactics of Christian Resistance*; North, *Backward, Christian Soldiers?*, 190.

20. North, *Theonomy*, xvi.

21. North and DeMar, *Christian Reconstruction*, xvii. He had come to this conclusion after interning for Senator Ron Paul. He viewed the inertia of national politics so large that change could only come from the grassroots.

22. McVicar, *Christian Reconstruction*, 182–87.

numerous times on Pat Robertson's CBN's *700 Club* during the 1980s, which was testimony to the success of his strategies, his increasing reputation within Reconstructionism, and the growth of Reconstructionism's influence on the wider evangelical consciousness.[23]

Schism and Reformation

During the early years of Tyler, North was still editing the Chalcedon journal, but he was to split ideologically with Rushdoony over the means for societal reformation and broke acrimoniously with him over a mix of personal and theological issues in 1981.[24] North was fired by Rushdoony, who, at the same time, also fired his fellow Tyler men Ray Sutton and James Jordan, who were on the Chalcedon staff. Sutton and Jordan had developed a radical ecclesiology as the means for societal transformation in opposition to Rushdoony's familial model, which became known as the "Tyler theology."[25] However, the Tyler church and divinity school had both unraveled by the end of the 1980s, being described by one important former member as an example of "Reconstructionist ecclesiolatry."[26]

The Tyler men eventually left to their own projects and think tanks, with Reconstructionism becoming an effective blend of Tyler, Bahnsen, and Chalcedon. Though much is made of the excesses of Tyler and the break with Chalcedon, North and the other Reconstructionists were still to reference Rushdoony through their own works.[27] Their tributes to him at his passing in 2001 are testament to the intellectual and personal debt they felt that they owed to him.[28] Thus, in the contemporary context,

23. North was far more polyvalent than Rushdoony when it came to engaging with the evangelical Christian world outside of Presbyterianism, going so far as to be involved with charismatics and Pentecostals. Rushdoony had been extremely critical of charismatic Christianity when he had written his *Institutes* but later joined North ministering to these groups as the influence of Reconstructionism grew.

24. McVicar, *Christian Reconstruction*, 192–94.

25. Rushdoony, "Christian Reconstruction as a Movement," 9.

26. Chilton, "Ecclesiastical Megalomania," para. 5.

27. With the coming and passing of the financial apocalypse predicted by North with Y2K, the more extreme survivalist rhetoric and Tyler extremism was quietly buried as he closed the ICE in 2001, though all its publications remain accessible at no cost at https://www.garynorth.com/freebooks/sidefrm2.htm. McVicar, *Christian Reconstruction*, 220–21; House and Ice, *Dominion Theology*, 18–19, 351–52.

28. Rushdoony et al., "Tribute to RJ Rushdoony."

alongside second-generation Reconstructionist Gary DeMar's stewardship of the American Vision foundation and the post-Bahnsen CMF, the three arenas of Reconstructionist thought might be now better thought of as complimentary rather than in an adversarial mode of relation, as was the case for a period in the early 1990s.[29]

The Diversification of the Movement

"The Enemy of My Enemy is My Friend"

An aspect of North's earlier thought, which brings us into the contemporary period of dominion theology, was his recognition and willingness to engage with what he felt was a major "convergence" between Protestant theologies that had been implacably polarized and hostile to one another. As both Tyler and Chalcedon pushed into the mainstream ideology of the New Right and began to heavily influence a new generation of Christian activists, both he and Rushdoony recognized that elements of Reconstructionism were being incorporated into revised fundamentalist, charismatic, and Pentecostal ideologies, far from Reconstruction's Reformed roots:

> [The] growing alliance between charismatics and Reconstructionists has disturbed Reformed Presbyterians almost as much as it has disturbed premillennial dispensationalists. It has led to accusations of heresy against both groups from all sides: pietistic Pentecostalism, pietistic Scofieldism, and pietistic Presbyterianism. The critics worry about the fact that Pentecostalism's infantry is at last being armed with Reconstructionism's field artillery. They should be worried. This represents one of the most fundamental realignments in U.S. Protestant church history.[30]

Both North and Rushdoony addressed charismatic conferences and seminars and developed personal contacts and friendships with charismatics, which would have been thought impossible when Rushdoony first wrote the *Institutes*, with its stinging criticism of charismatic Christianity. Both recognized a shift in the political and theological consciousness of evangelical Christians:

29. McVicar, *Christian Reconstruction*, 221; American Vision is found at https://americanvision.org/.

30. North, "Reconstructionist Renewal," 2.

> Younger charismatics and most of the independent Christian day schools are headed toward biblical law and away from the social and political policies of inaction that have been common in traditional, pietistic, dispensational circles since 1925. They are picketing against abortion clinics (legalized in 1973 by the U. S. Supreme Court, but not by God's Supreme Court). They are adopting ethics religion and abandoning the older escapist religion. The key word in this shift of perspective is "dominion." The secondary word is "resistance." Resistance to what? Secular humanism and its legal arm, the Federal government.[31]

There is little argument with North on this point. By the end of the 1980s, Rushdoony had estimated "20 million Christians [in the US] ascribed to some aspect of theonomical or Reconstructionist thinking.[32]

The Fundamentalist Dimension

Reconstructionism's movement into the mainstream was due to its influence on key fundamentalist and evangelical leaders. One of the hugely significant bridges between the previously hostile Reformed Reconstruction movement and what can be loosely called the "fundamentalist" and "broad-church" conservative movements were the Schaeffers.[33] Francis Schaeffer, the elder Schaeffer, was one of the important US cultural figures of the 1960s and 1970s, and even more so for the modern evangelicals; he had also studied under Van Til in the 1930s and had clearly taken some inspiration from him.[34] He is credited more than any other evangelical leader during the

31. North, *Unholy Spirits*, 12.

32. McVicar, *Rushdoony*, 201.

33. Dobson et al., *Fundamentalist Phenomenon*, 186–223. A succinct presentation regarding the Schaeffers is given by Edgar in "Francis Schaeffer." As both Edgar and Bahnsen note, Schaeffer's skill was to "translate every important theological concept into the vernacular" rather than in the academic rigor of his work; he did not write for the academy but for the laypeople. *L'Abri* was founded by him and his wife in 1955 as an experiment in communal living for the philosophical and religious pilgrims of the era, sitting intellectually somewhere between informal colleges and Christian communities. There are still eleven sites around the world: https://labri.org/.

34. However, Schaeffer never publicly acknowledged this, perhaps aware of the political and sectarian implications of doing so, though he was acknowledged by many important members of the Reconstructionist movement as doing "yeoman's service" for the cause (North, *Christian Reconstruction*, xiii). As Bahnsen critiques in his *Presuppositional Apologetics*, 241–60, Schaeffer's presuppositionalism was also qualitatively distinct from Van Til, owing far more to evidentialism than Van Tillianism.

1970s with rallying conservative Christian opinion in response to the "abortion on demand" ruling in the Roe vs. Wade ruling in 1973.[35]

The younger Schaeffer, Franky, was a filmmaker and took his father's words and turned them into films that reached a large audience and helped galvanize anti-abortion opinion.[36] However, Franky also wrote highly polemical works encouraging legal activism and worked with John Whitehead at the Rutherford Institute. Whitehead had been influenced and personally mentored by Rushdoony into legal activism and advocacy in the founding of the ACLJ, a conservative version of the ACLU. The focus was on defending religious liberty, the right to homeschooling, and preserving space for religious expression within the public sphere, which, as we have previously documented, had been under siege owing to the barely disguised radical socialism of the ACLU, and the legacy of the liberal Warren Supreme Court period during the 1950s and 1960s. Franky Schaeffer was brought into contact with Rushdoony's works, quoted them in his work and recommended Rushdoony's Chalcedon foundation to his evangelical audience.[37]

The Pentecostal Movements

However, what was more startling was the influence Reconstructionism began to exert on Pentecostalism. The twentieth-century Pentecostal movement that had started in Azusa Street around 1906 emphasized spiritual experience, the supernatural gifts of the Spirit, and was apocryphally related to the "enthusiasm" of the Welsh Revival of 1904–5.[38] Pentecostalism fundamentally changed the spiritual dynamics of a section of the Protestant church and became the putative heirs of eighteenth-century

35. McVicar, *Christian Reconstruction*, 173.

36. The anti-abortion *Whatever Happened to the Human Race* adaptation of the elder Schaeffer's book of the same name was particularly influential in generating activism amongst newly politicized evangelicals.

37. McVicar, *Christian Reconstruction*, 173–76. Franky suffered an existential crisis in the 1990s and retreated from his evangelical conservatism, offering public repentance for his previous radicalism. He tells his story in numerous works as seen in this *New York Times* profile: "To millions of evangelical Christians, the Schaeffer name is royal, and Frank is the reluctant, wayward, traitorous prince. His crime is not financial profligacy, like some pastors' sons, but turning his back on Christian conservatives" (Oppenheimer, "Son of Evangelical Royalty," para. 2).

38. Joyner, *Power to Change the World*, loc. 47; Johnson and Joyner, "Azusa Now Livestream 04.09.2016."

Arminian revivalism, emphasizing the role of free will and individual choice in salvation.

This revivalism precipitated an evolution of many new denominations during the twentieth century. First, the emergence of the "classic" Pentecostal denominations, such as the Apostolic Faith Church, AOG, COG, COGIC, Elim, and Foursquare, which were all founded before 1930. Secondly, the 1950s saw the emergence of the "big tent" healing revivals and the foundation of Oral Roberts University (ORU), which had close links with the Word of Faith movement under Dr. Kenneth Hagin, was founded in 1963.[39] Thirdly, during the 1970s and 1980s, the emergence of the "house church" and charismatic movements in both Britain, America, and Western Europe. It was also a time of a new wave of mission movements, such as the CCFC and YWAM. It continued to mutate and develop during the 1980s with the Kingdom Now movement and the birth of the distinctive neo-Pentecostalism of Central and South America[40] and the megachurches of Africa and Asia.[41]

Historical Pentecostalism had shared the theological emphasis of the modern revivalist movement that was inherited from the classical fundamentalists and their antipathy to social action, which meant that though many millions had "come into the kingdom," there was frequently little evidence of national change or positive influence of the massive numerical growth of the new churches. Such was the lack of social progress that by the mid-1970s, key leaders within the movements, such as C. Peter Wagner, Loren Cunningham, and Landa Cope, began to reflect on this wider cultural irrelevance and the political impotence of the Pentecostal and charismatic churches.

For example, in a documentary study related by Cope, it was found that in the most "Christianized" city of the United States (Dallas, Texas), there was found to be no improvement in drug addiction or homelessness,

39. The relation between Kenneth Hagin and the denominational Pentecostal movements was a tense one, though many American Pentecostals had worked with Hagin in his early days. As a "new wineskin," Hagin eventually founded Rhema Bible College, which is the strongest independent international Bible college today. Hagin also heavily influenced a wing of the emerging prophetic movement of Bill Hamon. He was also foundational to ministries such as Kenneth Copeland Ministries and the River Church movement under Dr. Rodney Howard Browne. See also Hamon, *Eternal Church*, 239–61.

40. Martin, "From Pre- to Postmodernity," 107.

41. Boonke, *Extra Impact*.

and divorce was at equivalent or greater rates than non-Christian communities.[42] What provoked Cope more than anything else was that when the local spiritual leaders of the community had been challenged regarding the decay of their communities, they held that none of this was their concern, for they were "spiritual leaders."[43] Thus, the paradox seen by Wagner, Cope, Cunningham, and others like them was that even though the Western church was numerically *stronger* than it had ever been, its *influence* politically and economically was *smaller* than it had ever been.

As a response, by the mid-1970s, they began to embrace Rushdoony's ideas of a "cultural mandate" in a slightly softened and repackaged form as the "seven mountains" mandate.[44] Notably, Wagner had explicitly adopted the language of dominion theology and was clearly influenced directly by Reconstructionism, though he attempted to distance himself explicitly from the extreme, theocratic elements of the Tyler theology.[45] In fact, the perceived similarity to Reconstructionism was so obvious that Wagner himself testifies, "Some wanted me ousted from Christendom—immediately!"[46] In reaction, it is arguable that he softened his view and rebranded his ministry to a degree in mitigation to the hostility aimed at him, but he remained clear that

> the underlying premise is that God wills his people here on earth [to] take dominion of the society in which we live, promoting the values, blessings and prosperity of His Kingdom . . . fear is . . . the principal driving [element] underlying the sincere opposition by some to Dominionism.[47]

Wagner is also important because of his links with John Wimber of the "power evangelism" movement, perhaps the most famous of the charismatic leaders during the 1980s and the first part of the 1990s. This, in turn, is important because Wimber is the spiritual father of what might be

42. Cope, *Old Testament Template*, 21–23. Where "Christianized" was defined as evangelical and attendance was mid-week as well as Sunday to distinguish it from traditional and formal attendance. It is also not without significance that radical Islam considers Texas to be "ground zero" in their colonization of the United States (Anderson, "Congressmen Call Texas 'Ground Zero'").

43. Cope, *Old Testament Template*, 23.

44. McVicar, *Christian Reconstruction*, 200.

45. Wagner, *Dominion!*, 12–17.

46. Wagner, *On Earth*, 7.

47. Wagner, *On Earth*, 8.

termed the contemporary "fifth wave" churches. These are churches that trace their genesis and inspiration to the 1994 "outpouring" of the Holy Spirit at what was then the Toronto Airport Vineyard Church with the Arnotts as leaders. This movement attracted a notoriety of such a degree that Wimber suspended the church from the Vineyard association, which provoked the corresponding response from the Arnotts of withdrawing themselves from the Vineyard covering completely, establishing a fully independent prototype church for the "fifth [charismatic] wave." Key members of this movement signed on to a "Reformer's pledge," which was a conciliatory articulation of Wagner's "dominionist" position in response to the criticism that had been leveled at it from within the charismatic and house-church movements.[48] Though not by name, the pledge itself obliquely mentioned the Reconstructionist movement, underlining the putative dependence of this "reform" movement on dominion theology and the Reconstructionists that went before it.

Summary and Concluding Remarks

We have seen that the movement seeded by Rushdoony was firmly established on the theonomical foundation of Bahnsen. With the economic and media expertise of North, a precocious and militant form of dominionism generated an enormous literary output that caused the movement to grow rapidly and extend its influence far beyond its Reformed roots. It became established within mainstream evangelicalism and was rather unexpectedly included in the Pentecostal and charismatic movements. Though the movement had split into factions, this diversification worked in its favor, and the hostility was generally short-lived. None of the main organizations are in an adversarial relation, and numerous hubs have remained easily recognizable as Reconstructionist, even if that terminology has fallen out of favor. Many other movements incorporated dominionist ideas during this period (we list some of these shortly.) The central conception remained that the gospel is relevant and necessary in every sphere of human life; it is the motivation, *modus operandi*, and unifying principle of the diverse conceptions of dominion theology now found within this broad and theologically diverse network. Rushdoony's ideas influenced key leaders within all these movements, whom, although they did not share his Calvinism, imported

48. Wagner et al., *Reformer's Pledge*.

his ideas whilst, like Wagner, distanced themselves from "extremism" by never publicly acknowledging the Reconstructionist influence.[49]

However, the controversy surrounding Rushdoony and his ideas has meant he has basically gone unacknowledged by those he inspired as they absorbed and morphed dominionism. Dominionism might now be better described as a *genus* and the associated terms (Reconstructionist, post-millennialist, dominionist, theonomist, Kingdom Now, Business as a Mission, Discipling Nations, New Apostolic Age, Christian nationalism, and some fellow travelers within the Hamonite prophetic movement) as *species*. The days of evangelical movements being politically neutral and considering sociopolitical involvement "unimportant" were largely ended during this period.[50] A whole new political consciousness amongst the evangelicals was born. The next chapter examines the extended and ferocious critiques of this newfound political consciousness amongst evangelicals and investigates why many Christians preferred to distance themselves, publicly at least, from dominonism.

49. "Never" may be too strong an adjective here, but only marginally so. A full-length book by a charismatic leader (Hamon, *Eternal Church*) purporting to be a modern history of the church gave Reconstructionism a single sentence; another book by a group of charismatic leaders on the imperative for societal reform (Wagner, *Reformer's Pledge*) gave a single obfuscated reference to the movement.

50. Though I argue in my *Politics* that a dangerous reaction to partisan political involvement amongst believers that sometimes places party before Christian principle is to slip back into a sophisticated, spiritualized, politically agnostic indifference that is of equivalent, if not, greater danger because of its reasoned basis. In particular, many British evangelicals find US Christian support for Trump, or right-wing conservatism generally, unacceptable. This, as I argue in my *Politics*, reflects the European addiction to socialism, which permeates the big government models of Europe.

The Critiques of Dominion Theology

Overview

DOMINION THEOLOGY WAS ALWAYS controversial and Bahnsen suffered a sustained attack over his *Theonomy* from its publication date in 1977; the dispute over the work eventually led to his "dismissal" from RTS.[1] However, that was a dispute over Reformed theology and localized in that movement. It was also a dispute regarding the praxis of a theological position regarding the status of the old covenant Mosaic law, a position that could legitimately claim to have formed a part of the Westminster Confession. What was "new" in the Reconstructionist program was its sociopolitical extension and the demands it made for the Christian participation in and redefinition of the *entirety* of culture; the quiet and unobtrusive toleration of Christianity at the behest of religious privileges granted by the state, situated at the outer limits of culture, was forcibly rejected as *apostate*. Consequently, it was attacked in a far more broad and systematic manner from 1987 to 1990, both from within lay Christianity and from within multidenominational seminaries. As McVicar demonstrates, these later attacks formed the basis of a critical narrative that was used in virtually every

1. Technically, Bahnsen was not dismissed, his contract was just not renewed—RTS, at the time, employed everyone on single-year contracts; but it was exceptionally unusual to be terminated outside of misconduct. Bahnsen had even been an associate professor there as a postgraduate student studying for a PhD from 1976; he graduated with his PhD in 1978 and was "dismissed" in 1979. His academic record was exceptional, and he was a gifted teacher; there were clearly deeper reasons. His own initially private and extensive account of what happened is found here: Bahnsen, "What Really Happened."

subsequent attack on Reconstructionism and dominion theology.[2] These attacked dominionism in two main ways:

a. It's optimistic eschatology.

b. It's theonomy.

This chapter considers these in turn and evaluates whether these criticisms have proved to be intellectually successful.

Eschatological Criticism

Dominionists of the Reformed tradition, such as Rushdoony and North, were exclusively postmillennial. Most modern dominionists, with a few exceptions, are postmillennial or maintain an "operational" eschatology that approximates to postmillennialism. As described in chapter 2, postmillennialism has historically been the most controversial of the eschatological groupings, so it is of little surprise that dominionists are attacked because they are or sound like postmillennialists. House and Ice, in criticizing Reconstructionism, make the blanket statement, "One cannot be a Reconstructionist and a premillennialist."[3] Similarly, Hal Lindsey, author of the most populist eschatological works of the 1970s and 1980s, wrote,

> There used to be a group called "postmillennialists." . . . World War I greatly disheartened this group and World War II virtually wiped out this viewpoint. No *self-respecting* scholar . . . today . . . is a "postmillennialist."[4]

Lindsey attacks dominion theology at book length by directly associating its prophetic viewpoint with the rise of the Holocaust:

> I believe we are witnessing a growing revival of the same false interpretation of prophecy that in the past led to such tragedy for so many centuries by a movement that calls itself either Reconstructionism, Dominionism and/or Kingdom Now.[5]

2. McVicar, *Christian Reconstruction*, 203–5.
3. House and Ice, *Dominion Theology*, 7.
4. Lindsey, *Late Great Planet Earth*, 164–65. Emphasis added.
5. Lindsey, *Road to Holocaust*, 25.

Walvoord, in a more scholarly fashion, cites the following central objections: "Postmillennialism in itself does not have the principle or method to attain a system of theology." He then enumerates his reasoning:

a. The viewpoint is "not apostolic," thus implicitly invalid for the Christian loyal to the historic faith.

b. Whitby-ism (after Daniel Whitby, the "founder" of postmillennialism) was philosophically humanistic, liberal, and non-Christian.

c. It is based on a subjective, figurative interpretation of prophecy.[6]

A famous and radical rejection of dominionism based on points (a) and (b) was found in Dave Hunt's 1980s triplet *Whatever Happened to Heaven*, *The Seduction of Christianity*, and *Beyond Seduction.* Hunt's thesis was that the dominion movement was adopting "worldly" aims of personal success using "carnal" methods of positive confession and self-fulfillment. These, he posited, were concepts borrowed from sociology and psychology, foreign to the classical pietism and the way of victory through suffering: "They misunderstand true victory. . . . Jesus conquers sin, death, and hell by allowing His enemies to kill Him."[7] The kingdom for Hunt was to be considered exclusively part of a new heaven and a new earth. On this basis, it is a misdirection of Christian energy, a distraction from the true mission of the church (which is evangelism), and is ultimately a demonic seduction to engage in culture with a view to transformation:

> Although the kingdom begins in the hearts of all who obey Christ as King, the outward manifestation of this kingdom will not come in its fullness until God has destroyed this present universe and created a new one into which sin will never enter.[8]

Hunt epitomized the mainstream evangelical theological reaction to dominionism. Modern evangelicalism in the 1980s was becoming increasingly dispensationalist in its commitments, and the "rapture" was a popular, publicly prominent article of faith, with many expecting the grand departure of the church in 1988.[9] This increasingly dominant stream of

6. Walvoord, "Millennium Issue," 23.

7. Hunt, *Beyond Seduction*, 262. A similar thought has been restated recently in Stark, *Prophets, Politics, and Nations.*

8. Hunt, *Beyond Seduction*, 224.

9. This was based on a specific interpretation of Matt 24:32–34. The "fig tree" is taken to symbolize the nation of Israel. The phrase "becomes tender and puts out leaves" refers

evangelicalism had inherited an instinctive suspicion of social programs and political involvement from the early fundamentalists, who had historically viewed it as a "distraction" from the work of evangelism. McVicar summarizes this view as representative of the belief that dominionism was a "hubristic . . . attempt to Christianize a chronically un-Christianizable world."[10] More sophisticated critiques employing the same basic ideas were presented to the neo-evangelical[11] academy and laity by a broad coalition of liberal and moderate evangelicals:

> At the turn of the century . . . Abraham Kuyper was elected prime minister of the Netherlands. His opponents voiced fears of theocratic oppression. Instead his administration was a model of tolerance and public pluralism . . . that the legitimate rights of all be fully represented. . . . If Christians today understood this distinction between the role of the private Christian citizen and the Christian in government, they might sound less like medieval crusaders.[12]

As Rushdoony had appealed directly to Kuyper for his philosophical and theological inspiration, this was a pointed attack.

Theonomical Criticisms

Neo-Evangelicals and Theonomy

The Reconstructionist belief in the continuing role of the Old Testament law as normative for the Christian provoked what North described as an "ecclesiastical war against biblical law."[13] Coverage within both the secular and Christian press became sensationalist, with even the more scholarly attempts at rebuttal sometimes reverting to evocative images of theonomists advocating capital punishment for homosexuals, adultery, the insane, and

to the reformation of the nation, which occurred in 1948. A "generation" in Israel was forty years, so the generation that sees the reformation of the state of Israel was the rapture generation—impeccable and full of prophetic insight, but catastrophically incorrect.

10. McVicar, *Christian Reconstruction*, 206.

11. The distinction between "neo-evangelical" and "post-evangelical" is examined in appendix A.

12. Colson, "Power Illusion," 34.

13. North and DeMar, *Christian Reconstruction*, xiii.

rebellious teenagers.[14] Much was made of Bahnsen's view that every "jot and tittle" of the law was binding for the New Testament believer, to the extent he formally responded to it on multiple occasions in subsequent editions of theonomy and also explicated the position further with two new books during the second half of the 1980s.[15]

Within the American context, there had been the suspicion that theonomical beliefs were incompatible with constitutional guarantees of religious freedom.[16] This idea had a powerful emotive imagery for the

14. Yurica, "Despoiling of America"; Longman, "God's Law," 41, 44; House and Ice, *Dominion Theology*, 63–64.

15. House and Ice, *Dominion Theology*, 20, 103. As I mentioned in an earlier chapter, the theonomical thesis originated with Rushdoony, but Bahnsen was the foremost exegete of it. Though the Tyler split initially affected the relationship between the two men, Bahnsen was later to consolidate his relationship with Chalcedon and Rushdoony. He was one of the few within the movement to have the standing to criticize Gary North of "logical fallacy" (Bahnsen, "Another Look at Chilton's *Days of Vengeance*") without a ferocious response from North.

Bahnsen's second edition of *Theonomy* appeared in 1984, seven years after the first edition; he added a lengthy second preface as a response to his critics, xi–xxxiii. He was to publish much longer rebuttals as *By This Standard* (1985) and *No Other Standard* (1991); the latter dealt more directly with the critics, the former was more of a lay summary of the academic *Theonomy*; however, in the foreword to the former, he mentions the latter, so there was a considerable delay in publication probably because of the drama surrounding his work and his struggles with his denomination.

His *magnum opus* was his *Van Til's Apologetic*, an extensive commentary on and readings from Van Til, which was completed shortly before his untimely death in 1995; it appeared in 1998. A further posthumous work *Presuppositional Apologetics* was in proofing when he passed and remained "lost" for over thirty years, only being rediscovered behind a filing cabinet when his office was cleared some sixteen years after his death. This was published in 2008 and was a development of chapters 10 and 11 of the multi-authored work *Foundations of Christian Scholarship* of 1976.

As these essays were written at the beginning of the controversy over his work, and Bahnsen worked on them as he went through the various controversies and emerged out the other side, the final editor of the manuscript viewed it as Bahnsen's most important work, the systematic interpretation of Van Til he had sought to bring out in the *Apologetic* (*Presuppositional Apologetics*, vii). On this point, Van Til considered Bahnsen to be the best representative of his position, and he was certainly the most rigorous philosophical and theological defender of the Reconstructionist positions.

16. In the contemporary context, the debate regarding Islam would appear to be significant and relevant here. Some are arguing very publicly for "secularism" in the public square as the only legitimate option to preserve Western values in countries that have allowed mass immigration from Muslim nations. Islam is very publicly both a religious and a political system; if Muslims become a majority in a country, they *will* dispense with democracy and minority rights as a matter of *principle* (for more on this, see Ali, *Heretic*, especially the chapters "Why Has There Been No Muslim Reformation," "How

American evangelical. The "democracy works" idiom was even articulated by charismatics who had otherwise adopted large portions of Reconstructionism's program.[17] Theonomists were thus portrayed as anti-*American* and anti-democratic rather than just defective on issues of theological principle.[18] It boiled over when Billy Graham's *Christianity Today* ran a cover story of an "extended exposé" on Reconstructionism, which labeled Rushdoony as a "heretic."[19]

It was argued that "theonomists" were unevangelical because of their emphasis on law, political, and civic engagement rather than "saving souls." This sounded very much like a recapitulation of Hunt's criticism and the criticism of House and Ice. In other words, *this* was the *central* objection to the Reconstructionist position. The pressure from mainstream neo-evangelicalism was such that Pat Robertson denied any formal links with the movement during his presidential bid of 1988, despite having hosted Rushdoony and North numerous times during the 1980s on his flagship *700 Club*.

Westminster Seminary and Theonomy

The single major attempt at a concerted *academic* response from within the same theological family as Reconstructionism to theonomy was attempted by Westminster Theological Seminary, where Van Til himself had taught.[20] It was ten years in the making and was thus intended and expected to be a theologically rigorous and authoritative critique of dominionism. We will

Islam's Harsh Religious Code Keeps Muslims Stuck in the Seventh Century," and "Jihad"; Ali, *Prey*, especially "Part 3: Clashing Civilizations, Revisited"; and Kassam, *No Go Zones*). The only obligation a Muslim has is to submit to the revealed word of God in the Qur'anic scriptures (this is the literal meaning of "Islam").

It is easy to confuse this with the theonomical position because is this not just what the Christian theonomists are arguing, the primacy of the old covenant law in the matters of jurisprudence? However, the *content* of the old covenant Scriptures given to Israel clearly delineate representational government and God exhorts his people to "govern themselves" in civil matters. It is in the practice of the religious cult where God declares and there is no debate.

17. Wagner, *On Earth*, 11–16.

18. McVicar, *Christian Reconstruction*, 202–5.

19. Clapp, "Democracy as Heresy." Graham was still actively involved in the magazine at this point, and this condemnation would have appeared authoritative to many evangelicals unsure about the movement.

20. Barker and Godfrey, *Theonomy*, 10.

evaluate this assertion in the section below when I consider the response of the dominionists to the book, but if the book can be said to have a coherent theological thrust, it is expressed with the Hunt-like appeal to piety, "[the] authority of the people of God is the authority of weakness," which was developed in the final chapter of the book with an appeal to the theonomists for a doctrinal and political pluralism:

> Such [a mix of religion and politics] warn evangelicals interested in a biblical view of society to give care to safeguard the formal principle of the Reformation. Do not mix the Gospel with an overly precise, potentially extra-biblical application of the Law . . . confusing revelation with tradition.[21]

Assessing the Criticisms

Eschatological Criticisms

We noted first that House and Ice, in criticizing Reconstructionism, made the blanket statement, "One cannot be a Reconstructionist and a premillennialist."[22] This, on the face of it, is a categorical statement that was theologically implausible even when it was written, for we have already argued classical premillennialism was triumphant in its eschatology; and many modern premillennialists within the Word of Faith and Pentecostal movements believe in social reform and do hold the two positions in an *operational* sense. The most we need to concede is that the theology of these latter movements may seem muddled and unintuitive to those like Walvoord and Pentecost, critiquing it from a premillennial perspective. This is reversible logic though as the reciprocal view has also been expressed: there have been plenty of Reconstructionists like Bahnsen and Gentry who have argued it is "schizophrenic" to claim to be Reconstructionist and yet to try to cling to a premillennial dispensationalism.[23]

Both sides of the argument, then, apparently converge in agreement. Either inflection of the argument might be considered as making the same logical error, but this is mitigated because the primary *theological* problem is the *dispensationalist* element rather than the premillennial aspect. Indeed, other premillennialists have explicitly argued that premillennialism

21. Davis, "Challenge to Theonomy," 398–99.

22. House and Ice, *Dominion Theology*, 7.

23. Bahnsen and Gentry, *House Divided.*

and reconstructionism are not fundamentally at odds with each other.[24] That is, for clarity, what should have been said was that "one cannot be a Reconstructionist *and* a modern dispensationalist," which, as we have seen, has as one of its central distinctives an intensely pessimistic and cynical perspective regarding culture generally. Modern amillennialism might also be a better fit in this same category, with its pessimistic cultural indifference, as might some modern "prophetic" viewpoints that argue for agnosticism to sociopolitical conditions.[25] Thus, in summary, the eschatological arguments are very weak and do not prove what they claim: it is perfectly permissible to be a premillennialist and a Reconstructionist. Indeed, with the extension of dominionism into the wider evangelical consciousness, it might be argued this is now the more *common* position amongst the Pentecostals and Word of Faith denominations.

Next, we considered Lindsey, the very popular writer of the 1970s and 1980s, and the *ad hominem* assault of his that no "self-respecting" scholar would be postmillennial. It is tempting to assert that this can be simply dismissed as an ignorant insult; there are plenty of "self-respecting" scholars who have been or are postmillennial. These scholars, and I count myself amongst them, feel that the overall arc of Scripture pushes in an optimistic and victorious consummation of the church prior to the return of the Lord as King, even if the premillennial thesis has the compelling feature of biblical literalism on its side. Indeed, it could readily be argued that Lindsey's apocalyptic prognostications of rapture and nuclear Armageddon through the 1970s and 1980s, all of which failed, render his scholarship as of insufficient quality that no "self-respecting" scholar would consider it worthy of serious attention, unless it was yet another case study in the sociological and psychological pathology surrounding the rapture and Armageddon.

However, his claim that it lends itself to antisemitism and a Jewish Holocaust requires further examination because of the seriousness of the charge. First, on Lindsey's own admission, he was merely picking up on the speculative appendix to House and Ice (who he quoted often) that the allegorical and symbolic prophetic viewpoint lends itself to a reduction in the importance of Israel as a nation and this, in turn, has been the historical root of antisemitism and the Holocaust.[26] Firstly, this has some

24. Schnittger, "Christian Reconstruction."

25. Stark, *Prophets, Politics, and Nations*. A critical response to this perspective was the basis of my *Politics*.

26. House and Ice, *Dominion Theology*, 397.

enormous leaps of logic, and it is hardly defensible that the "historical root" of antisemitism is principally or necessarily (in the logical sense) related to replacement theology. You can believe in replacement theology and have no animus towards the Jewish nation at all; indeed, you can conclude that evangelism of the modern state of Israel must be executed on the same basis as any other nation.

It is nonsense to assert that consistent amillennialists and postmillennialists find themselves pulled inexorably towards antisemitism; some *might* have been convinced by the polemics of Luther to move in that direction, but historically, antisemitism was added into Christian theology for other political or social reasons, often just an outright envy of the cultural successes of the Jews and a desire to appropriate their wealth with some pseudo-justification.[27] So, for example, Sloyan, as a Jewish intellectual and writer for the United States Holocaust Memorial Museum, establishes definitively that the roots of *modern* antisemitism are ethnic and racial animosity to the Jews, the religious component growing weaker with the passing of the centuries.[28]

Anti-Jewish hatred has often centered around the perceived *economic* advantage of the Jews that served as the template for the broader antisemitism. Hitler assaulted the Jews because he felt, in doing so, he would protect the racial, social, and economic integrity of the German republic that he believed had been hijacked by Jewish bankers; any religious element was subsidiary and only useful as providing some kind of moral compensation for the subsequent atrocity.[29] However, and more importantly, we now have the benefit of a gap of thirty-five years to test Lindsey's thesis that Reconstruction

27. Macneil, "Rise of Christian Anti-Semitism," para 5. A point I make in the introduction to this essay is that it is unlikely Luther would have intended his words to have been used as a justification for outright persecution and the killing of Jews. Both himself and Calvin felt that the Papist recourse to violence was one of the elements the Reformation needed to separate itself from and that there should be a degree of religious toleration, especially towards the Jews. It is true that they might have failed in their commitment to non-violence when trying to deal with the Anabaptists, and other dissident "radical Reformation" groups, but the point remains that it was highly unlikely that Luther intended his words to be misused in that way or the way that national socialism had exploited them.

28. Sloyan, *Christian Persecution*.

29. The popularity of the fictional *Protocols of the Elders of Zion* (1903), alleging that there was a worldwide Jewish conspiracy to control the world, was not limited to Russia, where it first appeared, but was popularized by some European and US industrialists (such as Henry Ford, whose "assembly line" was inspirational for Hitler), thus lending it credibility, despite it being quickly discredited as a forgery.

leads to "holocaust" and antisemitism; it has simply been shown in the years subsequent his positing of this thesis, as with his other eschatological theses considered above, to have been historically *incorrect.*

Whilst there are undoubtedly those who are dominionists that Lindsey presents as antisemitic in language, it seems equally true there are those who he does not mention, such as Schlissel, who are dominionists, Jewish, and have added an additional element to Reconstructionist theology that recognizes the importance of prophetic Israel.[30] In summary, Lindsey's attack was novel and ambitious but logically tenuous and seems clearly without theological rigor:

> Dispensationalists believe that the Jewish people have a title to the land that transcends virtually any other consideration. . . . The reconstructionist, on the other hand, makes a distinction. He believes that the Jewish people may exercise the title [to the land] only when they comply with the condition of repentance and faith. He has nothing against Jews living in "Eretz Yisrael" per se, but he recognizes that the far more significant question is Israel's faith. . . . If one's heart's desire and prayer to God for Israel agrees with the inspired Apostle's as recorded in Romans 10, can he thereby be called antisemitic?[31]

Of more substance were the academic critiques of Walvoord. The main assertion of Walvoord was that postmillennialism "cannot attain a system of theology." However, though argued at length by Walvoord, it has been demonstrated that it cannot be sustained on careful examination, and Walvoord's methodology itself became questionable under critique. Bahnsen characterized Walvoord's process as "newspaper exegesis" employing an abandonment of Reformed principles of exegesis to accommodate the "signs of the times."[32] He returns with interest Walvoord's dismissive theological criticism:

> By means of such newspaper exegesis, one could just as well discount the return of Christ in glory, saying "where is the promise of his coming?" (cf. II Peter 3:1–4). This *reductio ad absurdum* must be reckoned with. The fact that an era of gospel prosperity and world peace has not yet arrived would no more disprove the Bible's teaching that such an era shall be realized (in the power of God's

30. Schlissel, "Reconstructionism," 56–61.

31. Schlissel, "Reconstructionism," 59.

32. Bahnsen, *Theonomy in Christian Ethics*, 7, 96.

> spirit and the faithfulness of Christ's church to its great commission) than the fact that Christ has not yet returned disproves the Bible's teaching that such an event shall take place![33]

Bahnsen then argued further at great length that there was a prima facie case to recognize postmillennialism consistently within the history of the church.

Similarly, Bahnsen, Gentry, and Rushdoony all made the case that it is just *historically* disingenuous to present postmillennialism as the modern aberration when dispensationalism most certainly has a history and theology that can be traced back *no earlier* than 1820–30.[34] Most importantly, it becomes evident that the major error of Walvoord, in seeking to ensure the cogency of his critique, is that he seems to assume a seamless transition into dispensationalism from classical premillennialism, which is emphatically *not* the case, as we argued in an earlier chapter. Further, Gentry has also mounted a substantive theological and exegetical defense of postmillennialism.[35] Likewise, Bahnsen and Gentry have individual and joint works where they emphasized the novel character of dispensational thought and the poor quality of scholarship as characteristic of the modern dispensational premillennialism. Taken together, this body of work has certainly met the challenge of Walvoord to present a "system of theology."

Bahnsen is even more specific on this last point by highlighting important figures within the dispensationalist movement (Newton, Zahn, Darby) who had views that implicitly advocated an abdication of social responsibility, because it was an inevitable conclusion from their logic of an apostate Laodicean dispensation, to which the church had now entered. This became explicit with the first wave of fundamentalists denouncing it as a "distraction" from evangelism. The schism with classical premillennialism is obvious at that point; Christians were known throughout the early period of the church for both their premillennialism and their charity. There were even contemporary classical premillennialists such as Schnittger who claimed that dispensationalism had produced a deadly malaise within the arena of social and political action.[36] Schnittger, a premillennialist but also self-confessedly a Reconstructionist (and thus a living, breathing contradiction

33. Bahnsen, "Calvin and Postmillennialism," 10.

34. Bahnsen, "Calvin and Postmillennialism," 7; MacPherson, *The Rapture Plot*, viii.

35. Gentry, *He Shall Dominion*.

36. Schnittger, *Christian Reconstruction*, 9–10. This was originally a radio program pamphlet intended for a self-study group.

for some of Reconstruction's critics), in a few short pages, unconsciously exposes and refutes not only the dispensationalism of House, Ice, Lindsey, and Hunt but also undermines neo-evangelicalism's central attack that there is something inherently "unbiblical" or "unevangelical" about Reconstructionism or dominionism generally.

He elegantly makes the point that whilst he can judge the "postmils" as wanting in their allegorical use of prophecy, this does not invalidate the theological verity of their overall focus of the victory in Jesus and the increasing glory manifesting within the church as history progresses.[37] *This* focus, as we have also previously demonstrated, was the classical premillennialist view also.[38] Thus, an answer is also provided here to neo-evangelicalism's view that historical optimism or triumphalism reflects an import of non-Christian psychological ideas into the church. It was rather an expression of the Reformation that reestablished the principles of vocational domains and an ever-increasing glory within the church. In the light of this overall pattern of reasoning, the bankruptcy of the dispensationalist position is seen at its worst, as we consider that the neo-evangelical analysis of Hunt effectively places the Reformers in the place of deception, for the Reformers proposed a duty and obligation upon Christians to build the kingdom and establish secular authorities that honor God's law.[39]

However, some academic criticism is worthy of further attention. We must recognize the validity of Riddlebarger's qualification that there are issues of nomenclature that postmillennialists tend to minimize in order to claim many who may be more historically judged to have been amillennialists.[40] The obvious cases of questionable appropriation here are Augustine and the early reformers, Luther and Calvin.[41] This tendency is clearly seen

37. Schnittger, *Christian Reconstruction*, 6. Recent work by "postmils," such as Gentry and Mathison, is of a much higher exegetical quality.

38. Schnittger, *Christian Reconstruction*, 13.

39. It is of note that Hunt wrote a number of works directly attacking Calvin as a "tyrant" and Calvinism as misrepresenting God, principally *What Love Is This?* He had modern dominionism in mind as he wrote them; indeed, according to the back matter, it was *why* he wrote it.

40. Riddlebarger, "Princeton and the Millennium."

41. It might seem strange to assert that the early Reformers were his putative heirs with a gap of around a thousand years between them, but as Pawson, in his *Seminars* (audio), notes, Calvin might "merely" have been conceived of "writing down the theology of Augustine in a systematic manner" (Pawson, "Grace—Saving, Sovereign, and Free," 24:00–31:00). See also "Assessing Postmillennialism," 28.

in Bahnsen's essays, the work of Kik, and that of Boettner.[42] However, taking a step back, the debatable ascriptions can furnish further proof for *our* argument rather than detracting from it. The argument *we* have made is that there was a shift in thinking for both premillennialists and amillennialists away from their historical positions, emphasizing victory to culturally pessimistic and spiritually pietistic ones. Riddlebarger has correctly identified this change, but it does not defeat the central concept that the victorious mode of thinking now associated with postmillennialism had historical precedent within the history of the church, and in those figures especially. Bahnsen, for example, does an exceptional job in indicating the victorious expectation of a world subdued by the gospel in Calvin, regardless of whether his final status is better considered as amillennial.

We consider next the neo-evangelical Colson's attack on the dominionists, which was a stream well represented both within the academy and the popular Christian press. Firstly, Colson had a rhetorical pattern like that of Hunt, a fellow neo-evangelical, who we have mentioned earlier in the discussion. He had wanted to consolidate the impression within mainstream traditional evangelicalism of Reconstructionism as extreme and undemocratic. This clearly had traction amongst a section of the target readership of *Christianity Today*. It is also clear that there were evangelicals, charismatics, and Pentecostals who were initially persuaded by Jimmy Swaggart's concurrent accusation of Reconstructionism as "liberation theology in disguise." There were, and still are, those who fix an unscalable wall between religion and politics and whose faith is incidental to their "secular" activities.

Yet, Swaggart's condemnation of Reconstructionism seemed anachronistic, even as he made it, as his fellow charismatic and Pentecostal ministers were increasingly and actively embracing dominionism. He himself had even inadvertently recommended Gary DeMar's *God and Government* before realizing he was a postmillennial Reconstructionist. Robert Tilton's charismatic television ministry networked, by deliberate act, thousands of charismatic ministers with the Reconstructionists through conferences and satellite technology, with North's and Rushdoony's work finding its way into Oral Roberts University Law School and Falwell's Liberty University.[43]

42. Bahnsen, "Calvin and Postmillennialism"; Bahnsen, "Prima Facie Acceptability of Postmillennialism"; Kik, *Eschatology of Victory*, 3–15; Boettner, *Postmillennialism*, loc. 162.

43. North, *Unholy Spirits*, 392.

Secondly, we have already noted that Colson's appeal to the pluralism of Kuyper was novel and pointed, knowing the influence of Kuyper on Rushdoony, as was his important and correct distinction between the role of the private and the governmental. However, contra Colson, Rushdoony *had* clearly distinguished between Kuyper's theological and political legacies. He had also very clearly understood the distinction, like Lloyd-George after him, of the role of private Christian citizen and the Christian in government.[44] Far from being a modern crusader eager to impose a theocracy, Rushdoony was family-centric and believed in a small state focused solely on its primary tasks of providing a mechanism of justice and of securing the borders of the nation. He viewed families and communities accountable to God before the state or the church. Where Rushdoony was critical of modern Western democracies, it was because of their humanism rather than democracy *per se*.

Similarly, Rushdoony elsewhere had argued for a Christian basis for American history and his sociological prescription for reform was not an ecclesiocratic one.[45] This was not the revival of either a Catholic or Protestant hegemony. Rather this is a full participation in the processes of governance and the progress of the humanities and the sciences. For both Rushdoony and Lloyd-George, the Christian did not cease to be a Christian because he was in government, but his Christianity had to inform his very practice within government. This is also why Kuyper, at the opening of the Free University of Amsterdam, which he had founded, famously exploded the myth of the "secular" and the "religious," declaring, "There is not a square inch in the whole domain of our human existence over which Christ, who is Sovereign over *all*, does not cry: 'Mine!'"[46] Most pointedly, the focus of the university right from the beginning was not just on theological studies but on scientific and technological ones as well, reflecting Kuyper's philosophy of "sphere sovereignty."[47]

Likewise, Lloyd-George had argued vigorously through the 1960s for Christians who were both experts in their domains *and* scripturally literate;

44. Beyond the commentary below, we consider in some depth the work of Lloyd-George in our chapter on the philosophy of Christian involvement.

45. This being his chief distinctive from Gary North's reconstructionism, who broke with Rushdoony on this issue amongst others. See "Schism and Reformation," 86.

46. Bratt, *Abraham Kuyper*, 488 (emphasis original); a very brief but informative history is found on the university website at Vrije Universiteit Amsterdam, "History."

47. This is clearly exposited in his *Lectures on Calvinism* (1898) and an essay in Bratt's *Centennial Reader*, "Sphere Sovereignty."

it was the duty and task of the Christian professional association to work out how their Christianity should affect the working of their profession.[48] It might also be said that history has simply overturned the central charge of neo-evangelicals against dominionism of heresy because of their emphasis on social and political action. In most of the new churches within areas of the world where there has been little or no representative government, the church has had to address social and political issues as much as they have had to address spiritual ones. By necessity, they have adopted aggressive political activism and the rhetoric of victory and societal change.[49]

It can even be argued that the reconfiguration of the evangelical movement, because of the influence of dominionism, has meant that neo-evangelicalism itself has tended to have become marginalized as the primary Christian voice within the explosive growth experienced by these nondenominational churches. The rapidly growing neo-Pentecostal movement and the "fifth wave" postmodern experiential churches are often informed, admittedly, in sometimes a muddled or partially formed manner, by a dominion theology that asserts sphere sovereignty and seeks to transform and reform every aspect of culture.[50] This "new wine" dominionism may lack the coherence and abrasiveness of a Rushdoony or North, with their preference for a "compassionate Reformers" mantle, but it is now the new normal for the reformer or activist, be they evangelical, charismatic, or Pentecostal. Thus, for the neo-evangelicals of the Hunt and Colson ilk, their attack was ultimately based on straw man arguments.

Theonomical Criticisms Assessed

Of much greater significance theologically was the response to theonomy. The central force of the criticisms examined previously was that theonomy represents a reversion to pre-Christian legalism and a philosophical dogmatism, with the critics appealing instead to a pluralistic epistemology derived from natural law. For Bahnsen, it was almost trivial to dismiss the first part of this charge. *Legalism* is the saving by works but theonomy is seen as the *means* of the ministration of grace for sanctification:

48. Lloyd-George, *Romans: Exposition of Chapter 13*.

49. North, *Unholy Spirits*, 388–89.

50. Birch-Machin, *Speakers of Life*, 16; Coates, *Kingdom Now!*, 18.

> [They] fail to see the relevance of God's law as the way of sanctification and as the law of men and nations. They do not recognize God's law as God's plan . . . for godly authority and rule in every area of life. This anti-law attitude guarantees impotence and defeat to all churches who hold it.[51]

That is, he adeptly dealt with all the criticisms leveled at him with the simple assertion that the criticisms of him were normally substantial misunderstandings of what theonomy *was.*[52] Theonomy had never claimed to be a way of *salvation* but *was* the way of *sanctification.* Both Bahnsen and Rushdoony had anticipated this mode of criticism and had thoroughly refuted it in advance.[53]

The second part of the criticism was also swiftly dealt with. It is important to recognize that theonomy *was* the orthodox Reformed position held by both Luther and Calvin. Paradoxically, for the writers of Westminster's critique of theonomy, the founder of Westminster, nearly half a century earlier, had also asserted a theonomical pretext for his belief in societal reformation:

> It is perfectly clear what is wrong. The law of God has been torn up . . . and the inevitable result [what is wrong with the world] is appearing with ever greater clearness. When will the law be rediscovered?[54]

It seems the critics were chronically ill-informed or had deliberately chosen to ignore their own denominational catechisms and the epistemological foundation of their own seminary. The critique offered was anything but coherent, based on a fuzzy natural-law epistemology, as McDade also observes,

> Van Til was no pioneer in the field of ethics; he was *simply restating* the Reformed Faith of the Heidelberg Catechism . . . and the Westminster Larger Catechism.[55]

Bahnsen, in contrast, *had* understood the implications of Van Til's philosophy and the logical outworkings of Westminster's founding principles. This is evidenced by the fact that Van Til had recognized him as his most

51. Rushdoony, *God's Plan for Victory* loc. 200.
52. Bahnsen, *Theonomy in Christian Ethics*, xx–xxvii.
53. Bahnsen, *Theonomy in Christian Ethics*, 89, 297, 499.
54. Machen, "Importance of Christian Scholarship," 91.
55. McDade, "Problem with Christian Reconstruction," 2. Emphasis added.

able student and had wanted him to succeed him at Westminster. Bahnsen simply extended logically Van Til's restatement of the Reformed hermeneutic to the civil realm using Rushdoony's framework.[56] This he elaborated in the preface to his second edition of *Theonomy*, stating that when he spoke of the "jot and the tittle" of the law, he was not "requiring observance of ancient cultural details" but was applying the primary Reformed exegetical procedure that it is the underlying principles of the law, which "has abiding ethical validity."[57] This sense of "jot and tittle" is the Van Tillian axiom that every sphere and aspect of humanity's existence is subject to the law and jurisdiction of God as his creation: "All the facts of nature and of history are what they are, do what they do, and undergo what they undergo, in accord with the one comprehensive counsel of God."[58]

An autonomous realm of humankind is antithetical to the Reformed faith. Thus, theonomy, understood philosophically, is the theological, logical, and temporal continuity between *all* Scripture and *all* human life. That is, if someone consistently follows the logic of Scripture, the same conclusions about the implications of the law for Christian ethics can be arrived at by those not sharing the denominational Reformed heritage. Thus, Cope, one of the founders of YWAM, stated it thus:

> In Matthew 5 Jesus makes it clear that the entire Old Testament is the foundation for his message and his actions. . . . We do not reinterpret the Old Testament with the New, nor the New with the Old, but rather see them as a four-thousand-year line of thought that God is building. . . . In other words, greatness in the kingdom of God is being able to marry and live both Old and New Testament values. The Old Testament emphasizes nations and how we live together as a community here on earth, and the New Testament emphasizes the individual, salvation, and reaching the lost for a future in heaven. These must be married to see God and his kingdom clearly. . . . There is only one place to go in order to understand the specific definitions God gave to these terms. We must go to the law of Moses and the rest of the Old Testament. In Scripture, God has given us a set of values by which to measure and correct our own personal and cultural definitions of reality."[59]

56. Hence, the significance that Rushdoony wrote the preface to Bahnsen's *Theonomy* in 1971, though it never appeared until 1977. There was clearly an ongoing conversation between them. See North, *Theonomy*, 17.

57. Bahnsen, *Theonomy in Christian Ethics*, xiv–xv.

58. Van Til, *Christian Apologetics*, 127.

59. Cope, *God and Political Justice*, loc. 306, 484, 1190, 1199.

This is *precisely* what Bahnsen meant when he considered the law as the *means* of *sanctification*—the *correction* of our own personal and cultural definitions of reality.

Summary and Concluding Remarks

From a theological perspective, each of the criticisms we considered above appear to reduce to a variation on the classic fundamentalist position that somehow political involvement will "contaminate" the gospel message and Christians should avoid such involvement for that reason. Stated in that fashion, it should be clear that such a position is prima facie unacceptable and unscriptural; believers are called to be salt and light, and to "occupy [do the business of governing on my behalf] till [I, Jesus] come."[60] It is also true that virtually no major Christian thinkers in history have maintained that position and others, such as Machen and Finney, with very different theologies, have argued passionately against it; the withdrawal of the fundamentalist movement from the wider culture was an aberration in Christian history.

We can see that neither the attacks on the eschatology nor the attacks on the theonomy of dominionism were anywhere close to definitive or were even of sufficient force to undermine support for the movement. In fact, to the frustration of many critics, the controversy had the side effect of raising the awareness of mainstream evangelicalism to dominionism and disseminating its ideas even more widely, as "softer" versions more acceptable to the evangelical community developed. Thus, consequently, in the contemporary milieu, it is rare for the term "Reconstructionism" to be used, but its ideas and programs are very much alive.

When it came to Westminster's decade-in-the-making "critique" of theonomy, we must concur first with North that Westminster's attempts at refutation were simply the "worst writing" by any of the seminary staff who contributed to the book; second, with McDade in asserting that it simply showed they were not prepared to engage seriously with the political and social implications of their own historical Reformed heritage. The latter had been restated with logical clarity by their institutional founder and their first professor of apologetics, and worked out in detail sociologically by *their* finest students of a generation.[61] It is now a historical fact that none

60. See the discussion in the preface exegeting this term and justifying this amplification of the translation, xiii-xiv.

61. North, *Theonomy*, 11, 321–22. It is also of note that the publisher favored by the

of critiques of dominion theology that it included proved persuasive to any but the most partisan of reader. Theologically and rhetorically, the Reconstructionists had anticipated the criticisms and answered them quickly and forcibly in print. This academic response to Westminster's "critique" was of a far more rigorous and researched quality, as evidenced by the editors' extended rebuttal and exposure of the former's poor academic quality.[62]

However, that was not to say that the decade and a half of ferocious criticism had no consequences. Bahnsen was never to teach within a Reformed seminary after his dismissal, becoming an independent scholar and starting his own study center. After his premature death, some new colleges and seminaries did attempt to continue his legacy, and some of his most notable students are working today in Reformed contexts derived from those new institutions. The most noticeable, more general negative effects of the level of publicity generated by the criticisms were for some to disassociate from what were considered the most "extreme" of Reconstructionist views, with leaders such as the elder Schaeffer and Falwell failing to give the Reconstructionists any credit for the platform built on their foundation. Thus, it accentuated the differences between Reformed and the evangelical dominion theologies of, say, Wagner, with the latter clearly attempting to publicly distance themselves from the more controversial theonomical language, such as "theocracy" or "ecclesiocracy," and to adopt a softer idiom, even if these terms were being commonly misrepresented and misunderstood by the critics.

Nevertheless, in summary, the dominionist arguments have proved persuasive, survived, and thrived through the criticism. It should again be accepted that society cannot be changed or improved without political engagement and representation of the Christian view in the organs of power and at all the different levels of governance, from school, local community, county, state, and parliament. It is to how the Christian should engage that we now turn, with the help of the most distinguished British intellectual evangelical of the post-WWII period, Dr. David Martyn Lloyd-Jones (d. 1981), recognized as one of the finest expositional preachers ever. We develop our political philosophy with his assistance in the next chapter, and we demonstrate the scriptural basis for our involvement.

---

seminary declined to publish the work, and a non-Reformed publishing house associated with the neo-evangelical movement was used.

62. North, *Theonomy*. It is also noteworthy that it took less than a year for North to publish this collection of essays in contrast to the decade it took for the seminary to publish the critique.

Applying Dominion Theology—The Philosophy of Christian Involvement[1]

Overview and Prerequisites

In the previous chapters, we have explored the history and development of dominion theology, establishing its pedigree and its orthodoxy. The aim of this chapter is to build a case for a revival of the position that champions the active political and wider cultural involvement by those who hold to dominion theology, attempting to prove not just the divine prerogative of our involvement but what the governing principles of our involvement should be. Thus, we examine what is the locus of the practical problem for Christians: the role and interpretation of Rom 13. We have already learned that arguments as epistemologically self-conscious[2] Christians *must* be done on a scriptural basis at *every* step:

> [Christian philosophy] must always be based on an accurate interpretation of the teaching of the Scriptures. For some . . . there is a danger they may derive their knowledge more from [secular, unbelieving] philosophy than from a careful study of the Scriptures. They tend to extract just a certain number of great principles from the Bible and from there on they more or less forget the Bible and work the application out for themselves . . . True theology should always be based upon a careful and accurate exegesis and

1. This is a modified version of material found in both my "Politics" and *Foundations.*

2. What is meant by this term is worked out in my *Foundations*. In brief, the term implies we have a coherent Christian worldview where our metaphysics (our conception of the real), theory of knowledge (epistemology), and ethics (how we should then live) are logically consistent with each other.

> exposition and understanding of the Scriptures . . . we do not derive any theological principle from one scriptural statement only.[3]

Thereunto, we are in complete agreement with the *sense* of what Lloyd-Jones asserts; disputes of praxis need to be resolved by exegeting the objective text of Scripture rather than just preferring one version of subjectivity over another and then tagging on a few Scriptures we used to validate our argument, otherwise constructed from outside of Scripture.[4]

This is the governing principle for the simple reason that these matters at hand are needing to be settled. They are serious and are recognized as not just matters of preference, where we would accept individual Christian freedom and liberty and would admit a range of positions.[5] Rather, we are assuming that the questions before us are of the type that can, to a large degree, be settled. The issues are foundational, where we should be able to arrive at what is the scriptural position that is arguably binding in its essentials on all believers. They are not trivial issues of individual conscience (though we will recognize the important place of conscience) but admit of both philosophical and theological reflection and study.

3. Lloyd-Jones, *Exposition of Romans 13*, 16–17.

4. Whilst Lloyd-Jones maintains a strong distinction between philosophy and theology, which I have argued against in my *Foundations*, he does so in a way we can clearly understand with a clear rhetorical sense. As Calvin tells us, our aim is a *philosophy* constructed from Scripture, whilst most describe his works as works of theology. In the *Institutes*, Calvin frequently uses the Latin and French equivalent words for "philosophy" in both positive and negative senses, drawing a similar distinction as Lloyd-Jones does in rhetorical passages, often prefixing it with "profane." The Latin root of "profane" explicitly carried the sense of heretical and godless thought: "outside or before [pro-] the temple [-phane]." He clearly talks about "constructing a Christian philosophy" (*Institutes*, loc. 550) close to the head of the work. This is the sense in which my *Foundations* argued that philosophy should be conceived. Thus, I have no problem with the contextual interchange of the words "theology" or "philosophy," and it is a practice I shall follow occasionally in this chapter.

5. This is discussed in magisterial fashion in Lloyd-Jones, *Exposition of Chapter 14*. See also 1 Cor 1:12; Rom 14:1–23. His multi-volume commentary on Romans was one of the most notable achievements of twentieth-century Christian scholarship. A website that preserves his legacy is found at https://www.mljtrust.org/.

The Imperative for a Political Ethic

Is Political Involvement Legitimate?

A question that could be in some minds and that concerned me greatly a few years ago, as I became frustrated with what I considered insipid evangelical theology regarding our political and cultural positions (and indeed, what provoked me into an in-depth study of dominion theology) is whether it is right for Christians to be involved *at all* in the wider cultural or political processes. Are we not rather to be engaged in loading up the [Noah's] Ark of the church before we are removed either by the Rapture or the Second Coming? A famous radio preacher during the 1940s put it this way: "*you do not polish brass on a sinking ship*,"[6] and he has largely spoken for the subsequent generations of fundamentalists and evangelicals.

Thankfully, I believe we have already established the answer to that question in the previous chapters, but if you have come to this chapter directly, it is straightforward to answer this question with the text of the Bible *itself* (though I do strongly recommend a reading of our study). The apostle Paul had to write very early on in the life of the church to prevent people leaving their employment to wait for the coming of the Lord, despite that the second coming was considered imminent even by himself.[7] For even while having this eschatological conviction, he, at times, insisted both that believers should work and on his political and civil rights as a Roman citizen.[8] He had no problem addressing Agrippa in a political context and eventually appealing to Caesar to prevent his undoubted martyrdom at the hands of the Jews.[9] That is, we do not cease to have rights, a political relationship with, and a responsibility to and for our nation because we have joined the kingdom of God. Lloyd-Jones summarized it this way: "our citizenship is in heaven does not mean we do not stop being citizens

6. Quoted in Rushdoony, *God's Plan for Victory*, loc. 175.

7. 1 and 2 Thessalonians—the injunction "if one does not work, one does not eat" was made in the eschatological context within these letters; 1 Cor 7, 26–35.

8. Acts 22:25, 16:37.

9. Paul was certainly prepared to die for the gospel (and he did) but seems to have had a much bigger problem with suffering rank injustice at the hands of those that considered themselves just and civilized (Acts 25:16). Additionally, like Jesus, he took the greatest exception to hypocrisy, particularly the religious hypocrisy (Acts 23:3) of "the Jews." Like the Johannine use of the term, "the Jews" here refers to the Jewish authorities, which were an unhealthy political-religious hybrid, and it is not used as an ethnic slur. The authorities were the chief adversaries of both Jesus and Paul in their ministries.

[on earth] in contrast to various movements within the church. Thus, we should [remain] involved in politics."[10]

What we mean is this: the biggest problems in some "Christian" countries during the twentieth century, which have had almost continual revival for fifty to sixty years, is the prevalence of economic, social, and moral corruption in their societies. In some countries of Central and South Africa, which now have over 90 percent Christian populations, they are known for their mass poverty, corruption, and a lack of basic infrastructure, despite being some of the richest countries in terms of their natural resources.[11] However, far more dramatically, and with much more polemical force for our purposes here, Cope vividly describes how the most "Christianized" city in the US (the most "Christianized" nation in the world) failed to show any difference in many of the basic social indices that would make it a "good" place to live, in direct contradiction to the regenerating narrative of conversion preached by the evangelical churches.[12]

That is, this demonstrated a total failure of twentieth-century "revivalism" to reform societies because the believers failed to reform the political and social dimensions of their culture, dealing only with the saving of souls.[13] Our political philosophy is a "fake" gospel if it does not change the social and political character of the nations in which it is applied. Without such a political philosophy, we are just surrendering cultural real estate to secularism, humanism, and, most recently in the West, political Islam, failing in our primary objective of "discipling all nations."[14] Thus, what is argued in this chapter is a rejection, in principle, of any withdrawal from the marketplace, as advocated in some Christian convocations in lieu of reflections on the Trump era, and the building of

10. Lloyd-Jones, *Exposition of Chapter 13*, 17.

11. Nyagamago, "Top 10 Countries in Africa."

12. Cope, *Old Testament Template*, 21–27.

13. "Revivalism," in the modern sense, is a term most associated with the ministry of Charles Finney (1792–1875). However, he was extremely active in the political, educational, and wider cultural spheres; see my *Foundations* for a discussion of Finney and other pivotal figures within post-Reformation Christianity who were socially and politically active. They did not limit themselves to "spiritual matters," as was to become the habit of some of their imitators in the evangelical and fundamentalist movements of the nineteenth/twentieth century, most of whom believed any such engagement was a "distraction" from the real task of saving souls. See also, "Eschatological Criticism," 95–96.

14. Matt 28:19–20 (NAS).

the case for an informed, increased involvement, and commitment to see reform in the political realm.[15]

One Further Possibility—Political Neutrality

Before we can proceed though, it must be recognized that there has been a flurry of thought, scholarly and otherwise, in Christian circles on this issue triggered by the "Trump problem."[16] In one relatively recent convocation on political theology in which I was an invited participant, the discussion proper began by presenting an argument based on cultural relativism, the thrust of which was that our reading of Scripture is never neutral but colored by our cultural glasses. Fine, so far, I would broadly agree with that.

The application of this was then that politically, we had been unable to see that we had fallen in love with democracy and our way of doing things to the degree we had entered an inappropriate "syncretism" of our understanding of Scripture with the understanding of the political arena.[17] Consequently, we had incorrectly formed alliances or loyalties with particular politicians or parties.[18] Our closeness to particular ideologies had meant we were no longer capable of understanding God's perspective and articulating a Christian political philosophy.[19] The rest of the discussion was to present a "corrected" political theology that would restore to us this function. In brief, the principal feature of the position being advocated was a type of political agnosticism and detachment from the workings of the political world.[20] That is, God is indifferent to our political

15. Brown, *Evangelicals at the Crossroads.* Brown distills the issues down exceptionally well here; he has an earned doctorate (and it shows), as well as a substantial standing in the evangelical world.

16. For my extended use of this term, see Macneil, "Politics," appendix A.

17. In Macneil, "Politics," I discuss how the argument was made that democracy or Republicanism is no more God-ordained than, say, despotism or some other form of totalitarianism. Even the Nazis could be commended for "keeping order" if the alternative was violent anarchy. We *might* be prepared to countenance the last proposition, but we should remember the Nazis were voted *in*, and then they made very sure they could not get voted *out*.

18. In this case, Trump.

19. In this case, the ideologies were Republicanism and/or political conservatism.

20. The fullest statement of this argument is found in Stark, *Prophets, Politics and Nations.*

systems, and we should be, too, other than to trust he puts in the leaders *he* wants to fulfill his kingdom purposes.[21]

Now, that is problematic and seriously so. Despite its initial plausibility and spiritual sophistication as an argument, we must always remember that, philosophically, *any* argument based on asserting relativism and insurmountable cultural prejudice must *exempt itself* from its own analysis to have anything coherent to say. Otherwise, it, too, becomes just another culturally conditioned narrative, nothing more than a possibility in the sea of competing possibilities; as the meme goes, the argument "all judgments are relative" is rightly footnoted "*except* this one."

The very fact I assert we are suffering from cultural prejudice and zero objectivity in reading Scripture is asserting that I *can* stand *outside* of that prejudice and culture to make that assertion. *If* that is the case, *then* I have just refuted my own argument, which was predicated on the fact that the other person was unable to do what I have just done. This is my point about relativism above, the presenter proceeding to give us a political theology on their own analysis will be just as full of inescapable presuppositions and cultural prejudice; granted, they might be *different* ones but *present*, nevertheless. Thus, I believe such an argument is an illegitimate and retrograde step; the church has never improved any society by withdrawing from it but only when it was fully engaged in it.[22]

The Lack of a Shared Cultural Reference

The principal requirement for a Christian self-consciousness results now because of the collapse of a previously shared value base of Judeo-Christian origin in our wider culture, even if it was grudgingly maintained.[23] Indeed,

21. This "kingdom" language might seem a strange idiom to those outside of modern charismatic and Pentecostal Christianity. In brief, Jesus = King, dom = his domain, which includes the church but also his providential rule as "King of kings, Lord of lords" (Dan 2:37; Rev 19:16 NAS), which is explicitly dealing with the civil and political authorities.

22. Macneil, "Politics," §2.

23. I would say it arguably existed through to the mid-1980s, perhaps to the end of the Thatcher era in the UK (which itself finally petered out after a long, slow decline in 1990). The "sexual revolution" that began in the second half of the 1980s on the Left (when I was a member of various far-left groups and witnessed it firsthand) legitimized (culturally, at least) cultural ideologies with violently anti-Christian premises, which were a wedge to evict the ghost of Christianity from the public square.

However, even during the subsequent Blair era in the UK (both Labor leaders John Smith and Tony Blair were active members of the Christian socialist movement), certain

at the present time, the very *negation* of those previously held, common standards is considered praiseworthy and righteous.[24] Similarly, recent history has witnessed some watersheds in Christian culture that mandate a reexamination of Christian political philosophy. First, the polarizing influence of the Trump presidency demonstrated the antithetical and incoherent positions that were held by Christians regarding his first term as president. Second, the political tyranny of the COVID-era policies and the almost universal capitulation of the churches to what we will argue was the illegitimate use of authority by the national and international governments.

The Importance of Our History

A shocking discovery for many is that this is not the first time in Christian history that this subject has taken on an elevated importance:

> One of the most foolish aspects of modern life is the tendency to assume that all that has happened in the past is quite irrelevant and unimportant and that nobody knew anything until this present generation came.[25]

Thus, this means a good look at Christian history to understand the different views of the Christian understanding of and involvement in the political process. We would all benefit from a good history lesson and learning from our past, and we should see that the material of the previous chapters also serves this purpose well. We are not called to make an idol of the past or to canonize tradition, and we are called to "forget those things

---

moral matters were "banned" (unofficially) from journalists' questions, despite being newly "fashionable" for the radical (or liberal) left. A journalist who referred directly to the homosexuality of certain Cabinet members would no longer be "invited" to briefings (Marsden, "*Sun*'s Anti-Gay Attacks"; see also Wilson, "BBC Eases Privacy Edict").

The US situation is more complex in regard of "shared values," but it should be noted that Barack Obama publicly defended that marriage was for heterosexuals as late as 2008 to get the black evangelical vote. Since Trump took office, it is fair to say there has been increased tribalism and sectarianism, with some in the mainstream now openly speaking of democratic socialism as an alternative to the republicanism of the US, and seeking a complete remaking of the US without its constitution. It is rare, in public at least, to see those prepared to "cross the aisle" to work for what would be the common good in the US.

24. See for example, my blog, "Censorship—The New Normal"; Francis, "Cancelling Christians."

25. Lloyd-Jones, *Exposition of Romans 13*, 135.

[the excrement of religion] behind us,"[26] but that is something very different from ignoring the lessons of our history.

Basic Principles

Are We Called to Defend Truth?

Another strong statement made during the convocation was that as a matter of principle, "*we are not called to defend truth but relationships*." This takes some unpacking to counter its undoubted intuitive appeal and surface profundity; it has the distinctively anti-dogmatic, nonjudgmental, and postmodern flavor—we are to value the subjective relations and operations rather than being concerned about grasping that elusive nettle of "truth" and "being right."[27] Certainly, we can all accept that truth might be progressive for us and, as we support a pluralistic form of life, we do not need total agreement amongst ourselves to value each other's views and perspectives. In that respect, we can defend our relationships from unnecessary angst, particularly from those outside our immediate community. However, in the name of Christian epistemological self-consciousness, I am constrained to immediately question the proposition that we are not called primarily to defend truth in preference to relationships, even more so when the leader of our religion claimed the title of "the Truth."[28]

In addition, as with many things postmodern, it is difficult to locate precisely what is meant by "relationships" here, but our early fathers of the faith really had to work hard in sorting out our basic theology amid both internal schism and external philosophy. Perhaps more compelling from a pure exegetical perspective, our New Testament pattern demonstrates a radical stand for truth in the ministries of Jesus and Paul, and explosive confrontations to wit. Thus, despite being a painful and sometimes explosive process, the results of, say, the Council of Chalcedon or the Council of Nicaea are still with us.

26. Paul refers to "dung" in his famous "forgetting the past and pressing to the future" passage of Phil 3, which contextually dealt with his previous life in Judaism. The word he specifically uses in 3:8 was what we would call a "swear word"; it was only used in vulgar conversation.

27. One of the philosopher Rorty's famous quips was "take care of freedom and truth will take care of itself" (Rorty, *Take Care of Freedom*).

28. John 14:6 (NET): Jesus replied, "I am the way, and the truth, and the life. No one comes to the Father except through me."

This is even more the case in the political arena, with the forensic logic of Wycliffe, Huss, Luther, and Calvin, in challenging papal dogma with scriptural precedent that began and took forward the freeing *doctrinal truths* of the Reformation. The strength that came from taking a position and then defending it was of benefit to not just the church but the entire social and economic order. So, the Reformation did not only straighten out the logic of salvation but its determinism regarding the regularities of nature and God's covenantal operation in the world also broke the hold of the dogmas of Aristotelian metaphysics and made possible the scientific revolution.[29] Thus, it is in this sense of the power of free and critical thinking, that Christian political self-consciousness and a commitment to dominion theology must be robustly defended and argued.

The need for strong debate and the resolution of positions and issues is a recovery of what has been lost in the rush to postmodernity, rather than some radically novel innovation. In my *Foundations*, I have argued that Christianity is *objectively* defendable and presentable in such a way the unbeliever *understands* the challenge intellectually that is given to them. Only the spirit of God *saves* people, but Peter addresses us that we should be ready to give an *apologia*. An *apologia* is not simply a testimony but a *reasoned* defense of our faith—a defense by which we defend the truth by making a positive statement of our positions.[30]

In summary, then, although there are matters of subjective preference over which we need not divide, there is solid, objective ground on which most evangelical Christians should stand if they are thinking clearly. The testimony of Scripture for us *is* normative: we are called to be intelligently "dogmatic" in the face of challenge. If we are not defending truth, then apologetics is redundant, and our faith is arbitrary. Thus, this must also include a defense of a set of political principles.

29. The lack of progress in science (progress in medicine was perhaps the exception) was a notable feature of the medieval period until the Reformation, despite major advances in other areas of culture. This issue is examined comprehensively in Butler, *Philosophy of Science.*

30. BDAG defines ἀπολογία: (apologia) defense; as a legal technical term, a speech in defense of oneself; *reply, verbal defense* (2 Tim 4:16). BDAG emphasizes this is a *speech* in defense: it is a reasoned rather than inspirational or preached.

On Earth as It Is in Heaven

Hence, as issues of philosophy, theology, and methodology, we should be promoting the truth, and part of that truth is the political involvement of believers at every level of the political state to restrain the evil direction in which our political states are going.[31] We might formally agree that under *certain* sets of circumstances, partnership with politics *is* a form of idolatry, for it *is* God that raises up those he chooses and casts down others; and who are we to question God?[32] However, that does *not* mean that partnership with politics is *always* idolatry or that we should *always* accept powerlessness rather than influence, if we are not to make immediate nonsense of "mak[ing] disciples of all nations" and the kingdom coming "on earth as it is in heaven."[33] Again, this would seem self-evident that the kingdom does not come independent of the political realm; you cannot have kingdom standards in social and political matters without those who can understand and implement them in positions of power and influence.

Yet, some mystical iterations of Christian belief *do* dare to assert the contrary. This is normally rooted in a controlling, catastrophic pessimism regarding the human condition. In certain Gnostic heresies, this might also be the case; imported into this view was the Platonic conception of the inferiority, even the *evil* character, of anything physical. Thus, all human constructions and institutions would be considered temporal and a hindrance to perceiving the true reality, which is the spiritual. To this point, there are certain passages in the New Testament where the apostles urge upon us the importance of being heaven-minded and heaven-focused, e.g., Matt 6:33, John 3:31, Col 3: 1–2, which might appear in mystical apologetics.

However, in context, these tend to be made either as assertions of spiritual truths or as matters of Christian ethics to encourage faithfulness to the faith. Put another way, if you live your life in the shadow of the judgment of God before you enter eternity, you are likely to live a different life on Earth. Similarly, lest we become too mystical, we should also consider Paul's

31. This position, I believe, represents an orthodox Christian perspective. Granted, some might see our moral condition as the most enlightened or advanced that it has ever been and that our governments served with distinction in keeping us safe during COVID whilst simultaneously respecting law, life, and liberty.

32. Dan 4:17 (NET); Rom 9:17 (NAS). See also Rom 9. In my view, chapters 9, 10, and 11 of Romans contain some of the most complex and challenging logic of the Christian Scriptures.

33. Matt 28:18–20; Matt 6:10 (NAS).

signature for many of his letters: he made a point of mentioning spirit, soul, *and* body; he frequently addressed issues of immorality and misuse of the *body*. Certain forms of Epicurean and Gnostic philosophy advocated that because the body was doomed to destruction, you could wantonly sin. This could well have been the background to the problem at Corinth that Paul had to deal with at great length and in great detail, and the condemnation of both the Nicolaitans and Jezebel in Revelation.

In other words, the argument needs to be had not only about the legitimacy of certain principles but also in the details of working them out. This is what we will now proceed to undertake.

The Domains of Study

We require a strong, positive statement of scriptural principles. We are all members of the body of Christ, what Luther called the priesthood of all believers.[34] However, this is conceptually and practically distinct from those who work full time *in* the church as a ministerial calling. We tend to be very loose and vague in our common use of the term "church."[35] Thus, it should be immediately evident that there is a lot of theological and philosophical complexity to clarify such an important subject, so it requires us to cover a lot of philosophical ground by considering at a most basic level what the Bible tells us

a. about the relationship of ourselves as *individual* members of the body of Christ (the "church" as the fellowship of all believers) to the political state, and

b. of the relationship of the *institution* of the church (with its ministers, buildings, and governance) to the *institution* of the political state.

When we get those basics right, we can establish the necessary principles to both answer the questions and evaluate to what degree that which was presented to us is scriptural, complete, and defensible. The evaluation is only ever against Scripture and Scripture alone.[36]

34. Luther, *Selected Psalms II*, 332.

35. See Cope, *Old Testament Template*, 103–12.

36. Care should be taken here not to misinterpret this as to say any source of theology outside Scripture is illegitimate, otherwise all the philosopher or theologian could do was to copy out Scripture. It is rather that the rooting and grounding of our philosophy is in Scripture and hermeneutically in Scripture *as a whole*.

Our Civic Responsibility

As our previous chapters demonstrated, for those of us who are children of the Reformers, the sacred-secular distinction *should* be an untenable dichotomy that we should not accept, because it is certainly not a biblical one—there is *no* secular for the believer. If we do not argue on such a basis, we have already surrendered the conceptual ground to the secular-humanist opponents of Christianity. Our position should be rather at its *foundation* a distinctively *Christian* one, captured perfectly by Abraham Kuyper in an 1880 speech as he opened the university that he had founded:

> There is not a square inch in the whole domain of our human existence over which Christ, who is sovereign over *all*, does not cry: "Mine!"[37]

For Kuyper, there was no sacred or secular; *all* was sacred:

> Whatever man may stand, whatever he may do, to whatever he may apply his hand—in agriculture, in commerce, and in industry, or his mind, in the world of art, and science—he is, in whatsoever it may be, constantly standing before the face of God. He is employed in the service of his God. He has strictly to obey his God. And above all, he has to aim at the glory of his God.[38]

This emphasis is also found in J. Gresham Machen, who, like Kuyper, was concerned with the whole of culture and the transformational power of the gospel.[39] He was a passionate believer in the reformation of *all* culture by ensuring there could be Christian education at all levels rather than a centralized, state-controlled education.[40] This was his firsthand response to the noted anti-intellectualism, obscurantism, and narrow evangelistic focus of the emerging fundamentalist movement of the time. Unlike the fundamentalists, Machen had not just defended Scripture but the *entire* Christian worldview against liberalism and was concerned with the regeneration of *all* of culture. This was first seen in his "Christianity and Culture"

37. Kuyper, "Sphere Sovereignty," 488 (emphasis original).

38. Kuyper, *Lectures on Calvinism*, 45.

39. Machen was the founder of Westminster Theological Seminary in 1929 after the split with Princeton caused by the removal of the commitment to orthodox Christian theology as a requirement for ministers to graduate from the seminary.

40. Machen, *Education*. This was a collection of his speeches and essays, as well as an account of the founding principles of Westminster.

address, which was delivered on September 20, 1912, at the opening of the 101st session of Princeton Theological Seminary.[41]

His most famous work, his *Christianity and Liberalism*, had an introductory section that is invaluable reading as a restatement of a Christian conception of culture and immediately engages with the necessity of warfare in the cultural realm, specifically with socialistic political philosophies. It must be remembered Machen had witnessed the Russian revolution a mere five years prior to publishing this work and was contemporary to the greatest intellectuals of America, like John Dewey, who were laying the foundations of the "progressive" movement, which was to incubate American socialism.[42] This at once shows how basic in his thinking was his concern to engage and transform *all* of culture and how this eventually motivated him to break with Princeton and to found both WTS and the OPC. That is, despite this nominal thematic agreement with the emerging fundamentalist movement regarding the status of Scripture, Machen was not a fundamentalist under any interpretation of the term at the origination of its use.[43]

We can see this even more clearly chronologically when we consider that when Machen founded WTS, his first professor of apologetics (who was to remain over forty years in that post) was Van Til.[44] The earliest summary of Van Til, *By What Standard?*, was written by Rushdoony, so we can see the strong relationship between the thought of Machen and Rushdoony; he was undeniably concerned with the *entire* reformation of culture, the intellectual precursor of the modern dominion theology

41. Originally entitled "The Scientific Preparation of the Minister"; Machen, *Education*, 45–59.

42. Machen, *Christianity and Liberalism*, 1–13. It is arguable that the baby has *just* been born; it is only in the Trump era that American politicians in the *mainstream* Democratic Party and in the *mainstream* media were happy to campaign under the banner of "socialism," despite Marxism, in the guise of "critical theory," having been well established in the academies of the West since the 1960s.

43. As we have noted, Barr, in his *Fundamentalism*, commits this category error. Prominent fundamentalists at the time challenged Machen's "orthodoxy" as he never adopted dispensational premillennialism, which was considered the test of orthodoxy by the movement.

44. Van Til had taken Machen's chair at Princeton but resigned a year later with Machen and his colleagues. In the interim, he had been appointed to a prestigious pastorate within the Dutch Reformed church. Machen personally visited Van Til on two different occasions, eventually persuading him to leave his new appointment and join him in establishing the new seminary; Bahnsen, *Van Til's Apologetic*, 11.

movement. His was a theological position that has no reticence in taking political positions based on his understanding of the *implications* of Scripture. Machen was aggressive in his statement of the need to battle in the realm of intellectual ideas, believing correctly it was ideas that would come to dominate the political direction of a nation:

> We may preach with all the fervor of a reformer and yet succeed only in winning a straggler here and there, if we permit the whole collective thought of the nation or of the world to be controlled by ideas which, by the resistless force of logic, prevent Christianity from being regarded as anything more than a harmless delusion.[45]

We have seen through our study that through some noted professors of WTS, such as Van Til, and a second generation of students, such as Bahnsen, this cultural philosophy of full civic responsibility and engagement became foundational for the dominion theology movement that emerged into public view in the early 1970s with Rushdoony's *Institutes*. Within five years, by the time Rushdoony sponsored the publication of Bahnsen's *Theonomy*, it had begun to assert itself by equating civic responsibility with deference to the law of God found in the Hebrew Scriptures and had generated an enormous amount of controversy because of it.

However, we can now understand, because of our previous study, that it is only controversial to those who have forgotten that theonomy was central to the Reformed position and was the dominant influence in the Puritan confessions.[46] The Westminster Confession, with its exposition of civic responsibility and engagement, was not considered an innovation by the divines who wrote it but rather the renewal of patristic faith. The intellectual climate of Christian thought had become so dominated by the import of the *autonomous* mindset of non-Christian philosophy that it ceased to be authentically Christian. Our work, too, is, in many ways, a similar restatement and a set of corrective principles in our modern context. We might call this corrective "the theonomic imperative," and we consider this next.

45. Machen, *Christianity, Culture, and Liberalism*, 6.

46. It was rather the position, arguably, of Augustine and given its systematic expression by Calvin. It was developed by his successor Beza, by Bullinger, our own John Knox, and then the Puritan movement of the 1640s, to which modern Reformed theology owes most.

The Theonomic Imperative

As we have previously discussed, in vanilla Reformed social theory, "theonomy" (the law of God) is contrasted with "autonomy" (being the law to myself). Bahnsen's *Theonomy* was challenged as an aberration of the true meaning on the term as he applied it as a general social theory, but it is not difficult to demonstrate that a scholar from an entirely different background seeking a coherent political and social philosophy and practical program came to virtually identical conclusions. Cope was embarrassed by the lack of civic responsibility demonstrated by the evangelical church during the 1970s and was drawn to the same conclusions regarding what must be fundamental to building our political philosophy:

> The law given to Moses [is] to disciple the newly free nation of Israel. God begins to speak for himself and gives *clear*, *concise*, and very *specific* instruction for how to achieve justice in a community.[47]

In other words, we will all stand before the judgment seats of both the Father and the Son to give account, judged by the moral and social principles of this same law. Though we may have cultural idiosyncrasies, and we may need to probe beneath the application in ancient Israel to find the principle for our contemporary context, *God's* word is not rendered null and void by *our* culture. Again, Cope clarifies this for us whilst fully admitting our responsibility for establishing the application of the law in our culture:

> Remember that the truths of the Bible are told primarily in story form. We study the history and the context, but we will never be in the same circumstances as Moses and Israel, so their application will not necessarily work for us. The *principles*, however, are God's truth and are applicable in new and dynamic ways in any age, any set of circumstances in any nation.[48]

Importantly, with the postmodern apologist in mind, those "new and dynamic ways" do not extend to contradicting the explicit outworking of those principles in the nation of Israel that are given, as the apostle Paul tells us, "for teaching, for reproof, for correction, for training."[49] The main

47. Cope, *God and Political Justice*, loc. 231. Emphasis added.

48. Cope, *Old Testament Template*, 62. Emphasis added.

49. 2 Tim 3:16 (NAS).

philosophical point here is that you cannot be "corrected or reproved" in just any type of fashion for it to be non-arbitrary and to be in accordance with proper standards of justice; there must be *objective* standards of correction or reproof. It can only be *just* if it applies equally to all in morally equivalent circumstances.[50] It is God who defines the "morally significant" components of human reasoning through his Law—polygamy becomes no more morally acceptable, even if it is culturally normal among us. To argue otherwise is simply the Christian form of cultural relativism and needs to be dismissed as such.

To take a much more politically significant specific example, we can consider the social gospel movement, even the more "evangelical" version of it associated with evangelicals such as Ron Sider. It is often stated by apologists for that movement that God "told us not to steal" but "did not define 'stealing' for us." This is an outright fallacy; we have chapter upon chapter within Exodus, Leviticus, Numbers, and the restatement in Deuteronomy that establishes the principle of private property, your right to it, and that stealing is the illegitimate violation of those property rights. It further gives a penal code and authorizes the punishment of thieves; but equally, not all theft is treated as *criminal*; there are extenuating circumstances, but *all* theft is defined as sin and retribution is *always* made.[51]

As Cope argues, they are "dynamic" in the sense we do not talk about boundary markers and oxen when we talk about property rights, but the principles will apply to our cars and tax systems. This is not to deny that there are not places of ambiguity or of great challenge as to how we are to understand and apply God's word, but it becomes very clear whether our cultural practices measure up to his law or not, in many cases because of the fruit that they bear. Thus, we can see how theonomy is not just a theoretical or linguistic construct but provides a powerful tool for the mechanics—the

50. Even Sartre, the great existentialist philosopher famous for exhorting one should never act in "bad faith" by submitting to the will of others rather than deciding for yourself, accepted this piece of moral reasoning. He framed it in terms of a man having to choose between fighting in the Spanish civil war and taking care of his sick mother. *Whatever he chose, he would choose for all men*. The emphasis is on the "all" here; it is a misnomer to think existentialism *necessarily* equates with a lack of binding or universal ethics. One of Plantinga's earliest papers "Existentialist's Ethics" discusses this.

51. That is, there is a civic sanction associated with it. One example in Scripture is associated with the stealing of a small amount of fruit; restitution is made but there is no further punishment. In other cases, there is a fine, compensation, and restitution. It is an oft neglected feature of the law code in the Hebrew Scriptures that it encourages intelligent discrimination of the nature of a misdemeanor or a crime.

practical ethics of communal relations. However, what does theonomy say about the structures and broader frameworks of those relations, about government? Should we prefer republicanism over democracy, or democracy over monarchy? Should we dispense with human government completely as a construct of fallen humanity and advocate for Christian anarchism? We will consider these issues in the subsequent sections.

Theocracy or Representative Government

Some vocal critics of dominion theology argued it was urging the creation of a theocracy, where society is subject to the direct rule of the Creator.[52] However, such a view is a puerile distortion of the position, and Scripture itself mandates a theocracy *only* for the nation of Israel.[53] It is of note that even for the ancient Israelites, within such a theocratic society, the Lord instructed them to choose the wise amongst them to "govern themselves," with the law giving clear instructions for representative government and what we would call "checks and balances":

> You shall select out of all the people able men who fear God, men of truth, those who hate dishonest gain; and you shall place *these* over them *as* leaders of thousands, of hundreds, of fifties and of tens. Let them judge the people at all times; and let it be that every major dispute they will bring to you, but every minor dispute they themselves will judge.[54]

This, of course, is the *precise* reason why the American founders adopted the model of representative government they did.[55] This stratification of government recognizes that in practical terms, this side of omniscience, there are limits to what statecraft can accomplish. Politics

52. PRO-S.O.C.S., "Righteous Revolution."

53. On a practical note, we would do well to seek such a society, but it would be introduced based on consensus, not imposition. It is of note that George Washington, the first American president, dedicated the new nation to God in prayer after the presidential oath of office, representing the consensus of the Congress (Justice, "Anniversary of the First Inauguration," para. 1).

54. Exod 18:21–22 (NAU).

55. This story is vividly told in Barton and Barton, *American Story*, which is notable for its use and enumeration of primary sources. The scholarly standard for early American religious thought is Noll, *America's God*.

is not messianic, or Jesus would have perhaps started a political party or conquered the Roman Empire.[56]

Now, the second great principle that we must establish is that there is a clear distinction between what an individual Christian as a member of the state can do and what the church *as an institution* can do. The *individual* Christian can be a politician, and the church should be clear in its statement of principles over a political matter:

> The church keeps to the realm of principles and not detailed programs. She does not, as it were, enter into the arena either through preaching politics, or by sitting in the House of Lords . . . the business of the individual members of the church to work out these principles, *in detail*, for every aspect of life. Christians must not confine their Christianity to their own personal lives and piety and their own acts of worship. Christianity takes up the whole person. If men and women really believe the gospel, it must govern the whole of their outlook and thinking.[57]

Though we will later need to qualify Lloyd-Jones prohibition on the church with respect to the prohibition of "preaching politics," we can still agree substantively with the principles of involvement emerging here, again, not for theocracy but for participation and representative government:

1. The *church* is not to be involved in the details of a political program but is to teach principles and inform its congregants.

56. One stream of Jewish messianic thought had precisely this expectation, one that was evident even in his disciples (Acts 1:6). There was great disillusionment with Jesus for his political "weakness"; after welcoming him into Jerusalem, they were happy to shout "Crucify him!" a week later.

57. Lloyd-Jones, *Exposition of Romans 13*, 159. Emphasis added. The "House of Lords" is the upper chamber of the British Parliament. It has an important role in scrutinizing proposed legislation and can, in the extreme, delay legislative passage for up to one year. The Parliament Acts of 1911 and 1949 removed the lords' ability to veto a bill. Unlike the lower chamber, only 92 out of around 800 members are elected, with a mixture of inherited rights to sit in it (landed aristocracy), "honorary" peerages where the prime minister nominates someone as a "peer" that allows them to sit in the chamber, and 26 senior bishops of the official state church, the Church of England. Lloyd-Jones was objecting to this latter group that favored the state church, but to which he was also objecting in principle. Politicking can occur as prime ministers can appoint their political allies to alter the balance of power to increase the speed of the passage of legislation through the chamber, which is one of the reasons it has become so large; the elected lower chamber is 650 members.

2. The *individual* Christian is at liberty to be involved to whatever depth is necessary to ensure that the "powers that be" are "influenced in the right direction. It is their duty to do this, and they must not abdicate from their responsibility."[58]

So, in summary, we can accept with Lloyd-Jones and with Cope that a "perfect" society is not possible on Earth but that does not mean we cannot have the expectation of a *better* one more in line with the principles of the kingdom this side of any return of the Lord; we can accept that a complete reformation is only possible with the personal presence of Jesus, yet it *is* possible for us to be his government now because that is what *he* tells us in the Great Commission:

> Then Jesus came up and said to them, "*All authority in heaven and on earth has been given to me*. Therefore [you] go and make disciples of all nations, baptizing them in the name of the Father and the Son and the Holy Spirit, *teaching them to obey* everything I have commanded you. And remember, I am with you always, to the end of the age.[59]

Grammatically, in the Greek (the original language of the New Testament), the major imperative verb here is the *making disciples* rather than the teaching or the baptizing.[60] We should now be able to deduce that *making disciples* is precisely what the theonomical imperative enables us to do; dominion theology takes this commission seriously and explicates it as present in Scripture as a continuing inter-covenantal operation. That is, it is the discipling or *Christianizing* of our society, the reformation, salting, or whatever word we want to use, which is commanded and expected.

For the Christian though, there are important additions to the nation-building principles established in the Hebrew Scriptures. Though, as Cope correctly asserted, the focus of the Christian Scriptures is personal

58. Lloyd-Jones, *Exposition of Roman 13*, 159.

59. Matt 28:18-20, NET. Emphasis added.

60. The NET Bible exegetical note is informative here: "'Go . . . baptize . . . teach' are participles modifying the imperative verb 'make disciples.' According to *ExSyn** 645 the first participle (πορευθέντες, *poreuthentes*, 'Go') fits the typical structural pattern for the attendant circumstance participle (aorist participle preceding aorist main verb, with the mood of the main verb usually imperative or indicative) and thus picks up the mood (imperative in this case) from the main verb (μαθητεύσατε, *matheteusate*, 'make disciples')" (NET online: https://www.netbible.org/bible/Matthew+28). *Here, it is referring to Wallace, *Exegetical Syntax of the New Testament.*

salvation; the specific political and cultural context of the early believers as living under an often oppressive and hostile Roman rule meant apostolic input and precedent was required. This, of course, was the purpose of Paul's great exposition within Romans of the Christian life and specifically dealt with the imperial and state authorities as part of his argument. It is to the locus of this exposition, Rom 13, that we now turn.

Understanding Romans 13

Overview

Few passages of Scripture have created as much controversy as Rom 13, owing to the chronic lack of understanding of it in the modern Christian consciousness, despite there being substantive studies available in the history of the church over the last two centuries as the modern state evolved. So, for example, during the COVID lockdowns of 2020-21, an uncritical use of the passage was made to justify the unconditional surrender of religious freedom and civil liberty by most Christian leaders. Unfortunately, this demonstrates complete ignorance of the passage and demonizes all those over the centuries who found within the Scriptures a mandate for social reform, civil disobedience, and political revolution. It would indeed be perverse to rebuke a Luther, the abolitionist movement on both sides of the Atlantic, the American independence movement, or the apartheid activists within the South African church for a refusal to submit to the governing authorities.[61]

However, Rom 13 does require interpretation and contextualization to counter what some have argued is the plain sense of the text. That said, it is not my intention to do a verse-by-verse exegesis, as this has been authoritatively and competently completed by Lloyd-Jones, taking him 162 pages, which we cannot afford here.[62] That said, I incorporate most of his arguments in the following section and modify them as necessary with my own revisions as we draw conclusions from our present context. We will see that such revisions became necessary owing to the deterioration of the status of Christianity in our culture, and consequently, some of his assumptions and inferences were no longer valid for us. As noted, the early

61. In the dying days of apartheid, it was common for government ministers to quote Rom 13 to the dissident church centered around Archbishop Tutu.

62. Lloyd-Jones, *Exposition of Chapter 13*, 1–162.

Christians needed the apostolic input of Rom 13, 1 Tim 2, and 1 Peter 2 because the believers needed to know how to respond to pagan rulers who were often extremely hostile to the point of persecution and execution.[63] However, it is only necessary to consider Rom 13 extensively in this section, other than some relevant brief introductory remarks here.

Firstly, 1 Pet 2 is very much a recapitulation of the Pauline teaching of Rom 13; the testimony of Scripture itself shows Peter clearly took theological direction from Paul here and considered his works scriptural (2 Pet 3:15). Secondly, 1 Tim 2 has a significantly different focus; it has the primary subject of intercession for those in authority *that* the social and political conditions of effective evangelism and the discipleship of the nations might be possible. This is clearly still relevant to any comprehensive account of Christian political philosophy but not necessarily within the scope of understanding our relation to the state, which is our interest here. Hence, it will not be considered further here other than to emphasize such intercession was expected and *mandated* by Paul to *create* the conditions that would allow the execution of the political program in Rom 13. In practical terms, the enormous significance of 1 Tim 2 is that we are not to hide in our Christian ghettoes watching the reign of the Antichrist and waiting for the rapture. Thus, the principles of intercession and prayer for our governments form one of the central precepts of dominion theology.

The Context of Romans 13

It must be remembered that this section does not exist in isolation from the sections around it. This is important because some commentators seem to think it is an intrusion or clumsy insertion of thought. Yet, this is a new subsection in the section that began with chapter 12—the *application* of the doctrine laid down in the first eight chapters.[64] The great emphasis of chapter 12 is that of *living peaceably with other people.* Chapter 13 is, thus, perfectly in position, "[Government enables us] to live peaceably with one another, to maintain order, to avoid disorder."[65] The "vengeance of God" mentioned in 12 would then, arguably, be part of the function of the state

63. I deal with this passage more fully in Macneil, "Should I Obey My Government."

64. Chapters 9, 10, and 11 form a self-contained pericope on the problem of the Jews and their relationship to the gospel. There are still important principles in these passages, but the chapters are strongly focused on the Jews.

65. Lloyd-Jones, *Exposition of Romans 13*, 2.

and its laws. So, the first great conclusion we can draw from Rom 13 is the legitimacy of the state *in principle* as against those who reject all the institutions of men as fallen and illegitimate.[66] God has instituted it that the conditions of social peace might exist for the benefit of all:

> I urge, then, first of all, that requests, prayers, intercession and thanksgiving be made for everyone—for kings and all those in authority, that we may live peaceful and quiet lives in all godliness and holiness. This is good, and pleases God our Savior.[67]

However, (and I believe this is where many contemporary formulations regarding our rights, relationships with, and responsibilities to the state are at their weakest) based on this foundational principle, it then

66. This was one of Calvin's strongest criticisms of the Anabaptist post-Reformation movement (sometimes called the "Radical Reformation"), which became, progressively, to reject all forms of human (feudal) authority, and their agitation was making it easy for papist forces to justify attacking Reformed communities. A broad, revolutionary movement had coalesced in the time of Luther around Thomas Müntzer (c. 1489–1525), who, if not formally an Anabaptist, became allies with them and provided theological and logistical expertise to their radical reform program. The seeds of messianic Nazism and Communism are plausibly argued to have originated in their theology (Engels wrote extensively in praise of Müntzer), which had also justified violence against all nonbelievers (where the nonbeliever was widely conceived). He was later celebrated by the communists of the DDR (Müntzer was featured on a 5 Mark banknote) in the twentieth century. Müntzer was executed in 1525 after heading the Peasants Rebellion, and the movement itself was brutally suppressed after the attempt to create a commune failed in Munster in 1534.

Importantly though, the experience of the brutal suppression at Munster moderated their politics into its more moderate iteration, and the movement, though suppressed, did survive, such that the Amish, Mennonites, even Quakers and Baptists all lay claim to some kind of heritage from the Anabaptists. The English Civil War under Cromwell also had groups, such as the Levelers and the Diggers, which had clearly incorporated elements of egalitarian thinking from the Anabaptists, as had Cromwell himself. The Anabaptists *were* the first to assert that church and state should be governmentally separate, and this concept did find its way into mainstream Christian thinking and was given firm expression in the early US "wall of separation" between church and state.

In an important sense, all the Anabaptist groups remained social radicals but became committed to a *demonstration* rather than an *imposition* of Christianity. See Verduin, *Reformers*, for a historical review from within the Reformed community but with sufficient chronological distance to present a well-balanced view; see Broomfield, "Thomas Müntzer's Misunderstood Revolution," which provides additional biographical context, and Farrell, "Thomas Müntzer," which is a partisan pro-Müntzer account that helps strengthen the thesis that he was indeed inspirational to revolutionary movements of the left and right.

67. 1 Tim 2:1 (NAS).

becomes much too easy to give the state much *too much* authority over the church and the individual believer, to the degree that all the believer is entitled to is a weak, passive resistance or martyrdom. In contrast, we will find as we work through the chapter that there is a justification for a Christian taking part in a revolution to overthrow a corrupt government.

Obedience and Submission are Different Concepts

So, let us consider the first verse of Rom 13:

> Let every person be subject to the governing authorities for there is no authority except from God and those that exist are appointed by God. Therefore whoever resists the authority resists what God has appointed, and those who resist will incur judgement.[68]

Thus, it is straightforward to understand why many teach *unconditional* obedience to the state. This is reinforced by some commentators who note that the term translated "be subject" was originally a military term meaning "to rank under," but this is one of those occasions where we need to understand the semantics of the word have moved far beyond its original meaning, as witnessed in the Greek literature of that era, of which the Bible is an integral part. By overstressing the etymology, extremely severe interpretations of this passage that would admit *no* conditions for civil disobedience have arisen.[69] In contrast, as Lloyd-Jones explains, there are three other Greek words in common use during that period that would convey far more strongly the concept of "obedience," if that was what Paul had wanted to communicate. We must understand that "be subject to" does *not* simply mean "be obedient to," though the Greek verb in the middle voice had historically been used with this meaning, but that usage would have been already considered archaic and would be highly improbable at the time of Paul's writing.[70]

68. Rom 13:1–2 (this is my translation but it follows closely the NET).

69. Lloyd-Jones cites some of the most influential commentators of the nineteenth and twentieth centuries as having that view.

70. The Greek verb here is ὑποτάσσω (hupotasso) which is correctly rendered either subject or submit, rather than obey. BDAG, the academic "standard" reference work for the Greek language of this period, does not offer the meaning "obey," listing only the passive and active voice. *Vine's Expository Dictionary* (another standard work) lists "obey" as a possible but *minor* inflection in the passive or middle voice, noting the military origin of the word. The Strong's number is 5293 and Strong lists "obey" as a possibility for the

Thus, continuing our analysis, *subjection* rather implies a *reasoned* choice. For example, Eph 5:21 states, "*submitting* yourselves one to another in the fear of God," and it should be clear that in this case, there is a logical difference between subjection and obedience. Both parties cannot simultaneously *obey* one another if a difference arises, but they can respectfully resolve their differences by having a mental posture or attitude of *submission*. To not recognize this is to make this, and other examples of the usage of the word, logically contradictory.[71] Thus, Lloyd-Jones argues the context demands "*making room for*" or "*preferring out of respect*" as appropriate renderings.[72]

The Boundaries of Christian Resistance

Now, we must argue that a minister of the state demands unconditional respect and subjection only with regards to an *appropriate* execution of their office, and the ruler *must* behave in an honorable and just manner before the people, because those are the terms of their ordination before God: "He means the powers that are governing [well] and maintaining law and order."[73] In other words, they are following the prescription laid out in the following verses of Rom 13, punishing the *evil* doer, maintaining *justice*, defending the nation, and being fiscally responsible. If those conditions are not met, you are *not* bound.

However, this is not left just as conceptually defined in Scripture. The book of Acts provides the narratives for us of the conflict between the early church and the "authorities" that we might know there is no *unconditional* ethical mandate to obey our governing authorities.[74]

middle voice. Pertinently, the "middle" voice (often reflexive in nuance) was dying out during this period of the Greek language, adding to the improbability this was the sense intended.

71. Col 3:18; 1 Pet 3:1, 5.

72. Lloyd-Jones, *Exposition of Romans 13*, 20–22.

73. Lloyd-Jones, *Exposition of Romans 13*, 23.

74. Some might object that it was the religious authorities they came into conflict with, but Roman history does tell us that the Romans were shrewd enough to allow a degree of autonomy to their colonies in the sense they could keep their own civil and religious law *if* they recognized the supreme jurisdiction of Rome. In the Donatist controversy in the early church of North Africa, this was as simple as throwing some incense on the fire once a year; some believers compromised for the sake of political peace, but the Donatists would not and were severely persecuted by both the Roman authorities and

Additionally, both Kings and Chronicles also provide certain occasions where treaties and political cooperation with other nations, even between Israel and Judah, were condemned by the prophets on behalf of the Lord. This reinforces the presumption that the exercise of authority must be in accordance with the *terms* of its ordination before God—just because a government does something, that does not make it right or legitimate before God or the citizen. In fact, the pattern within Scripture was often that God empowered a rival power or individual to overthrow a ruler upon which judgment had been executed; this was his prerogative as "King of kings and Lord of lords." Most are familiar with this phrase from the book of Revelation (Rev 17:14, 19:16), but it also occurs in the much more interesting context of 1 Tim 6:15. We see at once in vv. 1–2 the call of "submission" of indentured servants to their masters, which must be matched with Col 4:1, which calls for masters to "submit" (in the sense of providing justice and fairness) to their servants.[75]

---

the church in Rome. We can glean this from the gospels and Acts, where the governors would rather that the Jews "judge according to their law" (Acts 18:15, 24:6) than get involved in such civil disputes. It was why Pilate was just plain reluctant to get involved in the trial of Jesus, and when he was forced to be involved, he refused to judge as justice demanded but rather in accord with what he perceived as public opinion.

75. It is worth noting that it was "indentured slavery" (voluntary service) and not "chattel slavery" (where the slave was the possession of the master) that was the normal sense of the word "slave," either within a Christian or a Jewish cultural context by the time of the New Testament, even though the Greek word δούλοις (doulois) did not distinguish between the two senses (this is why some translations use the word "slave" rather than "servant" in Paul's stylistic greetings). Paul might well have been playing idiomatically on this common sense of the word to emphasise how he viewed his service to God, as a matter of legal and moral obligation (I was redeemed and am now owned by Master and at his disposal). However, Paul also mentions elsewhere the privilege of being sons and daughters; John preferred to describe us as "children" of God or a "royal priesthood," and so, for either apostle, we can see something well beyond chattel slavery being expressed as descriptive of our intended relation to and with God.

More specifically, indenture was where a person would commit to serve a master in return for food, accommodation, return of appropriated property, debt release, and such like; this was also common in the days of the migration to the New World, where in return for passage, someone would commit to serve the landowner for a fixed period. Indentured slavery within Scripture was tightly regulated as a part of debt recovery and management—the Jubilee (seven and forty-nine years) was to be the release of those who had indentured themselves, historic debt cancellation, and the redistribution of property that had been sold back to its ancestral owners: "There shall be no poor among you" (Deut 15:4). Chattel slavery being not regulated stood morally condemned as lawless and the single, explicit mention of it in the Christian Scriptures was in Rev 18:13, where it refers to the excesses of the harlot Babylon. It is thus of no surprise that the abolitionist

Thus, it is pointedly *not* proven that every occupant of the office "has been ordained by God," and thus, we are not morally obligated to immediately obey them if they are *not* governing well. It is the *office* and not the person that is ordained by God. Particularly, we need to ask what we are to do with rulers who gratuitously abuse their position or are tyrannical. We need only think of Nero burning Christians coated in tar to light his feasts or of a Hitler orchestrating the Holocaust.

An answer can be suggested by an analogy. If our nation was attacked or was in imminent danger of being attacked, most of us would consider it perfectly just to sign up to fight if we were asked to, in addition to whatever diplomatic response there might be. We might even end up fighting for our nation and killing people of an aggressor nation to preserve our liberty and freedom. We would consider this "self-defense," and it seems a concept well-documented in the Hebrew Scriptures. For example, even though there was no scriptural mandate for a standing army in Israel, there were certainly borders, there were arrangements made for tribes to join with one another for national defense, and for the settling of disputes militarily if diplomacy failed.[76] The nation was instructed to live peaceably with its neighbors and to respect their territory, but they were to be equally vigorous in defending their own property, culture, and territory.[77] Thus, we should at least be able to ask the question, if those that attack us just happen to be members of our *own* nation and those in authority over us, should we not, too, have a right to self-defense?

The logic of the Second Amendment of the American Constitution was based on just that type of reasoning. The colonists and settlers had come from nations all over the Old World, where the monarchs and priests systematically oppressed the people and, in some eras, the people were systematically tortured and killed in the most brutal and public fashion, often at the behest of the papal hegemony that employed the surrogate army of the "Holy Roman Emperor."[78] They came to the New World in

---

movement began in a Christian context.

76. Deut 20:10–20; Josh 4:12; Num 32:6–25.

77. We leave aside the issue of the initial conquest of Canaan, which was a judicial decision by the Lord himself owing to the violence, corruption, immorality, and witchcraft that characterized the Canaanite tribes.

78. The "Holy Roman Emperor" was a title bequeathed by the Pope on one of the monarchs of Europe once the papacy had established its domination (c. AD 600). By the medieval period, this meant making that monarch's military resources available to the pope for dealing with "heresy" in any nation rebelling against his authority. The monarchs

search of religious freedom and political liberty. This is why Lloyd-Jones, who was something of an expert on the Puritanism of the early colonists, was able to write,

> Surely, as Christians, we are entitled to argue that if a state, a king, an emperor, a governor, a dictator or anybody else becomes tyrannical, then this state is violating the law of its own being and constitution as laid down in Romans 13:2.[79]

That is, the state was instituted, as 1 Tim 2:2 states, to ensure "we may lead a peaceful [tranquil] and quiet life in all godliness and dignity" (NET), the State exists to serve the people, not the people to serve the State. Thus, he continues:

> The moment . . . the State turns itself into a master and into a tyrant, it is disobeying the Law of God that brought it into being and it must itself be punished; and the form the punishment takes is that the government is *thrown out* and replaced by one that is prepared to abide by the teaching of Romans 13:1-7.[80]

This statement begs the question, what does "thrown out" mean? Are we permitted to fight with arms (as the American founders felt it necessary to mandate) to evict a tyrannical government? We have already seen the inadequacy of the unconditional submission position, and we can see that our options are much greater than simply passive resistance, but just what *are* the limits of our resistance?

Christians Can Be Revolutionaries

Within Christian war theory, the "just war" is defined as an extension of the duty of a magistrate to "restrain evil," and it is exactly this moral imperative to "restrain evil" that allows "[a Christian] to take part in a rebellion to change your government."[81] Whether that evil is internal or

were normally feuding with one another as well as trying to weaken the authority of the Pope over their nations. This was why some of the monarchs were sympathetic to the proto-Reformers, such as Knox, Wycliffe, and Huss, who vigorously asserted the political autonomy of nations and the superiority of the civil authorities over the church within the national boundaries.

79. Lloyd-Jones, *Exposition of Romans 13*, 46; Lloyd-Jones, *Puritans*.

80. Lloyd-Jones, *Exposition of Romans 13*, 46. Emphasis added.

81. Lloyd-Jones, *Exposition of Romans 13*, 69.

external to a nation, it is not an option for us to ignore it. However, such revolutionary action is the "last resort," as is going to war (the Lord spoke of multiple cycles of judgment against a nation before it was destroyed);[82] but as it was necessary to go to war against a Hitler, a Mussolini, or a Stalin for the purposes of restraining their evil, so it is necessary to resist the evil of our *own* leaders.

Indeed, this is not unusual in the history of the Protestant church and was a feature of the movement around Puritan Oliver Cromwell (the English Civil War) that spawned egalitarian groups, such as the Levelers and the Diggers, who prefigured many of the egalitarian policies that became associated with the later labor and trade union movements.[83] Christians were very active in these reform movements and the WEA, a Christian wing of the WMC movement (that was founded to promote literacy amongst working people), still exists in the UK today in accord with its original mission, whilst the WMCs are rather tatty, low-end social clubs.

So, it is also important to recognize that there are degrees of resistance between non-resistance and a full-blown rebellion that we can exercise. We start with dialogue and engagement with our elected representatives, but we cannot allow ourselves to be neutered when our representatives cease to represent us. We can protest, we can boycott, and we can take collective action, both as individuals and as congregations, to try and ensure social or political change. Importantly though, with congregational action, there are those specific issues that we considered earlier if we are not to confuse the individual and church institutional positions in relation to government.

However, in cases where oppressive government tyranny *is* directed at entire congregations, e.g., in the banning of public worship (as happened during COVID), the congregation should be able to respond collectively, and the church enunciates a political position as representative for its congregations. Where at all possible, we endeavor to keep our protest peaceful and respectful of the agents of the state; but where demonstrators are attacked or the conditions for demonstrating are made so restrictive, we are able to make our stand against that evil. It may be there are consequences for that stand, just as there were consequences for Paul before Festus in appealing to Caesar, or for the Jewish converts of the book of Hebrews in the confiscation

82. Lev 24:14–46.

83. See appendix C for a discussion of the English Civil War and the link with the founding of the United States.

of their property.[84] Yet, done under the guidance of the Holy Spirit, that can bring great victory to the church in the public square.[85]

Now, I hope it is understood that I am not asserting we are *immediately* revolutionaries; it is just that we need to understand we *can* be in the extreme. We can agree, as Lloyd-Jones puts it, "Christians should always be the best citizens in the country" and "good and peaceable" in their basic attitudes.[86] We have an ethical obligation to be the best citizens we can be *and* to be the most cooperative with the authorities over us as we can morally be. Even Stalin began to lessen the persecution of Christians because of the reputation for them being the best workers.[87]

Christians, by default, *are* on the side of law and order because they understand that sin has produced lawlessness among men and that lawlessness needs the sword of the state to restrain it; this is also why Paul makes the statement that it is an *"issue of conscience"* (v. 5) that we submit and even *pay taxes* to ensure the smooth operation of the state. However, Lloyd-Jones strongly and immediately qualifies this general orientation to the state after establishing it as a basic principle with this statement:

> There is a limit beyond which it [the submission to the State and its enactments] is not true. It is quite clear in the scriptures that *if the State should ever come between me and my relationship to God,* then I *must* not obey it.[88]

During the COVID-19 pandemic, this limit was undeniably violated throughout Europe as congregations were prohibited from congregational

84. Acts 25:12; Heb 10:34.

85. The River Church in Tampa Bay refused to obey the state COVID closure mandate to the degree the pastor was arrested. However, the enormous publicity that surrounded the event meant the mandate was overturned by the governor and the church was able to reopen at full capacity. There was a delay reopening because of attempted shootings and death threats, but within six weeks, the church reopened and has never shut since. It grew enormously through the pandemic as other churches shut permanently or went online, never to reopen physically. The pastor has since had his record expunged, the state attorney who charged him was dismissed by the governor because of political bias, and he has also met and prayed with the president on two separate occasions.

86. Lloyd-Jones, *Exposition of Romans 13*, 51.

87. This is a well-known paradox, even in today's Russia, where specific Christian ministries have access to and favor with the highest levels of the Russian government (I personally know of two) because of their reputation for honor and ethical conduct. Similarly, in some Islamic countries, Christians have access to TV stations because they are honorable and pay their bills on time.

88. Lloyd-Jones, *Exposition of Romans 13*, 52. Emphasis added.

worship and our almost universal failure to resist has cost us enormous space in the public sphere. Where there was or is substantive resistance, as was the case with the River Church in Tampa, Florida, and in some of the other US states where governors rejected federal mandates, the contrast could not be greater—they had full liberty to meet for worship, citizens traded freely with one another, they did not lose their businesses, and did not become reliant on federal welfare.[89]

Summary and Concluding Remarks

In this chapter, we have sketched how we apply the basic principles of dominion theology to our political philosophy, specifically, we established the principle of involvement and that it should be an involvement that is not passive or neutral. As a matter of principle, we are to defend truth rather than cede to postmodern subjectivity or cultural relativism, noting that the Reformation and Councils of the Church established prerequisites for culture in their catechisms. A strong view of truth also ushered in the scientific revolution. We asserted that it was an anomalous distinctive of twentieth-century evangelicalism to separate from wider political and cultural involvement. The Reformed church has had a history of political involvement since the days of Luther and Calvin through to modern figures, such as Machen, and the wider evangelical movement had the father of the modern revivalists Charles Finney as an example of intense political and cultural involvement.

We noted that for as long as there has been a Christian church, there has been political opposition to it as witnessed in the biblical narratives of Acts, in which there are recorded accounts of conflict. We also rejected that the correct Christian position was one of agnosticism to the political environment: 1 Tim 2 implies prayer for a social environment conducive to the

89. In the years since, there has been a move of millions of people from the repressive states into the states that did not lock down. The lockdowns were demonstrated to have been completely ineffective; there was no difference in outcomes from the strictest lockdowns in cities like New York to the least locked down cities in Florida (Zinberg, "Numbers Prove Cuomo's Lockdowns Hurt"). The utter hypocrisy during the pandemic of public officials who had locked down their cities was seen as they were caught at the same time holidaying in Florida, that was the first to remove any restrictions (Telegraph, "Under Fire for 'Fleeing' to Florida"; Bernstein, "'Not Surprised' Democrats Flee"). This is the perfect example of "authorities" that needed to be ejected from office at the first opportunity for failing in their duties under Rom 13.

preaching of the gospel and the discipling (Christianizing) of nations, which is correlative to a pluralistic political context and cultural transformation. We then dealt specifically with the contemporary, difficult issue of Rom 13, noting that because the biblical narratives record conflicts with the authorities for us, a simple surface reading of Rom 13 that demands unconditional obedience to the governing authorities is insufficient. In this regard, we considered in some detail the account of Rom 13 provided by the finest evangelical expositor of the twentieth century, Dr. Martyn Lloyd Jones. He drew the distinction between "honor," "submission," and "obedience" in considering the original Greek syntax and semantics of the passage.

His central position was that a State invalidates itself when it behaves in a tyrannical manner and when it intrudes into matters over which it has no jurisdiction, particularly in matters of religious practice and liberty. We established the principle from his work that only when the State is the minister of God, to bring order and punish moral evil, is obedience to the State required. We found that revolutionary activity by believers was permissible as an act of ejecting an immoral or tyrannical State that had delegitimized itself. We established further that the individual Christian is perfectly at liberty to be involved to any degree in political activity, but the domain of the institution of the church was separate to the political institutions. Its role was to be the moral guardian that would speak into these institutions rather than to be directly involved in the institutions of government.

We broadly agree with his position but note that he was writing during a time when the Judeo-Christian position was broadly accepted in all major political parties. Our qualification now is that this is no longer the case, and the church needs to recognize and expose the morally degenerate nature of "secular" politics and to sometimes publicly support those parties that support ethical positions more in line with the gospel. So, whilst we maintain with Lloyd-George that the church as an institution is not to argue for a theocracy, which was reserved for ancient Israel alone, we do now assert that it is to argue for a theonomical political position, seeing the scriptural principles of jurisprudence and government as immutable principles.

God, in his law, not only provides us with commandments as top-level principles but works out the application in detail in the succeeding narratives. So, for example, a party that aggressively campaigned on abortion, euthanasia, and sexual license would need to be challenged and proscribed on that basis.[90] This implies a greater level of involvement of the institution

90. The issue of "tactical voting" is a difficult one. The logic of the tactical vote is to

of the church in analysis of the political programs and its explicit support of parties or policies. However, the moral character of the individual politician should also be examined; some churches now do provide "voter guides" where they have tracked not just the party allegiance of a candidate but also their voting record. We conclude by reiterating that we cannot have kingdom standards in social and political matters without those who can understand and implement them in positions of power and influence.

---

cast a vote for the *least* evil of the candidates likely to win, even at the cost of a candidate in line with your principles. Or, as some communities of color in the US have decided to vote for Democrats who support anti-Christian positions because they believe on balance that the candidate can deal with other issues in their community more effectively that the alternative. Some Christians explicitly condemn not voting in line with your principles, i.e., if a Christian candidate was standing, you would be obligated to vote for them, even if they were in a constituency where they would have no chance of winning.

The relative merits of either of these options is also dependent on your voting system—for us in the UK we have a very limited democracy which does not employ a transferable voting system where you could indicate your choice of candidates as a rank. Consequently, the tactical vote is probably more appealing. The ethical dilemma is a bit like that associated with IVF; if the outcome is more children in the world, does it become a good thing even though fertilized embryos are often discarded during the process? Such ethical dilemmas would need to be considered in future work but are obviously not as simple as they may first seem; this is why Christians in their disciplines need to think through these issues.

Conclusion

Dominion Theology—Its History

In this book we, have traveled from ancient to modern eschatology, through the secularization of Western culture during the nineteenth and twentieth century, and demonstrated that the rise of modern dominion theology could be directly correlated with the situation in time and place of Christian thought. Thus, returning to the questions I posed in the summary in the introduction, I believe we can affirm with reasonable verisimilitude the two statements I wanted to test. Dominion theology has indeed been shown to have emerged from a postmillennial eschatological perspective in a distinctive sociological context with a definite philosophical heritage of presuppositional orthodox Reformed theology.

We can also confirm that it was the cultural crisis and conflicts of the late nineteenth and twentieth centuries, the failing of modernity and the emergence of postmodernity, that were shown to necessitate a new Christian response. It was a repudiation of both the decision to withdraw from culture, to ghettoize in a parochial Christian community, and to openly embrace socialism, as in the social gospel movement. Similarly, the program that was developed in a novel and penetrating fashion by Rushdoony expanded into a modern Christian sociological reform movement that allowed evangelicals more generally, not just the Reformed movement, to emerge from the intellectual marginalization. Pentecostals and charismatics, Word of Faith, Kingdom Now, and non-Western neo-evangelicals have all incorporated central elements of dominion theology into their social and political positions.

Lastly, we then demonstrated how dominion theology could form the basis for a coherent philosophy of Christian involvement. We argued that such a philosophy in all its key components has already had a long history within the Protestant church. We were reasserting the normative position after a period of aberration and apostasy in the late nineteenth and first half of the twentieth centuries. We built on the work of Lloyd-Jones, who gave a compelling exegesis of what was frequently the stumbling block for contemporary Christians to wider political involvement, Rom 13. We discovered a compelling case for a radical, even revolutionary, commitment both as individuals and as congregations to the political reformation of our nations.

Dominion Theology—Present and Future

The answer to my question regarding the status and future of dominion theology is more complex and subjective, but I believe some informed judgments are possible. Firstly, the evidence of the presence of dominion theology in an *operational*, if not doctrinal, form in most *growing* (as opposed to ossified) sections of the Church is established beyond doubt. Dominionism is part of the language toolkit of friend and foe alike. The dominionist arguments have proved persuasive, survived, and thrived through the criticism. It is, again, largely accepted that society needs improvement rather than abandonment by the redeemed, and it cannot be changed or improved without political engagement and representation of the Christian view in the organs of power and at all the different levels of governance, from school, local community, county, state, and parliament. Yet, it must be said that there are clear and substantive differences between the nature of that engagement within Reconstructionism with its roots in the Reformed communion, the Wagnerian NAR, charismatic Kingdom Now, Word of Faith "dominionisms," and the modern phenomena of Christian nationalism. Let us consider the key characteristics of each identified in the book to help with clarifying my final position.

In general terms, the Reconstructionist movement provided the clearest and most intellectually coherent philosophical and theological basis for dominionism in the work of intellectual figures such as Rushdoony, Bahnsen, DeMar, and North. These are now labeled "theonomists" because the distinctive feature of this brand of dominionism is the belief that God's law, not natural law, provides the epistemological basis for all knowledge and, therefore, all life should be predicated and informed by God's law as revealed to us in the Hebrew and Christian Scriptures. Faith necessarily embraces every sphere of culture and every aspect of the individual's relational and personal life. There is no realm of autonomous human existence. The Bible is considered a coherent whole, not dispensationalized into ages where the law is abrogated, but where the law is of continuous significance as a vehicle of sanctification and a guide to ethical conduct.[1]

There is also a position within the Reformed community that moderates this strict position but recognizes the continuity between the "new" and "old" covenants and the value of the law. These are those who emphasize the Hebrew Scriptures as a resource for principles to be applied in our current situation in time, but who argue against the validity of the civil case law of the Hebrew Scriptures as a basis for current civil law, as would be argued for by strict theonomists. Their epistemology tends to be far more situational and postmodern, with an emphasis on the ethical quality of the narrative in the Scriptures rather than seeing the Scriptures as a normative and exemplary source book.[2]

Next, dominionists like Kingdom Now or Word of Faith, which have a fundamentalist, Pentecostal, or charismatic heritage, are generally far less epistemologically self-conscious and tend to favor evidentialist apologetics, with its implicit confidence in natural law and reason to convince and convict. Where it is theologically informed, it often favors a "covenant neutral" epistemology, where "common grace" means truth is to be found in the redeemed and non-redeemed communities.[3] The Bible ceases to be a document of continuous revelation applicable in all ages but is to be viewed in a broad, dispensational sense. Ethics are essentially antinomian, emphasis is on the relational aspects of faith,[4] and "grace" is considered to have an antithetical relationship to law, "free from all external rules, but inwardly

1. I expand upon this philosophical position in my *Foundations*.

2. Cope, *God and Political Justice*, loc. 4427. Landa establishes the substance of her book on a theonomical basis with a thoroughly philosophically modern premise. I sense a change in emphasis to a more postmodern view as she attempts to demonstrate in later chapters how the apostles "interpreted" the law for their new situation.

3. Westminster Theological Seminary has been much criticized by Reconstructionists for moving in this direction, away from a presuppositionalist position. "Common grace" is a term associated with the Reformed movements, but the concept is present in evangelical theology more generally using different terminology.

4. God as my "Dad," pastors as "fathers," pastors' wives as "mothers," and together, we are "God's family."

prompted and enabled by the Spirit of truth."[5] These are also characteristic of the churches on the more mystical wing of the prophetic movement that often have weakly defined postmodern positions in their doctrines.

Finally, Christian nationalism is not really a distinct movement, coming into political parlance in the wake of Christian support for Trump, which I have examined in detail elsewhere.[6] It is generally used as a pejorative by opponents and tautologically by its proponents: "I love my nation and I am a Christian, therefore I am a Christian nationalist!" That is, Christian nationalists could be any of the above rather than a distinct category. Where it is becoming intellectually more sophisticated, it is recognizing the dangers to the Western Christian tradition by mass immigration (sanctioned and illegal) from nations with non-Western values. Recent immigrants from Islamic nations are seen to be particularly problematic as they have cultures frequently inimical to the West that deny freedom of speech, minority rights, the rights of women, and the separation of church and state. They do not believe assimilation into the host Western nation is desirable or required; it is these positions that are fertile ground for an emerging Christian nationalist movement as a political movement.[7]

Thus, in conclusion, I would assert that it is not possible to claim that dominion theology is a single theology any longer but is rather a collection of theologies with an idiomatic similarity and with varying degrees of semantic cross-pollination. It is my personal view that if dominion theology is not to degenerate into what one elder of the faith has described as "militant ignorance,"[8] it needs to rediscover its philosophical and theological basis in the Reformation tradition and have a renewed confidence in God's law and epistemological self-consciousness. My personal position is

5. Coates, *Not Under Law*, 58

6. Macneil, "Politics."

7. A case in point is Abdullah Hammoud, the current mayor of Dearborn, Michigan, the epicenter of Islamic culture in the United States. Though he is a second generation immigrant, he denies the entire concept of a "melting pot": Jonny C, "Dearborn Mayor Hammoud." He also labeled a Christian minister as "Islamophobic" that objected to the renaming of a street in honor of Osama Siblani, who has repeatedly expressed public support for Hezbollah, Hamas, and other Palestinian factions as "freedom fighters"; see Anti-Defamation League, "Osama Siblani." He publicly stated that he feels no obligation to use English in preference to Arabic and, only after extended opposition, decided to remove Arabic insignia from police uniforms and vehicles (Lepore, "Police in America's 'Muslim Capital'").

8. Landa Cope, speaking at the "Kingdom Solutions" conference hosted by Glasgow Prophetic Center, Sept. 19, 2014. Audio recording is available from GPA.

for a Christian political philosophy founded on the first two positions we considered here, the theonomical position but accepting something of the moderation of the second position, where there is the necessary extraction of principles outside of the cultural peculiarities of ancient Israel. In all fairness, most of the theonomists of the first position already grant this concession, but there are some that rigorously insist on the precise Mosaic formulations. Arguments over those details would need to be deferred to other more technical works but should not be an obstacle to advancing the rulership of God on Earth, hastening the return of the Lord, and the rule of the millennium.

Final Words

Thank you for persevering with me on this journey. It has been, in places, a tough climb, but I believe we can now see the Promised Land. Hopefully, you are now also armed, ready for battle in the political and cultural realms—get out there and be loud in whatever sphere of culture you are gifted and called to, unless you are part of clandestine operations! Some work unnoticed in a domain and achieve much more than if they were loud and advertised their presence, which is why we need the Holy Spirit to discern the signs of the times. We must remember to walk by faith and in the faith, not just by what might seem good or reasonable to us.

The recent assassination of Charlie Kirk for being a conservative Christian interested in societal reformation and the aggressive ingress of radical Islam into the West should make very clear that our very survival as a civilization depends on us embracing the social, political, spiritual, and wider responsibility for the whole of culture in the expression of our Christian faith. That is why I finished the discussion with the application of dominion theology with the outlining of a philosophy of Christian involvement; it is my belief that the believer who claims to be a prophet but does not vote or support those working to be in business, commerce, education, the arts, public service, or political offices understands nothing substantive about dominion.

Appendix A—Post-Evangelicalism

It is beneficial to distinguish between the neo-evangelical position and the post-evangelical position, the former we have mentioned repeatedly, whereas the latter has only been mentioned in passing. A "neo" evangelical is a broad designation that normally refers to evangelicals from non-traditional, often non-Western, jurisdictions that have had some kind of conversion, revival, or renewal to orthodox Protestant Christianity; for example, many Latin American Protestant and some non-classical Pentecostal churches[1] might be described in this way, but the core of the various diverse expressions and practices is still a commitment to a set of evangelical theological propositions. Post-evangelicalism was very different: its central concern is pastoral and relational, how Christianity should deal with culture. In this sense, it has something in common with dominion theology and, notably, the social gospel (which, as a historical movement, we considered in more detail in the main text) and, thus, is on the surface a potential competitor to them, which is why we take the time to mention it here.

Historically, there were some clear cultural and intellectual precursors to the view,[2] but it was Dave Tomlinson, a onetime leader within the British charismatic movement during the 1980s, who popularized this term in his 1995 book *Post Evangelical.* It is also important that a revised American edition came complete with a "critical" commentary by some who had attempted to import the movement into the US, where the sociological term "new emergent" had been applied; it was as an example of an

1. That is, those outside the historical Pentecostal denominations of the Assemblies of God (AOG), COG, COGIC, Foursquare, and Elim.

2. Loydell, "Evangelical Mind," para. 1.

exciting new movement that had emerged because of the shortcomings of the status quo. Thus, it was both driven by a pastoral dissatisfaction with evangelicalism and was intellectually interesting to the academy; Dave had initially hoped academics might pick the ideas up in this way and give some sort of rigorous expression to them.

The academy did, indeed, manage a small, single-volume set of six essays edited by Graham Clay in 1997 as *The Post Evangelical Debate*, and they were bona fide academic essays. With the intense interest showed in it at once-Christian festivals, such as Greenbelt (Dave relates how people crowded into a tent to hear him speak[3]), it appeared it was going to be a major movement; however, that did not materialize, and the potential threat to dominion theology, which was also asserting itself in the charismatic Christian conscience at the same time, evaporated. It is worthwhile understanding why this was the case.

As stated, as a matter of historical fact, it was Dave who really brought post-evangelicalism into the Christian mainstream consciousness because of his status and influence within British, American, Australian, and New Zealand charismatic Christianity. Dave, after leading a fifteen-person team and founding fifty charismatic churches for the best part of a decade, became "disillusioned by the theology and spirituality of the charismatic movement" and, in 1989, left and, not only that, became apostate from the charismatic movement more generally, which, at least formally, had maintained an evangelical commitment. Dave gives this compressed personal history,[4] which captures well the essence of his approach and the impetus behind the wider movement. To be clear, Dave still considers himself Christian and is now a Church of England minister, though on the (very) liberal, rather than the charismatic, wing of that broad church.[5]

To give him his due, spiritually, Dave, I believe, is someone with an apostolic mantle—whatever he will choose to build will grow as a gift from God. As the gifts and callings of God are without repentance, we can just as effectively build because it is the ability to build that is the gift from God, but in terms of this logic, what is built is not necessarily from God—in contrast to that which is established and successful because what is believed is sound theology reflecting metaphysical truths about the way the world really is, and is successful because of that. What I mean there is similar to

3. Tomlinson, *Post Evangelical*, ix.

4. Tomlinson, "Dave Tomlinson."

5. https://www.saintlukeschurch.org.uk/.

the paradox of the successful unbeliever, who, like Paul describes, has such a keen sense of conscience and, thus, in the understanding of the law of God, they are blessed and succeed on that basis.

Thus, for our purposes here, what makes this so interesting is that "post" is best understood for Dave and the post-evangelical "movement" as meaning "after," in the historical, sequential sense. Once, there was the evangelical, now we are "post" that movement and, most importantly, everything it intellectually stood for. So, for example, in Dave's 2012 book *How to Be a Bad Christian*, you will not find a statement of the imperative for repentance from the perspective that it is required for justification and, thus, salvation before a holy God, that we are required to believe the blood of Jesus was shed as an atonement for our rebellion (sin) against God, which places us under condemnation, and that we are required to believe in our heart and confess with our mouth to receive salvation as our means as deliverance from sin.[6] In other words, you will not find some kind of exposition of the gospel as distilled in just two verses from the first eight chapters by Paul in Rom 10:8–9.

Rather, for the post-evangelical, sin is not defined as something we need redemption from; in contrast, the mere use of the word "sin" becomes a narrative device, the purpose of which is pejorative; the focus on sin within Christian discourse for the post-evangelical becomes a stumbling block for some to receive the unconditional love of God. That is, the post-evangelical prescription is to throw any theological clarity into the bin of that historical religion and tradition that has gotten in the way of a relationship with the loving God, who loves all without prejudice and precondition; it is never defined as the mindset and heart condition that separates us from God and that it is required of us to repent to receive freedom, which would then allow us to experience the operation and working of the love of God. Repentance for Dave is recast as a psychological exercise necessary for mental hygiene, which, of course, it is, but it is also a necessary spiritual transaction, a precondition of our justification before God.

We would perhaps say that Dave's book really is a manual for the "bad Christian" because it never clearly states the "good news" of the gospel as deliverance from the dominion of the said "sin," preferring the sentimental "unconditional love of God" as a substitute for it. God's love in the salvific sense is *not* unconditional, rather it is *freely available* to all those who meet his *conditions* of repentance. The "good Christian" recognizes

6. Tomlinson, *How to Be*.

that God so loved the world, he gave his Son for the purpose that those who repent and believe would be saved; a failure to comply with these preconditions really does mean permanent separation from God and an eternity in hell, regardless of the removal of hell from the Alpha course and the evangelical consciousness, let alone the liberal Christians who excised it a century or two ago.[7]

So, as a wider theological method, post-evangelicalism, with its nonjudgmental acceptance of all, is brutally defective in terms of basic Christian theology; but this was unimportant to the post-evangelicals themselves because it has always been much more about the practice of Christianity than any theoretical or theological account of it—a relaxed, non-confrontational, supremely liberal, friendly, "inclusive" approach that creates a "community where all are welcomed and accepted." This passive stance, in thoroughly postmodern fashion, wants to parade its wares in the markets of the public square and hope that someone midway between the clothes and music stalls might stumble across our bench and then realize they had found what they were really looking for. In other words, all that post-evangelicalism had to offer is a sort of rarefied Alpha-course experience, which itself had faced criticism as a sanitized, hell-free Christian option for professionals looking to actualize their spiritual life with this optional add-on of Jesus.

This, of course, is where we see the contrast with dominion theology most dramatically and the explanation as to why dominion theology has and will endure. For the dominion theologian, it is about a complete, integrated intellectual and spiritual worldview, a practice flowing from a coherent and cogent theology that presents a narrative for every sphere of human culture. The subjective spiritual experience is fortified by the objective knowledge from the Scriptures.

In contrast, post-evangelicalism, at its very best, has a fuzzy subjective concept of the Scriptures as an important relic worthy of veneration, but subject to the enlightened intellect and practices of the modern world, free of all those ancient prejudices, bigotry, and arguments about the content of

7. One reaction to liberalism, the neo-orthodox movement of Barth and Brunner in the 1930s, also equivocated on the concept. Brunner was more forthright in his renunciation of the doctrine than Barth, who was more ambiguous and frequently redefined theological terms (as he often did) to mean something than their historical meaning. The concept is psychologically offensive to most thinking people and would seem to be at odds with the "God of love," of the Scripture, but that forgets the same book also teaches "God is just."

Scripture, and then further about the canon of Scripture. With respect to the issue of canonicity, a genuine church merely *recognizes* the canonicity of books; it does not *decide* on them; the prerogative with regards to Scripture is always with the author, not with humanity.

Thus, on analysis, post-evangelicalism becomes the religion of personal and collective preferences and survives based on its toleration by the hosting culture; it has no power to change or to set culture in its intellectual definition, or, more correctly, it is unable to direct culture because of its lack of any such definition. However, not wishing to take anything away from the post-evangelical mindset, it is certainly of note as a subcultural phenomenon of sorts that has some affection for an unoffensive "quiet" Christianity in the public square, which once mythically existed in the Judeo-Christian past cultural consensus of Western nations. However, in contrast to dominion theology, it has lost the intellectual essence of Christianity, trading it for the innocuous and ultimately false gospel of unconditional love, acceptance, and inclusion.

Appendix B—The Late Jesus

This was an article I had written for a Christian publication summarizing many of the themes of this book but proceeded to fold before it was published!

FIRSTLY, IT MUST BE admitted that there are and have been some fine scholars (Walvoord, Chafer, Pentecost) who have defended dispensationalism as an innovation of premillennialism. It cannot be denied the system has provided some genuine prophetic insights and scarcely a radical preacher will not accuse the current church of "Laodicean lukewarmness," a concept birthed in dispensationalism viewing the containing passage of Rev 3 as a particular "sub-dispensation" within the church age. However, on the contrary, there are also fine scholars (Gentry, Mathison) who have objected on an exegetical basis, historians (Macpherson) who have thoroughly repudiated it as an orthodox development of premillennialism, reclassifying it as a mystical, unorthodox innovation, and missionologists (like Cope) who have repudiated it on a theological level. The latter is what I am interested in here first and then to consider the theological credibility of the favorite "blessed hope" of the dispensationalists, the "rapture" doctrine. I include some references at the end for the other categories if you are interested.

With regards to the eschatological tenor of dispensationalism, Landa Cope, one of the founders of YWAM in the 1970s with Loren Cunnigham, asserted that "theologies of imminent return" have repeatedly emerged as the church began to take on its social and political kingdom-building role and have led to its premature termination and surrender of culture to the secular humanists, with disastrous consequences for culture as a whole.[1] She views Hal Lindsey's *The Late Great Planet Earth* as "the one for our

1. Cope, *Old Testament Template* and *God and Political Justice.*

generation," as the evangelical church began to emerge in the 1970s from over fifty years of self-imposed cultural ghettoism to asserting itself again in the cultural sphere. She argues Peter and Paul expected return in their lifetimes and every Christian generation since has had those who adopted a similar position.

Yet, we must hold this important scriptural imminence in tension with our social responsibility as believers in line with the scriptural admonition to "occupy until he comes." In her words, we must "build the kingdom" and not worry about the return, for Jesus told us not to; we are to be about the King's business and be ready to give an account of our works (Luke 19:13–27).[2] In my words, it should not distract us from exercising dominion and subduing the earth to God's law. To bastardize Vernon McGee's dispensationalist quip, "You don't polish brass on a sinking ship,"[3] I say, "Let us get an army of marine maintenance men and women if it helps the ship stay seaworthy."

Now, the second issue I would like to consider is the illogical nature of the favorite doctrine of classical dispensationalism, "the rapture." The valley of decision for the rapture was 1988 and its final burial, if there had been any lingering doubts, should have been 2007—the two dates featured prominently in the dispensationalist's calendar for "sound prophetic reasoning." The year 1948 was the foundation of the state of Israel, "the budding of the fig tree" (Matt 24:32–34) and forty years is a generation of Israel. Edgar C. Whisenant allegedly sold 6 million copies of "88 Reasons Why the Rapture is in 1988,"[4] basing his logic on detailed mathematical calculations and prophetic principles (this is still available on Amazon), and his failure did not discourage him from predicting 1989, 1990, and 1991. I have in my collection recordings from the late 1980s of otherwise rational and sane preachers I would happily recommend, thoroughly convinced the rapture was *days* away, and their audiences shrieking in ecstasy. One friend of mine believed a minor earthquake that occurred in North Wales in 1990 (where we were both living at the time) was the "trumpet call" in Revelation—he

2. The KJV uses this phrase; most modern translations would say "do business"; the verb literally refers to the business of trading and making money. The KJV translators were perhaps trying to capture the wider context of the passage where it is talking about a King and his subjects—"occupy till I come" is a military idiom referring to a king leaving his occupying force to rule in his absence. In this instance, I think the KJV translators made a good call.

3. Rushdoony, *God's Plan for Victory*, loc. 177.

4. This is available from Whisenant, "88 Reasons Why."

sold his profitable and successful business and waited to be caught up! His sad spiritual story since, despite his enormous intelligence, is a lesson for any believer. Yet, he simply, with a greater degree of conviction, believed and acted on a lot of the traditional teaching in British Pentecostalism that I, too, had received and been sincerely taught.

For some, the rapture could legitimately be delayed until 2007, for 1967 was the first time that Jerusalem had been in the hands of the Jews for two thousand years, this clearly being a prophetic marker of some kind for anyone with true prophetic discernment (obviously). However, these passed as did the apocalypses predicted by the pagan astrologers with the unusual and rare alignment of all nine planets at around the same time. Even now in 2025, with a healthy dose of Jewish mysticism, some believe that the rapture will be on September 21, 2025. (Prudentially, I am editing this on that very date, and subsequently, November 13, 2025, so we can safely assume the rapture did not occur unless Starmer is in fact the antichrist's UK government representative, and I really was "left behind.") The Jewish prophet Jonathan Cahn explains forcefully why this is really a very weak mode of reasoning, making the point that other very similar prognostications just bring shame and disrepute on the church, and it should be stated that he believes in a rapture![5]

However, dispensationalism and its predilection for predictions and "signs of the times" has somehow survived. In the last few years, planetary convergences, comets, and consecutive "blood moons" on Passover/Jubilees that have not occurred for millennia have all been posited as signs of the end and our imminent removal by otherwise sane and competent ministries. Unless I missed something, nothing of note has happened, except the sales of lots of DVDs and MP3s of their "prophetic packages for [mis]understanding the end times"—but I hasten to add, I could have missed whatever was supposed to have happened. There has always been a tendency amongst dispensationalists of "special revelation" and prophetic insight concealed from the rest of us "Moabite evangelicals."[6]

Remarkably, there are still able scholars committed to the view who can maintain a critical view of the failures of their forerunners as "rapturists" or suffering from "rapture mania." One such able scholar was Chuck Missler who I thoroughly recommend on most subjects.[7] However, it was

5. Cahn, "Whether the Rapture Will Happen."

6. MacPherson, *Rapture Plot*, 55–85.

7. Chuck has passed since I wrote this article; he went onto glory on May 1, 2018.

notable in his late work there was no mention of the "budding fig tree" as the reformation of Israel that has featured predominantly in previous prophetic iterations. According to his final position, the marker for the forty years and the last generation is the rapture *itself.* In other words, he has foreclosed the issue of trying to predict the date in any specific way, though he was still comfortable predicting it was "possible within the next twelve months," though that was during the long-past and otherwise excellent 2011 Strategic Perspectives conference. He separates previously dispensationalist harmonized "end time" passages between Luke and Matthew into pre- and post-tribulation events, posits specific psalms as additional sequences of prophetic events that have previously been "missed" (Ps 89—see his "Perilous Times" and "Planet in Jeopardy" series) and separates pre- and post-restoration events. This increasing granularity in dealing with the text to extend the prophetic time frame is befitting to the resilience of the position against all the odds after 1988.

Notwithstanding this attempted academic reorientation of dispensationalism, there is still a huge appetite for rapturist psychological escapism bred by it, if the *Left Behind* series is anything to go by, which made millions for its creators in the 2000s and was still having "behind the scenes" YouTube videos made about it in 2018. I contend there is clearly something seriously amiss with such an attitude of a Christian with regards to their educational, social, and political responsibility. It is about as far from the Reformation call of Luther and Calvin to redeem society and establish godly secular states as one could get, and these teachings should now be in disrepute.

I believe it is a sign of maturity in the believer to take their place as heavenly ambassador in an earthly kingdom by fully engaging with their social responsibility and not retreating into mysticism, even when dressed up as the fashionable prophetic lingo "God's government in the heavenlies" or "we are God's government in session this evening." Maybe there is a place for climbing to the tops of mountains and proclaiming to the powers and principalities the judgments of God, but I struggle with this; it would be far better if prophetic direction, admonition, and maybe even rebuke could be given to our own apostate rulers. Let us think clearly and build the kingdom on Earth and within our vocations, without distraction or condemnation that we are being "worldly."

His personal website is still available (https://chuckmissler.com/) and the ministry he founded is still active: https://www.khouse.org/.

Further Reading

Cope, Landa. *An Introduction to the Old Testament Template: Rediscovering God's Principles for Discipling Nations.* 2nd ed. Seattle: YWAM, 2011(2006).

———. *God and Political Justice: A Study of Civil Governance.* Seattle: YWAM, 2015.

Lindsey, Hal. *The Late Great Planet Earth.* Grand Rapids: Zondervan, 1970.

Macneil, Michael. *Dominion Theology.* Eugene, OR: Wipf & Stock, 2026.

MacPherson, David. *The Rapture Plot.* 2nd ed. Simpsonville, SC: Millenium III, 2000.

Missler, Chuck. *Christianity's Most Preposterous Belief—the Rapture.* Coeur d'Alene: Koinonia House, 2014.

Appendix C—The English Civil War and the Founding of the United States

AS WE LEARNED FROM our study of Rom 13, the duty of a magistrate is to *restrain evil*, and whether that evil is internal or external to a nation, it is not an option for us to ignore it. Revolutionary action is the "last resort" as is going to war; but as it was necessary to go to war against a Hitler, a Mussolini, or a Stalin, for the purposes of restraining their evil, so it is necessary to resist the evil of our *own* leaders. Indeed, this is not unusual in the history of the Protestant church and was a feature of the movement around Puritan Oliver Cromwell (the English Civil War) that spawned egalitarian groups, such as the Levelers and the Diggers, who prefigured many of the policies that became associated with the later labor and trade union movements.

The history around these groups and their relationship to Cromwell is contested history and all did not go well, but there was a strong element of novel, egalitarian Christian political thinking in all these groups, and religious tolerance was a distinctive of Cromwell's general political philosophy (being the first to explicitly grant the Jews protection and religious freedom) despite his conflict with the Catholic forces. The English Civil War was actually three conflicts between 1642–51; the final conflict of 1650–51 was probably the most significant event that was a catalyst for the Puritan migration to the New World, as it marked the period of the betrayal and brutal suppression of King Charles II, who had fought Cromwell with the support of the Scots Presbyterians on the promise of spreading Scots Presbyterian influence through the realm in preference to the English Puritan republicans supporting Cromwell. Owing to the historic alliance of Scotland with France against England, the "moderate" Scots Presbyterian party had chosen a political alliance with Charles (who had exiled to France) over a spiritual one with Cromwell.

The Scots were deceived in this matter, considering the English republic a bigger threat to Scotland as a nation than the compromising Charles II, who had clear Catholic sympathies, even seeking assistance from the pope to get him back into power after Cromwell had executed his father (Charles I) and established the protectorate. They took what they believed was a political shortcut to the propagation of Presbyterianism throughout the realm by the royal patronage of Charles in return for their support. Charles had initially been crowned King of Scotland as an act of defiance against the new English republic under Cromwell but was quickly defeated by Cromwell and went into exile until the restoration of the monarchy following Cromwell's death. Scotland had been incorporated into the English protectorate under Cromwell, so the desire to reassert political independence was a strong stream in Scots' thinking amongst the political leaders.

Furthermore, the alliance of the Scots with Charles was a paradoxical alliance, as the Scots Presbyterians and English Puritans were of a common spiritual ancestry: both stood against the Catholic hegemony, were reformers of nominal state Protestantism, and should have been unified against Charles and with Cromwell in common cause to create a new British republic with its common law constitution, much like the United States was to become. Like his father (and most of the other European monarchs, who were intriguing against one another as well as against the Pope, who was constantly looking to reassert his authority throughout Europe through alliances with the local potentates), Charles II lied and, after his victory and the restoration of the monarchy in 1660, brutally suppressed both his Scots Presbyterian supporters and the English Puritans, exhuming Cromwell's body from Westminster Abbey, beheading it, and placing his severed head on a spike (where it remained for twenty-five years) as a sign of the new regime's triumph.

The failure of the strategy of compromise for Scots Presbyterianism to maintain independence from England was completed when the Scots parliament was dissolved on May 1, 1707, following the Act of Union, which created the kingdom of Great Britain.[1] To complete his iniquity,

1. Though I am generally critical of Stark's *Prophets,* one emphasis of her thinking is to avoid the unholy political alliances in preference to the purposes of God, a principle that should be considered carefully and might well apply in this scenario, but which I have also argued in the book can too easily lead to an indifferent agnosticism regarding fighting for just political government.

Charles later entered a secret treaty with Catholic Louis XIV of France, gaining subsidy in return for publicly converting to Catholicism (re-opening the door for papal subjugation of the entire realm); but he only publicly converted to Catholicism on his deathbed when there was no political risk of conflict with parliament. He had obviously only indicated support for Presbyterianism as a means to his desired end: his restoration to the throne and the restoration of the monarchy. To this point, the British monarchy and its hegemony have remained ever since, with only the post-WWII settlement and the subsequent loss of the empire seeing a reduction in the political influence they exerted behind the scenes, despite the alleged ascendency of parliament. Even now, any bills passed in the British Parliament still need "royal assent" before they pass into law. Often thought of as merely a formality, it was only a few years ago that senior figures of the British establishment and army argued that such assent be withheld if radical leftist Jeremy Corbyn had come to power in 2019.[2] British democracy has only ever dangled by a thread, quickly washed away should the people dare to speak too loudly.

However, taking the long view, the ascension of the US as the premier Christian nation with its republicanism, traditions of religious freedom and tolerance (after Roger Williams, a reformer of Puritanism), in preference to the European nations with their state churches, has its roots in this period as the Puritans struggled to reform English and Scottish Protestantism; many of them later became key voices in the Puritan colonies. Nevertheless, it pains me to think, as a Scot, that the Scots betrayed the Protestant cause for Britain and probably the rest of Europe, but our betrayal did lead to the foundation of the American republic and its vision of a free people under God; we can rest in this marvelous example of divine providence that we see in the foundation of that new republic of the United States.

2. Jeremy Corbyn was unexpectedly elected leader of the British Labour Party in 2015 as the Labour Party "lurched to the left" (as it had often done in the past) after its electoral defeat. Corbyn was incredibly popular with the grassroots of the party and dramatically increased party membership, but he was *loathed* by the *Parliamentary* Labour Party who were "uniparty" loyalists—a true democratic socialist but also a member of the Christian socialist movement, an exceptionally unusual combination for a British democratic socialist. He was later ousted in a party coup, nominally over the failure to deal with antisemitism in the party and was ejected from the party altogether in 2024. He has, however, remained as an MP and has just formed a new socialist party in the UK but suffered the immediate humiliation of the cofounder metaphorically knifing him in the back on all sorts of party structure issues, policy issues, and even the party name—welcome to the world of democratic socialism!

I also talked about this on YouTube[3] and combined some further comment into a blog post.[4]

3. Macneil, "American Thanksgiving."
4. Macneil, "English Civil War."

Bibliography

Where a year appears in parentheses, this refers to the date of the publication of the original edition and where there is substantive divergence between the editions, or where there has been a subsequent digitization of a classic work.

Ali, Ayaan Hirsi. *Heretic: Why Islam Needs Reformation Now.* New York: HarperCollins, 2015.

Ali, Ayaan Hirsi. *Prey: Immigration, Islam, and the Erosion of Women's Rights.* New York: HarperCollins, 2021. Kindle ed.

Allis, Oswald T. *Prophecy and the Church.* Philadelphia: P&R, 1945.

Almond, Gabriel A., et al. *Strong Religion: The Rise of Fundamentalisms Around the World.* Chicago: University of Chicago Press, 2003.

Amazon. "Frank Schaeffer." https://www.amazon.co.uk/stores/author/B000AP9HNQ.

Anderson, Adrian. "Joachim of Fiore: Social Upheaval from Biblical Prophecies." Rudolf Steiner Studies. http://www.rudolfsteinerstudies.com/free-ebooks/Joachim%20of%20Fiore.pdf.

Anderson, Erin. "Congressmen Call Texas 'Ground Zero' in Fight Against Sharia." Texas Scorecard, Feb. 4, 2026. https://texasscorecard.com/federal/congressmen-call-texas-ground-zero-in-fight-against-sharia/.

Anti-Defamation League. "Osama Siblani and the Arab American News." Apr. 15, 2013. https://www.adl.org/resources/profile/osama-siblani-arab-american-news.

Augustine. *The Complete Works of Saint Augustine.* Translated by Marcus Dods. Luxembourg: Amazon Media EU S.à r.l., 2013. Kindle ed.

Ayer, Alfred J. *Language, Truth and Logic.* 2nd ed. New York: Dover, 1952.

Bahnsen, David. "Greg Bahnsen and the Auburn Avenue Controversy." In *Danger in the Camp: An Analysis and Refutation of the Heresies of the Federal Vision,* written by John M. Otis, 431–52. Corpus Christi, TX: Triumphant, 2005. eBook.

Bahnsen, Greg L. *By This Standard: The Authority of God's Law Today.* Powder Springs, GA: American Vision, 2008 (1985).

———. "Calvin and Postmillennialism." *PostmillennialWorldview* (blog), Oct. 24, 2023. https://postmillennialworldview.com/2023/10/24/calvin-and-postmillennialism/.

———. *No Other Standard: Theonomy and Its Critics.* Tyler, TX: ICE, 1991.

———. *Presuppositional Apologetics: Stated and Defended.* Edited by Joel McDurmon. Nacogdoches, TX: American Vision, 2008.

———. "The Prima Facie Acceptability of Postmillennialism." *Journal of Christian Reconstruction* 3.2 (1976–1977) 32–96.

———. "Review: 'Another Look at Chilton's *Days of Vengeance*.' *Journey* 3:2 (March–April 1988)." Covenant Media Foundation. https://thebahnsenbibleacademy.com/wp-content/uploads/2024/02/PB075-Another-Look-at-Chiltons-Days-of-Vengeance-Journey-3-2.pdf.

———. *Theonomy in Christian Ethics.* 2nd ed. Phillipsburg, NJ: P&R, 1984 (1977).

———. *Van Til's Apologetic: Readings and Analysis.* Phillipsburg, NJ: P&R, 1998.

———. "What Really Happened at Reformed Theological Seminary." Apr. 1979. https://store.americanvision.org/products/greg-bahnsen-what-really-happened-at-reformed-theological-seminary-rts.

Bahnsen, Greg L., and Kenneth L. Gentry. *House Divided: The Break-Up of Dispensational Theology.* Tyler, TX: ICE, 1989.

Barker, William S., and W. Robert Godfrey, eds. *Theonomy: A Reformed Critique.* Grand Rapids: Acadamie, 1990.

Barr, James. *Fundamentalism.* 2nd ed. London: SCM, 1984 (1977).

Barton, David, and Tim Barton. *The American Story: The Beginnings.* Aledo, TX: Wallbuilder, 2020.

Bauer, Walter, et al. *A Greek–English Lexicon of the New Testament and Other Early Christian Literature.* 4th revised and augmented ed. Chicago: University of Chicago Press/Cambridge University Press, 1952.

Berkhof, Louis. *Systematic Theology.* Grand Rapids: Eerdmans, 1996 (1929).

Bernstein, Brittany. "DeSantis: 'Not Surprised' Democrats Flee to Florida to 'Enjoy Life' without 'Draconian' Covid Policies." Yahoo!, January 3, 2022. https://www.yahoo.com/news/desantis-not-surprised-democrats-flee-200900978.html.

Bethell, Nicholas. *The Last Secret: The Delivery to Stalin of Over Two Million Russians by Britain and the United States.* New York: Basic, 1974.

Beveridge, William. "Social Insurance and Allied Services." Parliamentary Archives, BBK/D/495. London: HMSO, 1942.

Birch-Machin, Mark. *Speakers of Life: How to Live an Everyday Prophetic Lifestyle.* Maidstone, UK: River, 2015.

Blackburn, Simon. *Ruling Passions: A Theory of Practical Reasoning.* Oxford: Clarendon, 1998.

———. *Truth: A Guide for the Perplexed.* London: Penguin, 2006. Kindle ed.

Boettner, Loraine. *The Millennium.* Phillipsburg, NJ: P&R, 2012 (1958).

———. *Postmillennialism.* Luxembourg: Amazon Media EU S.à r.l., 2011. Kindle ed.

Boonke, Reinhardt. *Extra Impact* (newsletter). Feb. 2008. Christ for all Nations (CfaN).

Bratt, James D., ed. *Abraham Kuyper: A Centennial Reader.* Carlisle, UK: Paternoster, 1998.

Broomfield, Matt. "Thomas Müntzer's Misunderstood Revolution." *Nation*, Nov. 19, 2024. https://www.thenation.com/article/culture/thomas-muntzer-biography-drummond/.

Brown, Michael L. *Evangelicals at the Crossroads: Will We Pass the Trump Test?* Concord, NC: Equal Time, 2020. Kindle ed.

Bultmann, Rudolf. *History and Eschatology: The Gifford Lectures 1955.* New York: Harper & Row, 1957.

———. *History and Eschatology: The Presence of Eternity.* New York: Harper Torch, 1962 (1957).

———. *Jesus Christ and Mythology.* New York: Charles Scribner's Sons, 1958.

Butler, Christopher. *Postmodernism.* Oxford: Oxford University Press, 2002.

Butler, Michael. *Philosophy of Science.* Audio Series: MB100-MB121. Nacogdoches, TX: Covenant Media Foundation, n.d. https://store.cmfnow.com/The-Philosophy-of-Science-p258401225.

Cahn, Jonathan. "Jonathan Cahn on Whether the Rapture Will Happen on the Feast of Trumpets Sept 23, 2025? | Prophetic." Jonathan Cahn Official, Sept. 3, 2025. YouTube video, 8:13. https://www.youtube.com/watch?v=L1BYtEl-PZo.

Calvin, John. *Institutes of the Christian Religion.* Translated by Henry Beveridge. N.p.: Fig, 2012 (1539). Kindle ed.

Carnap, R., et al. *Wissenschaftliche Weltauffassung, der Wiener Kreis.* Translated by Friedrich Stadler and Thomas Uebel. Vienna: Artur Wolf Verlag, 1929.

Chadha, Jagjit. "Might the UK Really Need a 1970s-style IMF Bailout?" Economics Observatory, Sept. 25, 2025. https://www.economicsobservatory.com/might-the-uk-really-need-a-1970s-style-imf-bailout.

Chilton, David. "Tyler, Texas: A Taped Lecture." Preterist Archive. https://web.archive.org/web/20171020223851/http://www.preteristarchive.com/Modern/1992_chilton_tyler.html.

———. "The Work of the Ecclesiastical Megalomania." Word MP3, audio recording. https://www.wordmp3.com/details.aspx?id=181.

Clapp, Rodney. "Democracy as Heresy." *Christianity Today*, Feb. 20, 1987. https://www.christianitytoday.com/1987/02/democracy-as-heresy/.

Clarkson, Frederick. "Christian Reconstructionism." *Public Eye Magazine* 8.1 (March/June 1994). http://www.publiceye.org/magazine/v08n1/chrisre1.html.

Coates, Gerald. *Kingdom Now!* Eastbourne, UK: Kingsway, 1993.

———. *What on Earth Is This Kingdom.* Eastbourne, UK: Kingsway, 1983.

Coates, Gerald, and Hugh Thompson. *Not Under Law.* Eastbourne, UK: Kingsway, 1975.

Colson, Charles. "The Power Illusion." In *Power Religion: The Selling Out of the Evangelical Church*, edited by Michael Scott Horton, 30–50. Chicago: Moody, 1992.

Colson, Charles, et al. *Power Religion: The Selling Out of the Evangelical Church?* Edited by Michael Scott. Chicago: Moody, 1992.

Cope, Landa. *God and Political Justice: A Study of Civil Governance.* Seattle: YWAM, 2015.

———. *An Introduction to the Old Testament Template: Rediscovering God's Principles for Discipling Nations.* 2nd ed. Seattle: YWAM, 2011 (2006).

———. "OTT Business Seminar: Business and Economics." Template Institute, 2011. Audio recording.

———. "OTT Business Seminar: Law and Government." Template Institute, 2011. Audio recording.

Dabney, Robert L. *Systematic Theology.* Luxembourg: Amazon Media EU S.à r.l., n.d. (1878). Kindle ed.

Dallek, Robert. "Roosevelt's Relationship [sic] Stalin." WW2history.com. http://ww2history.com/experts/Robert_Dallek/Roosevelt_s_relationship_Stalin.

Davis, D. Clair. "A Challenge to Theonomy." In *Theonomy: A Reformed Critique*, edited by William S. Barker and W. Robert Godfrey, 389–402. Grand Rapids: Acadamie, 1990.

DeMar, Gary, and Peter Leithart. *The Reduction of Christianity: A Biblical Response to Dave Hunt.* Atlanta: Dominion, 1988.

Dobson, Ed, et al. *The Fundamentalist Phenomenon*. Edited by Jerry Falwell. New York: Doubleday, 1981.

Docherty, Thomas. "Postmodernist Theory." In *Twentieth Century Continental Philosophy*, edited by Richard Kearny, 474–503. London: Routledge, 1994.

Dodd, C. H. *The Parables of the Kingdom*. Revised ed. Welwyn, UK: James Nisbet, 1961 (1935).

Doherty, Brian. *Radicals for Capitalism: A Freewheeling History of the Modern American Libertarian Movement*. New York: Public Affairs, 2007.

Düsterdieck, Friedrich Hermann Christian. *Kritisch exegetisches Handbuch über die Offenbarung Johannis* [Commentary on the apocalypse of John]. Göttingen, DE: Vandenhoeck und Ruprecht, 1859.

Edgar, William. "Francis Schaeffer and His Global Influence." *To the Ends of the Earth* 3.2. https://wm.wts.edu/magazine-articles/francis-schaeffer-and-his-global-influence.

Edwards, Jonathan. *The Works of Jonathan Edwards*. 2 vols. Edited by Edward Hickman. Luxembourg: Amazon Media EU S.à r.l., n.d. Kindle ed.

Farrell, Jenny. "Thomas Müntzer and the German Peasants' War." Culture Matters, May 30, 2025. https://www.culturematters.org.uk/thomas-muntzer-and-the-german-peasants-war/.

Festenstein, Matthew. "Dewey's Political Philosophy." In Stanford Encyclopedia of Philosophy Archive. Spring 2014 ed. http://plato.stanford.edu/archives/spr2014/entries/dewey-political.

Feyerabend, Paul. *Against Method*. 4th ed. London: Verso, 2010.

———. *The Tyranny of Science*. Cambridge: Polity, 2018.

Fish, Stanley. *There's No Such Thing as Free Speech: And It's a Good Thing Too*. New York: Oxford University Press, 1994.

Flew, Antony, and Roy Abraham Varghese. *There Is a God: How the World's Most Notorious Atheist Changed His Mind*. New York: HarperOne, 2008.

Francis, Lizzie. "Cancelling Christians: Billy Graham Wouldn't Be Welcomed into Britain Today." Critic, June 14, 2021. https://thecritic.co.uk/cancelling-christianity/.

Geehan, E. R., ed. *Jerusalem and Athens: Critical Discussions on the Philosophy and Apologetics of Cornelius Van Til*. Phillipsburg, NJ: P&R, 1980.

Gentry, Kenneth L. Jr. *He Shall Have Dominion: A Postmillennial Eschatology*. Tyler, TX: ICE, 1992.

Gould, Steven Jay. *Punctuated Equilibrium*. Cambridge, MA: Belknap, 2007.

———. *The Structure of Evolutionary Theory*. Cambridge, MA: Belknap, 2002.

Hamilton, Floyd E. *The Basis of Millennial Faith*. Grand Rapids: Eerdmans, 1955 (1942).

Hamon, Bill. *The Eternal Church: A Prophetic Look at the Church—Her History, Restoration, and Destiny*. 2nd ed. Shippensburg, PA: Destiny Image, 2003 (1981).

Heelas, Paul, et al., eds. *Religion, Modernity, and Postmodernity*. New York: Wiley, 1998.

Hillerbrand, H. J. "Martin Luther and the Jews." In *Jews and Christians: Exploring the Past, Present, and Future*, edited by James H. Charlesworth, 147–57. New York: Crossroad, 1990.

History.com. "New Deal." http://www.history.com/topics/new-deal.

Hobbes, Thomas. *Leviathan or the Matter, Forme, and Power of a Commonwealth Ecclesiastical and Civil*. Overland Park, KS: Digireads, 2014 (1651). Kindle ed.

Hodge, Charles. *Systematic Theology*. Louisville: GLH, 2015. Kindle ed.

Holder, R. Ward. "John Calvin (1509–1564)." Internet Encyclopaedia of Philosophy. http://www.iep.utm.edu/calvin/.

Hopkins, Samuel. *A Treatise on the Millenium: Shewing from Scripture Prophecy, that It Is Yet to Come; When It Will Come; in What It Will Consist; and the Events Which Are First to Take Place, Introductory to It*. Luxembourg: Amazon Media EU S.à r.l., n.d. (1811).

Horner, Barry. "The Reformed Eschatology of William Hendriksen." Future Israel Ministries, Jan. 15, 2015. http://web.archive.org/web/20150308234357/http://futureisraelministries.org/files/william_hendriksen.pdf.

House, H. Wayne, and Thomas Ice. *Dominion Theology: Blessing or Curse? An Analysis of Christian Reconstructionism*. Portland: Multnomah, 1988.

Hunt, Dave. *Beyond Seduction: A Return to Biblical Christianity*. Eugene, OR: Harvest House, 1987.

———. *Whatever Happened to Heaven*. Eugene, OR: Harvest House, 1988.

———. *What Love Is This?: Calvinism's Misrepresentation of God*. 4th ed. Bend, OR: Berean Call, 2018 (2002).

Hunt, Dave, and T. A. McMahon. *The Seduction of Christianity: Spiritual Discernment in the Last Days*. Eugene, OR: Harvest House, 1985.

Ice, Thomas, and Kenneth L. Gentry Jr. *The Great Tribulation—Past or Future? Two Evangelicals Debate the Question*. Grand Rapids: Kregel, 1988.

Isoje, Agnes. "6 Times Pastors Predicted Rapture and Got It Wrong." Pulse, September 24, 2025. https://www.pulse.ng/story/joshua-mhlakela-rapture-prophecy-20250924 13504940542.

Ito, Suzanne. "Demanding Respect for All Religious Louisianans." ACLU, Aug. 15, 2007. https://www.aclu.org/news/national-security/demanding-respect-all-religious-louisianans.

Joachim. *Expositio in Apocalypsim*. Frankfurt am Main, DE: Minerva G.M.B.H., 1964 (c. 1196).

Johnson, Bill, and Rick Joyner. "Azusa Now Livestream 04.09.2016." Contend Global, Apr. 9, 2016. YouTube video, 11:55:00. https://www.youtube.com/watch?v=ZK2DkDKej cs&feature=youtu.be.

Jonny C. "Dearborn Mayor Hammoud: 'The Entire Point of America Is Not Assimilating to Culture and the Language.'" Newsbreak, Nov. 18, 2025. https://www.newsbreak.com/jonny-c-224527595/4353430088816-dearborn-mayor-hammoud-the-entire-point-of-america-is-not-assimilating-to-culture-and-the-language?s=ws_native.

Jordan, James B. "A Theocratic Critique of Theonomy." Basileian Lectures Complete Recordings 1988–1997 (4 MP3s). https://www.wordmp3.com/product-group.aspx?id=322.

Joyner, Rick. *The Power to Change the World: The Welsh and Azusa Street Revivals*. Fort Mill, SC: Morning Star, 2010 (2006). Kindle ed.

Justice, Ethan. "Today is the Anniversary of the First Inauguration: George Washington's Prayer and the Need to Rededicate America to God." 917 Society, Apr. 30, 2025. https://www.917society.org/post/today-is-the-anniversary-of-the-first-inauguration-george-washington-s-prayer-and-the-need-to-reded.

Kant, Immanuel. *Religion Within the Limits of Reason Alone*. Translated by Theodore M. Greene and Hoyt. H. Hudson. New York: Harper Torchbooks, 1960.

Kassam, Raheem. *No Go Zones: How Sharia Law Is Coming to a Neighborhood Near You*. Washington, DC: Regnery, 2017.

Kik, J. Marcellus. *An Eschatology of Victory*. Phillipsburg, NJ: P&R, 1971.

Kliefoth, Theodor Friedrich Dethlof. *Die Offenbarung des Johannes* [The revelation of John]. Leipzig, DE: Dörffling und Franke, 1874.

Kuhn, Thomas Samuel. *The Structure of Scientific Revolutions*. 4th ed. Chicago: University of Chicago Press, 2012.

Kuyper, Abraham. *Lectures on Calvinism*. Luxembourg: Amazon Media EU S.à r.l., n.d. (1898). Kindle ed.

———. "Sphere Sovereignty." In *Abraham Kuyper: A Centennial Reader*, edited by James D. Bratt, 461–90. Cambridge: Paternoster, 1998.

Lawrence, Bruce. *Defenders of God: The Fundamentalist Revolt Against the Modern Age*. San Francisco: Harper San Francisco, 1990.

———. "From Fundamentalism to Fundamentalisms: A Religious Ideology in Multiple Forms." In *Religion, Modernity and Postmodernity*, edited by Paul Heelas et al., 88–101. New York: Wiley, 1998.

Legal Information Institute. "First Amendment." https://www.law.cornell.edu/constitution/first_amendment.

Lepore, Stephen M. "Police in America's 'Muslim Capital' Backpeddle After Sparking Fury for Introducing New Badge Featuring Arabic." Daily Mail, Sept. 8, 2025. https://www.dailymail.co.uk/news/article-15078643/Muslim-capital-new-badge-Arabic.html.

Lindsey, Hal. *The 1980s: Countdown to Armageddon*. King of Prussia, PA: Westgate, 1980.

———. *The Late Great Planet Earth*. Grand Rapids: Zondervan, 1970.

———. *The Rapture*. New York: Bantam, 1983.

———. *The Road to Holocaust*. New York: Bantam, 1989.

Lloyd-Jones, David Martyn. *The Puritans: Their Origins and Successors*. Edinburgh, UK: Banner of Truth, 1996.

———. *Romans: Exposition of Chapter 13*. Edinburgh, UK: Banner of Truth, 2015.

———. *Romans: Exposition of Chapter 14:1–7 Liberty and Conscience*. Edinburgh, UK: Banner of Truth, 2017.

———. *What Is an Evangelical?* Edinburgh, UK: Banner of Truth, 1992.

Longman, Temper III. "God's Law and Mosaic Punishments Today." In *Theonomy: A Reformed Critique*, edited by William S. Barker & W. Robert Godfrey, 41–58. Grand Rapids: Acadamie, 1990.

Loydell, Rupert. "The Evangelical Mind." Ships of Fools, May 26, 2024. https://shipoffools.com/2024/05/the-evangelical-mind/.

Luther, Martin. *The Martin Luther Collection*. N.p.: Waxkeep, 2012. Kindle ed.

———. *Selected Psalms II*. Luther's Works 13. Edited by Jarislov Pelikan. St. Louis: Concordia, 1956.

———. "Efficacy of the Gospel." In *Sermons of Martin Luther*, vol. 3, edited and translated by John Nicholas Lenker et al. Ada, MI: Baker & Baker, 2007.

———. "Vorrede auff die Epistel S. Paul an die Romer [Preface to the letter of St. Paul to the Romans]." In *D. Martin Luther: Die gantze Heilige Schrifft Deudsch 1545 aufs new zurericht*, vol. 2, edited by Hans Volz and Heinz Blanke, translated by Brother Andrew Thornton, 2254–68. Munich: Roger & Bernhard, 1972.

Lyon, David. *Postmodernity*. 2nd ed. Oxford: Open University, 1999.

Lyotard, Jean-François. *The Differend: Phrases in Dispute*. Translated by Georges Van Den Abbeele. Manchester: Manchester University Press, 1989.

———. *La condition postmoderne: rapport sur le savoir*. Paris: Minuit, 1979.

———. *The Postmodern Condition: A Report on Knowledge*. Translated by Geoff Bennington and Brian Massumi. Manchester: Manchester University Press, 1984.

Machen, J. Gresham. *Christianity and Liberalism*. Grand Rapids, Eerdmans: 2009 (1923).
———. *Christianity, Culture, and Liberalism*. Louisville: GLH, 2009.
———. *Education, Christianity, and the State*. Edited by J. Robbins. Hobbs, NM: Trinity Foundation, 1995.
———. "The Importance of Christian Scholarship." In *Theonomy: An Informed Response*, edited by Gary North, 89–111. Tyler, TX: ICE, 1991.
Mackie, J. L. "Evil and Omnipotence." *Mind* 64.254 (1955) 200–212. https://www.jstor.org/stable/2251467.
Macneil, Michael. "American Thanksgiving and the English Civil War." Planet Macneil, Nov. 27, 2025. YouTube video, 18:22. https://www.youtube.com/watch?v=tOifrSHJOHk.
———. "Censorship—The New Normal." *Planet Macneil* (blog), Aug. 21, 2021. https://planetmacneil.org/blog/censorship-the-new-normal/.
———. "The English Civil War and the Founding of the United States." *Planet Macneil* (blog), Nov. 27, 2025. https://planetmacneil.org/blog/the-english-civil-war-and-the-founding-of-the-united-states/.
———. "Examine Why Augustine and Plantinga Both Considered the Problem of Evil as a Primary Challenge to the Rationality of Christian Belief. Does Plantinga's Free Will Defence Constitute an Effective Development of the Arguments Presented by Augustine?" Coursework essay for MA studies in philosophy and religion, Bangor University, June 2015. https://www.researchgate.net/publication/325828197_Examine_why_Augustine_and_Plantinga_both_considered_the_problem_of_evil_as_a_primary_challenge_to_the_rationality_of_Christian_belief_Does_Plantinga's_Free_Will_Defence_constitute_an_effective_develop.
———. "Fake (but Peer-Reviewed) Academic Papers Published by Fake (but Famous) Journals." *Planet Macneil* (blog), Sept. 24, 2023. https://planetmacneil.org/blog/fake-but-peer-reviewed-academic-papers-published-by-fake-but-famous-journals/.
———. *The Foundations of Philosophy: Epistemological Self-Consciousness*. Eugene, OR: Wipf & Stock, 2025.
———. "Fundamentalism as a Modernism." *Planet Macneil* (blog), Nov. 6, 2011. https://planetmacneil.org/blog/fundamentalism-as-a-modernism/.
———. "The Fundamentals and Fundamentalism." *Planet Macneil* (blog), Apr. 25, 2024. https://planetmacneil.org/blog/the-fundamentals-and-fundamentalism/.
———. "'The Great COVID Caper—Hoax or Greatest Public Health Emergency in Peacetime?' A Dissertation on the COVID-19 Novel Coronavirus, its Global Management and How to Survive the Next Pandemic." Nov. 2020. doi:10.13140/RG.2.2.14767.15528/2.
———. "HAMAS vs Israel—Understanding the Conflict." *Planet Macneil* (blog), Dec. 21, 2023. https://planetmacneil.org/blog/hamas-vs-israel-understanding-the-conflict/.
———. "A Holistic Context for Understanding the Categories of Religion and State." Conference paper presented at University of Aberdeen, Sept. 2015. https://www.researchgate.net/publication/325807168_Creating_a_holistic_context_as_a_basis_for_a_defensible_understanding_of_the_categories_of_religion_and_state.
———. *Macneil's Guide for the Spiritually Perplexed*. https://planetmacneil.org/Documents/Content/Macneils-Guide-for-the-Spiritually-Perplexed.pdf.
———. "Politics, Church, and State in the Post–Trump Era." Apr. 2021. doi:10.13140/RG.2.2.16282.16325.
———. "The Rise of Christian Anti-Semitism." *Planet Macneil* (blog), Mar. 8, 2008. https://planetmacneil.org/blog/the-rise-of-christian-anti-semitism/.

———. "Scripture and the Post-Darwinian Controversy." *Planet Macneil* (blog), June 14, 2015. https://planetmacneil.org/blog/scripture-and-the-post-darwinian-controversy/.

———. "Should I Obey My Government—Civil Disobedience in the COVID-Era." *Planet Macneil* (blog), Mar. 1, 2020. https://planetmacneil.org/blog/should-i-obey-my-government-civil-disobedience-in-the-covid-era/.

MacPherson, David. *The Rapture Plot.* 2nd ed. Simpsonville, SC: Millenium III, 2000 (1994).

Mangalwadi, Vishal. *Truth and Transformation: A Manifesto for Ailing Nations.* Seattle: YWAM, 2012 (2009). Kindle ed.

Marsden, Chris. "The *Sun*'s Anti-Gay Attacks on the British Labour Government." World Socialist Web Site, Nov. 20, 1998. https://www.wsws.org/en/articles/1998/11/sun-n20.html.

Marsden, George M. *Reforming Fundamentalism: Fuller Seminary and the New Evangelicalism.* Grand Rapids: Eerdmans, 1988.

Martin, Bernice. "From Pre- to Postmodernity in Latin America: The Case of Pentecostalism." In *Religion, Modernity and Post Modernity*, edited by Paul Heelas et al., 102–46. Oxford: Blackwell, 1998,

Masselink, William. *Why a Thousand Years?* Grand Rapids: Eerdmans, 1953 (1930).

Mathison, Keith A. *Dispensationalism: Rightly Dividing the People of God.* Phillipsburg, NJ: P&R, 1995.

———. *Postmillennialism: An Eschatology of Hope.* Phillipsburg, NJ: P&R, 1999.

McDade, Paul. "The Problem with Christian Reconstruction." Dec. 24, 2014. http://www.calvinjones.com/3spheres/articles/ProblemReconstruction.pdf.

McGrath, Alister. *A Passion for Truth: The Intellectual Coherence of Evangelicalism.* Leicester, UK: Apollos, 1996.

McGrath, Alister, and Joanna Collicutt McGrath. *The Dawkins Delusion?: Atheist Fundamentalism and the Denial of the Divine.* London: SPCK, 2007.

McVicar, Michael J. *Christian Reconstruction: R. J. Rushdoony and American Religious Conservatism.* Chapel Hill: University of North Carolina Press, 2015.

Missler, Chuck. "America's Challenge." Strategic Perspectives Conference. Coeur d'Alene: Koinonia House, 2012. MP3 download.

———. *Christianity's Most Preposterous Belief—the Rapture.* Coeur d'Alene: Koinonia House, 2014.

Moore, G. E. "A Defense of Common Sense." In *Contemporary British Philosophy*, edited by J. H. Muirhead, 193–223. London: Allen and Unwin, 1925.

Niebuhr, Reinhold. *The Nature and Destiny of Man.* 2 vols. Westminster: John Knox Press, 1941–1943.

Nietzsche, Friedrich. *Der Wille zur Macht: Versuch einer Umwerthung aller Werthe (Studien und Fragmente, Nachgelassene Werke).* Edited by Ernst Horneffer, et al. Leipzig, DE: Druckerei C. G. Naumann: 1901.

Noll, Mark A. *America's God: From Jonathan Edwards to Abraham Lincoln.* New York: Oxford University Press, 2002.

North, Gary. *Backward, Christian Soldiers?* 2nd ed. Tyler: ICE, 1986.

———. "Cutting Edge or Lunatic Fringe?" *Journal of Christian Reconstruction* 11.1 (1978) 1–2.

———. "The Importance of the 700 Club." *Biblical Economics Today* 5.1 (1982) 10–13. http://www.garynorth.com/freebooks/docs/a_pdfs/newslet/bet/8202.pdf.

———. "Reconstructionist Renewal and Charismatic Renewal." *Christian Reconstruction Newsletter* 7.3 (1988).
———, ed. *Theonomy: An Informed Response*. Tyler, TX: ICE, 1991.
———. *Unholy Spirits: Occultism and New Age Humanism*. Tyler, TX: ICE, 1994 (1988).
North, Gary, and Gary DeMar. *Christian Reconstruction: What It Is, What It Isn't*. Tyler, TX: ICE, 1991.
North, Gary, et al. *The Legacy of Hatred Continues: A Response to Hal Lindsey's* The Road to Holocaust. Tyler, TX: ICE, 1989.
———, et al. *Tactics of Christian Resistance*. Tyler, TX: Geneva Divinity School, 1983.
———, et al. *The Theology of Christian Resistance*. Tyler, TX: Geneva Divinity School, 1983.
Nyagamago, Maxwell. "Top 10 Countries in Africa with the Largest Christian Populations: 2025 Rankings." Pulse, Nov. 5, 2025. https://www.pulse.com.gh/story/africa-largest-christian-populations-2025-2025110516480794783.
O'Daly, Gerard J. P. *Augustine's City of God: A Reader's Guide*. Oxford: Clarendon, 1999.
Oppenheimer, Mark. "Son of Evangelical Royalty Turns His Back, and Tells the Tale." *New York Times*, Aug. 19, 2011. https://www.nytimes.com/2011/08/20/us/20beliefs.html.
Otis, John M. *Danger in the Camp*. Corpus Christi, TX: Triumphant, 2005.
Packer, J. I. *Fundamentalism and the Word of God*. Grand Rapids: Eerdmans, 1958.
———. *An Introduction to Covenant Theology*. N.p.: Fig, 2012. Kindle ed.
Pawson, David. "Grace—Saving, Sovereign and Free: IHOPKC May 2011." 1:27:11. https://www.davidpawson.co.uk/search/?mediaID=3728&t=Grace%20-%20Saving,%20Sovereign%20and%20Free.
Pelletier, Joel. "The Movement." American Fundamentalists, Oct. 9, 2004. http://www.americanfundamentalists.com/movement.html.
Pentecost, J. Dwight. *Things to Come*. Grand Rapids: Zondervan, 1964.
Peters, George N .H. *The Theocratic Kingdom of Our Lord, Jesus Christ as Covenanted in the Old Testament and Presented in the New Testament*. Vols 1–3. New York: Funk & Wagnalls, 1884. https://archive.org/details/TheTheocraticKingdomPetersVols1-3.
Plantinga, Alvin. *The Analytic Theist*. Edited by James F. Sennett. Grand Rapids: Eerdmans, 1998.
———. "An Existentialist's Ethics." *Review of Metaphysics* 12 (1958) 235–56.
———. *God, Freedom, and Evil*. Grand Rapids: Eerdmans, 1977.
———. *Warranted Christian Belief*. New York: Oxford University Press, 2000.
———. *Warrant: The Current Debate*. New York: Oxford University Press, 1993.
———. *Warrant and Proper Function*. New York: Oxford University Press, 1993.
———. *Where the Conflict Really Lies: Science, Religion and Naturalism*. New York: Oxford University Press, 2011.
Poythress, Vern S. *Inerrancy and Worldview: Answering Modern Challenges to the Bible*. Wheaton, IL: Crossway, 2012.
Price, Roger. "The Millennial Issue: The Three Views." Chichester Christian Fellowship, 1979. Audio casette, 60 min.
———. *The Millennial Issue*. Supporting poster STS 7–10. Chichester Christian Fellowship, 1978.
———. "Premillennialism." Chichester Christian Fellowship, 1979. Audio casette.
PRO-S.O.C.S. "The Righteous Revolution—Could There Be a Theocracy in America's Future?" 1996. http://prosocs.tripod.com/riterev.html.

Puplava, James. "The Impending Financial Collapse." Strategic Perspectives Conference. Audio recording. Coeur d'Alene: Koinonia House, 2011. MP3 audio.

Quine, W. V. O. "Two Dogmas of Empiricism (1953)." In *From a Logical Point of View*, 20–46. Cambridge, MA: Harvard University Press, 1980.

Rauschenbusch, Walter. *Christianity and the Social Crisis in the 21st Century*. New York: HarperCollins, 2007 (1907). Kindle ed.

———. *The Social Principles of Jesus*. New York: Woman's, 1917.

———. *A Theology for the Social Gospel*. New Haven, CT: Yale University Press, 1917.

Rhodes, R. "Absolute Truth in an Age of Uncertainty." Strategic Perspectives Conference. Coeur d'Alene: Koinonia House, 2011. MP3 audio.

Rhodesia and South Africa. "Terrorist Sponsorship." http://www.rhodesia.nl/wccterr.html.

Riddlebarger, Kim. "Princeton and the Millennium: A Study of American Post-millennialism." Mountain Retreat: Reformed Christian Eschatology. https://www.mountainretreatorg.net/eschatology/princetonmill.html.

Rorty, Richard. *An Ethics for Today: Finding Common Ground Between Philosophy and Religion*. New York: Columbia University Press, 2011.

———. *Philosophy and the Mirror of Nature*. Princeton: Princeton University Press, 2018 (1979).

———. *Take Care of Freedom and Truth Will Take Care of Itself: Interviews with Richard Rorty*. Edited by Eduardo Mendieta. Stanford: Stanford University Press, 2006.

Rushdoony, Mark R. *Rousas John Rushdoony: A Brief History of the Life and Ministry of My Father*. Vallecito, CA: Chalcedon, 2025.

Rushdoony, Mark R., et al. "A Tribute to RJ Rushdoony." *Chalcedon Report*, Apr. 2001. https://chalcedon.edu/magazine-issues/a-tribute-to-r-j-rushdoony.

Rushdoony, R. J. *By What Standard?* Fairfax, VA: Thoburn, 1974 (1959).

———. *Christianity and the State*. Vallecito, CA: Chalcedon, 1986. Kindle ed.

———. "Christian Reconstruction 1." Chalcedon Foundation, 1960. RR155A1, MP3 audio, 45 min.

———. "Christian Reconstruction 2." Chalcedon Foundation, 1960. RR155A2, MP3 audio, 45 min.

———. "Christian Reconstruction as a Movement." *Journal of Christian Reconstruction* 14.1 (1996) 9–20.

———. "The Death of the Old Humanist Order." Presented at the annual conferences of Christian Reconstruction. Chalcedon Foundation, n.d. RR177A2, MP3 audio, 45 min.

———. *God's Plan for Victory: The Meaning of Postmillennialism*. Vallecito, CA: Chalcedon, 1997. Kindle ed.

———. *The Institutes of Biblical Law*. Phillipsburg, NJ: P&R, 1973.

———. "Money, Inflation, and Morality." Presented at the annual conferences of Christian Reconstruction. Chalcedon Foundation, n.d. RR175A2, MP3 audio, 37 min.

———. *The Mythology of Science*. Vallecito, CA: Ross House, 2001 (1967).

———. "Noncompetitive Life." *Faith and Freedom*, vol. 1 no. 6. Mises Institute archive. 1950.

———. "Postmillennialism in American History 1." Chalcedon Foundation, n.d. RR199A1, MP3 audio, 35 min.

———. "Postmillennialism in American History 2." Chalcedon Foundation, n.d. RR199A2, MP3 audio, 35 min.

———. *Van Til and the Limits of Reason*. Vallecito, CA: Chalcedon/Ross House, 2013 (1960). Kindle ed.

Russell, Bertrand. *History of Western Philosophy*. 2nd ed. London: Routledge, 1991 (1946).

———. "Logical Positivism." In *Logic and Knowledge: Essays 1901–1950*, edited by Robert C. Marsh, 365–82. London: George Allen & Unwin, 1991.

———. *Logic and Knowledge, Essays 1901–1950*. Edited by Robert Charles Marsh. London: George Allen & Unwin, 1956.

———. *The Problems of Philosophy*. New York: Cosimo, 2007 (1912).

Ryle, J. C. *John Wycliffe and His Work*. Luxembourg: Amazon Media EU S.à r.l., n.d. Kindle ed.

Schlissel, Steve M. "To Those Who Wonder if Reconstructionism Is Anti-Semitic." In *The Legacy of Hatred Continues: A Response to Hal Lindsey's The Road to Holocaust*, edited by Gary North, 56–61. Tyler, TX: ICE, 1989.

Schnittger, D. *Christian Reconstruction—from a Pretribulational Perspective*. Oklahoma City: Southwest Radio Church, 1986.

Schweitzer, A. *The Quest of the Historical Jesus*. London: SCM, 2000.

Scofield, C. I. *Rightly Dividing the Word of Truth*. Luxembourg: Amazon Media EU S.à r.l., n.d. (1896). Kindle ed.

Selbrede, Martin G. "First Major Book About R. J. Rushdoony." *Faith for All Life* (May/June 2015) 4–13.

Sennett, J. F., ed. *The Analytic Theist—an Alvin Plantinga Reader*. Grand Rapids: Eerdmans, 1998.

Sloyan, Gerald S. *Christian Persecution of Jews Over the Centuries*. United States Holocaust Memorial Museum. https://www.ushmm.org/research/about-the-mandel-center/initiatives/religion-holocaust/resources/christian-persecution-of-jews-over-the-centuries.

Smith, John H. *Dialogues Between Faith and Reason: The Death and Return of God in Modern German Thought*. Ithaca, NY: Cornell University Press, 2011.

Stadler, F., and Thomas Uebel, eds. *Wissenschaftliche Weltauffassung, der Wiener Kreis*. Reprint of original edition with translations. Vienna: Springer, 2012.

Stark, Emma. *Prophets, Politics, and Nations: Understanding the Vital Role that Prophetic Voices Play in Shaping Nations*. Shippensburg, PA: Destiny Image, 2024.

Stein, Gordon, and Greg Bahnsen. "The Great Debate: Does God Exist? Dr. Greg Bahnsen vs Dr. Gordon Stein." University of California Irvine, 1985. Biblia 7, June 9, 2013. YouTube video, 2:13:57. https://www.youtube.com/watch?v=anGAazNCfdY.

Stoll, David. *Is Latin America Turning Protestant? The Politics of Evangelical Growth*. Berkeley: University of California Press, 1990.

Stott, John. *Involvement: Being a Responsible Christian in a Non-Christian Society*. Vol. 1. Old Tappan, NJ: Fleming H. Revell, 1985.

Straight Arrow News. "Oracle's Larry Ellison Sees AI Supervision Keeping Citizens on 'Best Behavior.'" Sept. 16, 2024. YouTube video, 1:41. https://www.youtube.com/watch?v=sQqQtgRdjZU.

Sunstein, Cass R. "Justice Breyer's Democratic Pragmatism." *Yale Law Journal* 115.7 (2006) 1719–1743. https://doi.org/10.2307/20455667.

Swinburne, Richard. *The Existence of God*. 2nd ed. Oxford: Clarendon, 2004.

Taylor, James E. "The New Atheists." Internet Encyclopaedia of Philosophy. http://www.iep.utm.edu/n-atheis/.

Thiselton, Anthony C. *Hermeneutics: An Introduction*. Grand Rapids: Eerdmans, 2009.

Telegraph. "Alexandria Ocasio-Cortez Under Fire for 'Fleeing' to Florida amid Lockdown in Home State of New York." Jan. 4, 2022. https://www.telegraph.co.uk/world-news/2022/01/04/alexandria-ocasio-cortez-fire-fleeing-florida-amid-lockdown/.

Tomlinson, Dave. "Dave Tomlinson." Work of the People. https://www.theworkofthepeople.com/person/dave-tomlinson.

———. *How to Be a Bad Christian . . . and a Better Human Being.* London: Hodder & Stoughton, 2012.

———. *The Post Evangelical.* London: SPCK, 2014.

Torrey, R. A., and A. C. Dixon, eds. *The Fundamentals: A Testimony to the Truth.* Grand Rapids: Baker, 2008 (1917).

Toy, Eckard V. "Spiritual Mobilization: The Failure of an Ultraconservative Ideal in the 1950s." *Pacific Northwest Quarterly* 61 (Apr. 1970) 77–86.

Turrentine, Jeff. "The Supreme Court Ends Chevron Deference—What Now?" NRDC, June 28, 2024. https://www.nrdc.org/stories/what-happens-if-supreme-court-ends-chevron-deference.

van Oort, Johanne. "The End Is Now: Augustine on History and Eschatology." *HTS Teologiese Studies/Theological Studies* 68.1 (2012) a1188. https://hts.org.za/index.php/hts/article/view/1188.

Van Til, Cornelius. *Christian Apologetics.* 2nd ed. Phillipsburg, NJ: P&R, 2011.

———. *Christianity and Barthianism.* Phillipsburg, NJ: P&R, 1974.

———. *The New Modernism: An Appraisal of the Theology of Barth and Brunner.* Phillipsburg, NJ: P&R, 1946.

———. *The Protestant Doctrine of Scripture.* Phillipsburg, NJ: P&R, 1967. Kindle ed.

Verduin, Leonard. *Reformers and Their Stepchildren: Fighting Amongst the Brothers.* Grand Rapids: Baker Academic, 1980. Kindle ed.

Vine, W. E., et al., eds. *Vine's Complete Expository Dictionary of Old and New Testament Words.* Nashville: Thomas Nelson, 1996.

Vrije Universiteit Amsterdam. "History." https://vu.nl/en/about-vu/more-about/history.

Wagner, C. Peter. *Dominion!: How Kingdom Action Can Change the World.* Grand Rapids: Chosen, 2008.

———. *On Earth as It Is in Heaven.* Ventura: Regal, 2012.

Wagner, C. Peter, et al. *The Reformer's Pledge.* Edited by Ché Ahn. Shippensburg, NJ: Destiny Image, 2010.

Walvoord, John F. "The Millennium Issue in Modern Theology." *Bibliotheca Sacra* 106 (1948) 430.

———. *The Millennial Kingdom.* Grand Rapids: Zondervan, 1959.

Warfield, B. B. *Writings of BB Warfield.* Vol. 2. Edited by Johnson C. Philip and Saneesh Cherian. N.p.: Philip Communications, 2013. Kindle ed.

Whisenant, Edgar C. "88 Reasons Why the Rapture Will Be in 1988." https://ia801303.us.archive.org/19/items/ReasonsWhyTheRaptureWillBeIn1988PDF/14080011-88-Reasons-Why-The-Rapture-Will-Be-in-1988.pdf.

Wilson, Jamie. "BBC Eases Privacy Edict." *Guardian*, Dec. 21, 2000. https://www.theguardian.com/media/2000/dec/21/broadcasting.uknews.

Wittgenstein, Ludwig. *Culture and Value.* Revised ed. Edited by G. H. von Wright. Oxford: Blackwell, 1998.

———. *Tractatus Logico-Philosophicus.* New York: Cosimo Classics, 2007.

Wright, David F. "The Edict of Milan." *Christianity Today* issue 28, 1990. http://www.christianitytoday.com/history/issues/issue-28/313-edict-of-milan.html.

Yurica, Katherine. "The Despoiling of America: How George Bush Became the Head of the New American Dominionist Church/State." Yurica Report, Feb. 11, 2004. http://www.yuricareport.com/Dominionism/.

Zinberg, Joel. "The Numbers Prove Cuomo's Lockdowns Hurt NYers on EVERY Metric—While Florida Flourished." Paragon Health Institute, Feb. 16, 2023. https://paragoninstitute.org/public-health/lockdown-analysis-new-york-vs-florida/.

Index of Names

Subject Index

Index of Scriptures

www.ingramcontent.com/pod-product-compliance
Lightning Source LLC
LaVergne TN
LVHW050629100826
845148LV00011B/1791
* 9 7 9 8 3 8 5 2 6 8 0 2 3 *